THE ORIGINS OF BRITISH BOLSHEVISM

RAYMOND CHALLINOR

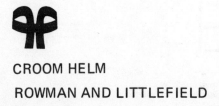

CROOM HELM

ROWMAN AND LITTLEFIELD

© 1977 Raymond Challinor
Croom Helm Ltd, 2-10 St John's Road, London SW11

British Library Cataloguing in Publication Data

Challinor, Raymond
    The origins of British bolshevism.

    1. Revolutionists – Great Britain   2. Great
    Britain – Politics and Government – 1901-1936
    I. Title
    322.4'2'0941   DA566.7

ISBN 0-85664-448-X

First published in the United States 1977
by Roman and Littlefield, Totowa, New Jersey

Library of Congress Cataloging in Publication Data

Challinor, Raymond
    The origins of British bolshevism.

    Bibliographical notes
    Includes index
    1. Communism—Great Britain—History.   2. Socialism
    in Great Britain—History.   I. Title.
    HX243.C43 1977   335.43'0941   77-3576

ISBN 0-87471-985-2

Printed in Great Britain by offset lithography by
Billing & Sons Ltd, Guildford, London and Worcester

CONTENTS

1 THE GREAT DIVIDE

British revolutionary socialism was born in Paris on 27 September 1900.
There, at the congress of the Second International, delegates fiercely
debated the propriety of Alexandre Millerand and two other French
socialists joining the government of Waldeck-Rousseau. It was not merely
that the government was pledged to administer capitalism, and would
therefore inevitably carry out anti-working class measures, but the
Cabinet contained General Gallifet, the butcher of the Paris Commune.
Twenty thousand communards had been murdered at his command.
This made left-wing delegates even more incensed. They heckled Jean
Jaures, the veteran French socialist, when he put the case for participation in the Government. He argued that the public would condemn the
French Socialist Party, regarding it as an abdication of responsibility,
if they shut the door in Waldeck-Rousseau's face. Religious and military
reactionaries threatened the Republic. The duty of French socialists
was to unite with others to defend parliamentary democracy and
freedom.

Speeches for and against were made amid cheers and counter-cheers
until Karl Kautsky put forward what he hoped would be considered a
compromise resolution. It condemned, in general terms, participation
by socialists in capitalist governments, but nevertheless argued that in
exceptional circumstances this might be necessary. When congress
passed the resolution, the left exploded with anger. They taunted the
supporters of Millerand with shouts of 'Vive la Commune' and 'Go to
Chalons' — a reference to the place where French soldiers had recently
killed strikers.[1]

Among the vociferous opposition stood a solitary member of the
British delegation. All the rest had supported Millerand and voted for
the Kautsky resolution, but George S. Yates quite unequivocally
opposed class collaboration. He returned to Britain determined to
continue the struggle against all Millerands, be they French, British, or
any other nationality. Yates was a talented young man. He spoke fluent
French and German, had an impressive knowledge of socialist theory,
and was a dedicated internationalist. Indeed, he returned from Paris
with the words and music of *The Internationale*, which he introduced
into Britain.[2]

Yates visualised the struggle in a world-wide context. 'A big wave of opportunism is passing through the ranks of the international socialist party.' He cited Sweden, where a section of the Social Democrats kept the Liberals in office, as well as Italy and Britain, where socialists dropped their principles to make alliances with non-socialists. Even the conduct of the Second International exemplified this trend. Significantly, he referred to the Kautsky motion in the same terms as Lenin: it was a 'caoutchouc' — that is to say, India rubber — resolution that could be stretched in any direction. Most of the pressure, Yates observed, was liable to come from right-wingers, anxious to establish for themselves a cosy niche within capitalism. Hence he thought it necessary to build 'a new party, as we have no ambition to swim with the tide.'[3]

Like most British Marxists, Yates belonged to the Social Democratic Federation. It was within this organisation that he first unfurled the flag of revolt. The initial task was to establish a nationwide list of contacts. Then they could come together and publish a paper. This would not simply give them an organ for expressing their views; it would act as an organiser, bringing closer contact and regular activity.

In his efforts, Yates received valuable help from James Connolly, the Irish revolutionary, later to be the leader of the 1916 Easter Uprising. For a long time, Connolly had been exasperated by the half-hearted, compromising policies of British socialists. The Paris congress merely served as the final insult. It was not only the Kautsky resolution — Connolly pointed out that since Millerand joined Waldeck-Rousseau's cabinet 12 strikes had been smashed by the military — but also the attitude adopted towards Ireland. The British delegation had argued that the Irish Republican Socialist Party, of which he was a leader, did not have a right to separate representation at the congress. Ireland was part of Great Britain, not an independent country. While congress did not accept this argument, such conduct simply served to convince him of the extent to which imperialist conceptions had corroded the socialism of the British delegation.

In May 1901, James Connolly sailed to Scotland to help George Yates with his campaign. In a sense, he was just repaying a debt. Four years before, Yates had gone over to Dublin and assisted the IRSP with its demonstrations against Queen Victoria's Diamond Jubilee celebrations. When clashes occurred between socialists and loyalists, Yates figured prominently in the mêlée and, as a result, lost his job. Although compelled to return to Scotland, Yates still remained in Connolly's high esteem and arranged Connolly's speaking tour for him.

This took place at a time when a quickening interest was being shown

in socialist ideas. The presence of Connolly gave the SDF in Scotland a
boost, adding to recruitment and attendance at meetings. Very quickly,
he acquired a reputation. Typically, the Press Officer of the Leith SDF
reported:

> Comrade Connolly is certainly one of the best propagandists we
> have. While his lectures are scientifically accurate, they are at the
> same time so simple even the biggest dunce of his hearers cannot
> fail to grasp their meaning. Like our Falkirk comrades, we can
> recommend the English branches to secure his services. [4]

Wherever Connolly went, he denounced the class collaborationist
policies of Millerand and his English equivalents. Both the success of his
meetings and the clarity of his arguments influenced the Scottish SDF
district council, persuading it to support George Yates' policies. But,
equally, Connolly's impact was a reason why the SDFs national leadership shunned him, not wanting to see his speaking itinerary extended to
England, as it would probably exacerbate the discontent rumbling
inside the Federation. Yet, despite official discouragement, Connolly
secured speaking engagements in Lancashire, Oxford, Reading and
London.

A general malaise afflicted the Social Democratic Federation,
making it highly vulnerable to left criticism. Originally formed as a
middle-class radical organisation in 1881, it became avowedly socialist
two years later. Since then, its message invariably fell on stony ground.
Years of hard work and sacrifice achieved practically nothing. The SDF
possessed a few branches and little influence. It recruited new members
but proved incapable of holding them. In 1894, Frederick Engels estimated that these birds of passage almost certainly exceeded 100,000.
In 1896, delegates to the SDF conference were told the number
exceeded a million.[5] While it seems improbable that the figure was that
high, there can be no doubt that the membership turnover remained
large.

The underlying reason for the weakness of the SDF was the immense
might of British capitalism, seemingly invincible and unassailable, which
appeared to make any talk of socialism futile nonsense. At the turn of
the century, Britain had an empire upon which the sun never set.
Britannia ruled the waves, with the biggest navy in the world. Although
some other countries had made rapid industrial advances, Britain still
remained one of the foremost industrial nations, renowned for the high
quality of its engineering products. Also, Britain was the world's leading

trading country while London had become the most important banking
and financial centre of the world. All told, these achievements gave
considerable confidence and assurance to the ruling class. The rest of
society, enjoying generally rising standards of living, remained inclined
to echo the paeans of praise for capitalism, the system from which it
appeared all blessings flowed.

As a consequence, it was not surprising that socialists found the
general public unreceptive. Jim Connell, who wrote the words to the
song 'The Red Flag', lugubriously complained: 'For over 20 years, we
have been trying to convert people to Socialism, and we found that to
keep them we must re-convert them 365 times each year.'[6]

Inevitably, the lack of success and isolation left its scars on the SDF:
it tended to become dogmatic and sectarian. At the same time as it
antagonised workers, the SDF failed to satisfy serious Marxists. This
was because the Federation's leaders faced the ever-present pressure to
take an illusory short cut to socialism by discarding some of their
principles for the sake of immediate gain. Clearly, given the SDFs
small size, they must have been sorely tempted. In 1900, the SDF
claimed to have 96 branches and 9,000 members. But it was largely
on paper. Many of the branches failed to pay their subscription while
membership fees, involving a negligible penny a month, were paid in a
haphazard, erratic fashion. Probably in 1900, the Federation had about
50 functioning branches with an active membership of about 1,000.
This could hardly be regarded as a good harvest after almost 20 years
of campaigning.

In these disheartening circumstances the SDF shuffled around,
looking for possible roads to quick success. One possibility was to woo
the trade union leaders. Admittedly, these gentlemen, ultra-respectable
and cautious, were almost all anti-socialist, but perhaps, with gentle
persuasion, they could be prevailed upon to drop their prejudices. Then
the trade unions, with all their financial and organisational strength,
would be at the disposal of the socialist cause. A second possibility was
to fuse with the Independent Labour Party. The ILP, formed in 1893,
had in its few years' existence attracted more members and sunk deeper
roots into the working class. The problem was that the ILP had a
distinctly Nonconformist, anti-Marxist bias. Many of its speakers were
like Philip Snowden who usually ended his address with a 'Come to
Jesus' appeal that won the ILP new members. As his biographer
declared: 'Snowden and his audiences thought of Socialism as a practical application of the New Testament.'[7] Naturally, with visions of
heavenly harmony, the ILP eschewed the class struggle.

The political disagreements were considerable but the majority of the SDF did not think they necessarily constituted an unsurmountable obstacle to fusion with the ILP. It was thought that unity would greatly enhance the appeal of socialist ideas to the general public. Moreover, within the common organisation, it was hoped that the SDF members would win the ILP members over to more correct positions.

Both the overtures made to the ILP and the trade union leaders required of the Social Democratic Federation adjustments in its approach. It would have to discard its criticisms of these other bodies since a few misplaced words could endanger unity. As a consequence, SDF propaganda lost what incisiveness it had, and soft-pedalling became the accepted custom. A blind eye was turned to craft prejudices and to union officials betraying their members, while confused and sentimental nonsense uttered by Ramsey MacDonald and other ILPers remained unchallenged — all in the interests of greater unity.

As it fitted in with their conception of politics, the SDF leaders were prepared to make ideological concessions to right-wing forces. For their approach was based on drawing a distinction between practical day-to-day issues and long-term objectives. The SDF leaders saw as their ultimate aim the establishment of a socialist society, but that did not stop them, in the here and now, from entering into alliances that had not the remotest connection with socialism.

The quest for unity created strains within the SDF between the leaders and a section of the rank-and-file. Members like Yates and Connolly did not like the swamp of compromise into which the SDF was drifting. In contrast, the leaders did not like the leftish statements of Yates and his friends. These constituted an acute embarrassment to the Federation at a time when tact and diplomacy were required if unity was to be achieved. The growing incompatibility of the two approaches became increasingly evident, eventually leading to a split.

It was not merely a difference of outlook but also of age. Most of those who held official positions had been in the SDF virtually since its inception. They were middle aged and middle class, unable to attune themselves to the fresh stirrings among the workers. The person who illustrated this most clearly was H.M. Hyndman, the founder and main spokesman of the SDF. Within his bulky frame, Hyndman embodied the contradictions of Victorian society. An aged businessman, he became a socialist after reading Marx's *Capital* while sailing back from America. Once the SDF had been formed, he plunged into activity, making many speeches and writing many books. Much of the credit for popularising socialist ideas in Britain must go to Hyndman. But this did not endear him to Marx and Engels, both of whom regarded him as a self-satisfied, garrulous individual, who had grafted a few socialist ideas on to his essentially conservative outlook. Marx's hostility was aggravated further by Hyndman's plagiarisms of *Capital* for his own book, *England for All.*[8] The reason given by Hyndman for failing to acknowledge his indebtedness was that British people would not accept ideas if they knew these ideas came from foreigners. Proud to be British, Hyndman looked with disdain on all aliens, particularly Jews. He also believed in Britain maintaining strong armed forces.

As the years went by, Hyndman's bourgeois background asserted itself more and more. Increasingly, he tended to view British workers in the same jaundiced way he had hitherto reserved for foreigners. His outlook was fundamentally élitist. The toiling masses needed distinguished persons, like himself, to guide them, and it was base ingratitude on their part that they did not recognise how lucky they were:

> I don't mind saying that I am utterly disgusted with workers here in general and with our party in particular. Neither deserve to have men of ability from the educated classes to serve them. It is a waste of life. They are not worth the personal sacrifice and continual worry.[9]

Hyndmann confided these sentiments to Neil Maclean, secretary of the Glasgow Clarion Scouts, in a letter dated 3 September 1900. It may have influenced Neil Maclean, who subsequently played a central role in the schism and became the first general secretary of the Socialist Labour Party.

Through its experience, the left came to understand the widening gulf that separated its politics from those of Hyndman and his colleagues. What started as a dispute on a single issue — how British delegates voted over Millerand at the Paris congress — extended until it covered a gamut of issues. One of the sources of contention was the SDFs attitude to the Boer War (1899-1902). Although the Federation had adopted an anti-war stance, its position was somewhat sullied by racialist remarks. Hyndman and his colleagues were a long way from expressing an international socialist opposition to the war. James Connolly criticised the approach of *Justice*, the organ of the SDF:

> *Justice*, instead of grasping the opportunity to demonstrate the unscrupulous and bloodthirsty methods of the capitalist class, strove to divert the wrath of the advanced workers from the

capitalists to the Jews; how its readers were nauseated by denunciations of 'Jewish millionaires' and 'Jewish plots', 'Jewish-controlled newspapers', 'German Jews', 'Israelitish schemes', and all the stock phrases of the lowest anti-semitic papers until the paper became positively unreadable to any fair-minded man who recognised the truth, viz., that the war was the child of capitalist greed and inspired by men with whom race or religion were matters of no moment.[10]

Even this equivocal opposition was dropped. In July 1901, Hyndman persuaded the executive of the SDF that further anti-war agitation was 'a waste of time and money'. In his opinion, the best outcome of the conflict was a British victory.[11] As this was a period in which humanitarian feelings were being aroused because of Britain's creation of concentration camps in South Africa, the SDFs new line met opposition. At least 40,000 women and children died in the camps, and many socialists considered it was not a time to remain quiet. Disregarding the decision of the national executive, the Scottish district council continued to oppose British imperialism. Some idea of the tone and approach adopted can be gained from this report of how Falkirk SDF responded to the celebrations of Britain's final victory:

> While on all sides of the street the harlot, Capitalism, was decked in horrible array of all possible and impossible colours, there was projected from the windows of the SDF a transparency of five feet, giving the statistics of deaths in war, deaths in concentration camps, the numbers of paupers, the number of unemployed in Britain, the famine deaths in India, and the famine deaths, emigration and evictions in Ireland.[12]

A subsidiary reason why Hyndman was loath to become involved in opposition to the Boer War was that, if he did, he would have to associate with members of the Liberal Party, and this was something that he did not wish to do. For Hyndman and the rest of the Federation's leaders considered the Liberal Party to be the greatest obstacle to the advancement of socialism. So determined has the SDF been to scupper the Liberals that in 1885 it had accepted money from an agent of the Conservative Party to finance the contesting of constituencies where it was hoped to embarrass the Liberals. The result was that the SDF gained a derisory number of votes and acquired the stigma of having received 'Tory gold'. While the Federation's policy mellowed slightly, at its 1899 conference it still passed a resolution declaring that socialists should aim to cause 'the extinction of Liberal candidates by the votes being cast steadily on the Tory side'. The SDF executive then sought to get branches to organise as many people as possible to vote Conservative. In its report to the SDF conference in 1900, the executive complained: 'It is regrettable that the branches of the SDF have, with a few exceptions, shown so little interest in a question of such manifest importance.' [13]

Naturally, the left opposed these electoral manoeuvres. Almost instinctively, it rebelled against the notion of voting Tory. Underlying this was often an attitude of disgust towards conventional political processes. Too often electioneering degenerated into unprincipled vote-catching. When George Lansbury, the SDF candidate at Bow, deliberately played down his socialist commitment so that he could make an electoral alliance with non-socialists, the left accused him of 'cow-trading', making sordid deals 'to obtain some of the fleshpots of office and influence.' [14]

But then, Hyndman and the rest of the SDF leadership placed much more store by conventional political institutions than did their left-wing critics. When, in 1902, Edward VIIs coronation took place, the SDF seized the opportunity to send an 'Open Letter to the King'. This declared that the 'great and growing popularity of the king is not undeserved.' It asked His Majesty to use his position 'to improve the well-being of Englishmen at home and to save from utter ruin their greatest dependency abroad.' Thereby the king could secure for himself 'a name in history which mankind will look back to with admiration and respect.' [15] In a rather different vein, the statement of the Scottish left-wing referred to 'the little corpulent man who is the legal head of the capitalist state of Great Britain', and ended: 'Away, kinglet. Hie you home and set your house in order. Soon we, the workers, shall come to visit your palace and on the topmost turret we shall raise the red flag of the Socialist Republic.' [16]

Such contrasting attitudes inevitably led towards a split in the SDF, the culmination of a process of growing internal friction. It started, as we have seen, with George Yates attending the Paris congress in 1900. By March 1901, largely due to Connolly's efforts, the Scottish district committee had been captured by the left. The committee resolved as soon as possible to publish its own journal. This, presumably, was because it was dissatisfied with *Justice*, the official organ of the SDF, which rejected left-wing articles. But without wealthy backers, it was difficult to start a paper. While they slowly and painfully raised the money, left-wingers had to look elsewhere to find a vehicle for their views. The American Socialist Labour Party provided the assistance, opening the columns of its *Weekly People* to British contributions.

Links between Scottish and American socialists were first established by J.P. Doull. He visited the United States in 1898 and brought back some American SLP literature. Some of the Scottish SDF were attracted by the simple and clear way in which socialist ideas were expressed, especially in the writings of Daniel De Leon. They were also interested by the way American SLP attached greater importance to the industrial than to the purely electoral struggle. William Walker, of the Edinburgh branch, wrote to De Leon for advice, and on 3 February 1898 De Leon replied to him, outlining what he thought the correct line on trade unionism happened to be.[17] A band of Scottish socialists quickly fell under the influence of De Leon. By 1900, his pamphlets and the *Weekly People* were quite extensively sold by left-wingers. Quite understandably, they sought help from the American SLP when other channels of expression had been denied them.

Another source of outside assistance came from Ireland. As far as he could, James Connolly used the *Workers' Republic*, organ of the Irish Socialist Republican Party, to assist his Scottish comrades. He appears to have counselled them not to be pushed out of the SDF prematurely. He seems to have thought that, given the opportunity, many English members of the SDF could be won over to a left standpoint.[18] The Scottish left tried to follow his advice.

As a consequence, the SDFs 21st annual conference, held at Birmingham Town Hall, on 4-5 August 1901, turned out to be a stormy affair. George Yates, the delegate from Leith, challenged the official policy on the Kautsky motion at the Paris congress. A resolution from Leith on this issue had been excluded from the agenda by the executive. Nevertheless, Leonard Cotton, of the Oxford branch, managed to by-pass this obstacle. He moved an amendment from the floor that, in effect, repudiated the action of the SDF delegates at the Paris congress and declared that opposition to the entry of socialists into capitalist governments was a question of principle, not of tactics. Besides being supported by Yates, Cotton's amendment was backed by William Gee, the SDFs Scottish Organiser, and by John Carstairs Matheson, a Falkirk schoolmaster, who had previously been described by *Justice* as 'one of the best educated and best informed men in the whole movement.'[19]

Cotton's manoeuvre angered the SDF leaders. When Harry Quelch replied upon their behalf, he was obviously shaken by this challenge to official policy:

He (Quelch) maintained strenuously that we were not impossibilists, and circumstances must determine our policy. We must adopt any and every means to realise Social Democracy. He himself was in favour of any means, from the ballot box to the bomb, from political action to assassination. (Cheers) Oh, yes, the movers of the resolution cheered assassination, but they would not allow a socialist to enter a Ministry.[20]

There was no evidence that Quelch's critics favoured acts of individual terrorism any more than Quelch himself was prepared to adopt any means to secure socialism. Yet his speech, with a tinge of extremist phraseology, had the required effect. Cotton's amendment was lost by 37 votes to eight.

Undaunted by defeat, Yates went on to challenge the SDF leadership over control of the journal *Justice*. Although it acted as the official voice of the SDF, *Justice* was privately owned. It belonged to the Twentieth Century Press, a company in which Hyndman and his friends held a majority holding and thereby could see to it that the journal was slanted their way. Yates' resolution to get the SDF to take over *Justice* was defeated by 41 votes to 17. His motion opposing further unity negotiations with the ILP was also lost.

The left made tangible progress at the Birmingham conference, extending its influence to England. Contacts there arranged a speaking tour for James Connolly. Wherever he went, he tried to explain what he meant by revolutionary socialism. 'The necessity for the revolution in England,' he told workers in Salford, 'was demonstrated by the fact that the industrial supremacy of this country was fast disappearing.' Confronted by mounting discontent, the capitalists would concede reforms. At a London meeting, Connolly predicted that: 'If the workers ask for the capitalist baker's shop, he will throw the loaves at them to keep them out.' Connolly told them not to be content with a few more slices of bread — what they wanted was the entire bakery.[21] But to achieve such an immense transformation, he said, a much greater level of socialist consciousness needed to be attained. For this reason, he always encouraged his listeners to read the *Weekly People*, buy the Marxist classics being published by the New York Labor News Company, and start economics classes to get down to serious study. In this way, Connolly hoped not merely to make converts, but also to have workers who, being more knowledgeable and trained, were likely to be of greater effectiveness in the struggle.

Connolly's activities, stimulating the growth of centres of opposition

within the SDF, could not fail to arouse mutual hostility between the
Hyndman leadership and himself. This was further aggravated in
January 1902 when *Justice* failed to publish the manifesto of the Irish
Socialist Republican Party. The ISRP suspected this was because the
editor, Harry Quelch, was contesting the Dewsbury by-election and
thought publication might lose him votes. Later, Quelch denied that
this was the case but Connolly did not accept this explanation, saying
it had been done 'on obvious grounds of opportunism.' He added that:
'But for the loss to the socialist cause, he would have been glad Quelch
lost.'[22] The Irish manifesto appeared in American, French and German
working-class papers before *Justice* was prodded into printing it.

By March 1902, when the SDFs annual conference was held at
Blackburn, the official leadership was confronted by a much
strengthened opposition, which conducted a running battle throughout
the proceedings. First, Anderson (Edinburgh) and T. Fraser (Glasgow)
moved that a verbatim report of conference be made. This, an attempt
to counteract the tendentious reporting of previous conference, was
defeated by 41 votes to 11. Next Yates (Leith) and J. Fitzgerald
(Burnbank) sought to oppose the continued unity negotiations with the
ILP. Supported by J. Kent (West Ham Central) and J.T. Cox
(Southampton), their resolution was lost by 54 votes to 22. Similar
fates awaited numerous other motions, which sought to establish trade
unions with a definite socialist orientation, to prevent SDFers from also
belonging to other political organisations, and to obtain more clear-cut
policies. Usually they gained about 20 votes against about 50 for the
platform. The official report stated:

> At the conclusion of the conference, and in the midst of the some-
> what acrimonious turn which the discussion had taken, H. Quelch,
> on behalf of the executive, proposed that the thanks of the con-
> ference be given to the Blackburn comrades . . . He thought that
> conference was one of the best and most successful that had been
> held. There had been exhibited wide and deep differences, but it
> had been made abundantly manifest that these differences were
> only due to a small knot of extremists.

He ended with the threat the extremists 'must either fall into line or
fall out altogether.'[23]

The magnitude of the disagreements at the Blackburn conference
probably made the SDF leaders decide to perform an act of drastic
surgery. Their first expulsion was Percy Friedberg, of the Finsbury

Park branch. A letter he wrote to *Justice*, correcting inaccuracies in its
Blackburn conference report, remained unpublished so he submitted it
to the *Weekly People*. When Friedberg's branch resolved to stand by
him, the executive made it plain that all would be expelled unless the
expulsion was implemented. This placed the left-wingers in a quandary.
Some of the London comrades, led by Jack Fitzgerald and Con Lehane,
believed it was vital to stay inside the Federation. At the Blackburn
conference, they had won three seats on the executive. More gains
might accrue from remaining within the SDF and exposing the weaknesses of the Hyndman group. Equally cautious advice came from the
ISRP, but the Finsbury Park branch did not heed it. Not being prepared
to expel Friedberg, all its members were thrown out.

Meanwhile, in Scotland the left continued to acquire strength.
Supporters and money increased in modest amounts. Even so, it
became clear that they were within reach of accomplishing the aim
they set themselves in March 1901 — the publication of their own paper.
James Connolly agreed to arrange for its publication by the Workers'
Publishing Co, Dublin. The first issue of *The Socialist*, organ of the SDF
Scottish district council, was shipped over from Ireland and appeared
on sale in August 1902.

Both in tone and content *The Socialist* was at variance with official
SDF policy. Precisely the politicians Hyndman and his supporters
wished to court were denounced in its columns each month. The
second issue contained an editorial by George Yates entitled 'The
Labour Lieutenants of Capital'. It espoused what he regarded as the
revolutionary attitude to existing labour leaders:

> He sees the labour leader as the political agent of capital among the
> workers, carefully extinguishing every spark of class-consciousness
> as it arises, betraying and misleading his class at every juncture,
> and where independent class action cannot be hindered, capturing
> it and rendering it futile and worthless.

To underline his opinion, elsewhere in the same issue Yates had another
article, headed 'Capitalist Stoolpigeons', in which he denounced the ILP
for not supporting the recent carters' strike and for making no statements against the monarchy during the coronation of Edward VII.

In following months, *The Socialist* subjected many other working-
class leaders to critical scrutiny. Robert Blatchford, editor of the
widely-circulated *Clarion*, was castigated not only for supporting re-
armament and the Boer War, and remaining silent about United States

aggression against Cuba, but also for not adopting a proper class line on domestic issues. In his book, *Britain for the British*, he declared: 'I do not wish to stir up class hatred.' This aroused *The Socialist* to riposte: 'No, we ought to love the class who send miners to die in the pits from firedamp and workers in the workshop, in the pottery, and in the chemical works.'[24]

Robert Smillie, the Scottish miners' leader, was another target. As parliamentary candidate at North-East Lanarkshire in 1901, he promised to support 'every item' of the Liberal programme.[25] What angered *The Socialist* even more was when Smillie used 'the most contemptible of all dodges . . . his exploitation of race-hatred in his attack upon the Polish miners of Lanarkshire.' He advocated new legislation to keep them out.[26]

Also singled out for chastisement was Keir Hardie. Socialism to him was 'the kingdom of God upon earth'. Having such vague and confused ideas, Keir Hardie possessed the advantage of pliancy, an ability to disregard political disagreements, and to make alliances that involved discarding political principles. In February 1903, he told the third annual conference of the Labour Representation Committee:

> They all, Liberal, Tory and Socialist alike, rejoiced at the magnificent conference got together in this hall. What was the principle that enabled them all to come together and discuss this matter? Independence. If they, the Socialists, had insisted that all should be Socialists, there would be no such gathering. Had the Liberals insisted that all should be Liberals, they would have had a like result. They had fixed upon a common denominator that, when acting in the House of Commons, they would neither be Socialists, Liberals, nor Tories, but a Labour Party.[27]

With disarming frankness in the same debate, John Ward, of the Navvies' Union, expressed the prevalent view. He declared: 'They wanted to get their feet well planted in the House of Commons, and he believed they should not be a bit particular about the way in which they did it.'

The formation of the Labour Representation Committee launched a tidal wave of opportunism. Will Crook, its successful candidate at the Woolwich by-election in March 1903, confessed himself to be a man of 'robust imperialism', 'an opponent of the claptrap of Socialism.'[28] Yet the ILP, along with the Liberal Party, supported him. His election was greeted with enthusiasm by leading industrialists, as well as by members of the aristocracy, as Crook was proud to point out.[29]

The fact that the ILP supported candidates like Crook, participating in their election campaigns without attempting to spread the ILPs own distinctive socialist policies, could not fail to have an effect on the party's whole outlook. When its representatives won a seat, they had become so inured to back-pedalling, to expressing consensus politics, that they rarely, if ever, used their positions to campaign for socialism. Joe Burgess, one of the leaders of the Glasgow ILP, admitted the swing to the right:

> The recent record of the ILP had shown that, whatever it might have been at its early stages, whatever pugnacity it might have shown, and whatever its policy had been, it was now manifesting a desire to sink itself into, or be absorbed by, the great labour forces of the country.[30]

The drift of the ILP rightwards had repercussions on the SDF. Whatever appeal unity once possessed had now vanished. Insofar as the ILP looked for political allies, it sought them inside the Labour Representation Committee. At the same time, trade union officials also tended to turn their attention to the Labour Representation Committee, and consequently had become less susceptible to the blandishments of the SDF. Clearly, the tactic of Hyndman and the rest of the SDF leaders, of seeking unity with the ILP and union leaders, lay in ruins. While it would be wrong to blame the left-wingers inside the Federation for the débâcle, they could at least be said to have contributed to it. To Hyndman and his followers, they were 'impossibilists'. By their doctrinal insistence on socialist purity, they made it utterly impossible for the SDF either to win elections or even to secure worthwhile allies. Obviously, they would have to be expelled.

Hyndman and the Old Guard nominated the 23rd SDF annual conference, at Shoreditch Town Hall, on 10-12 April 1903, as the place of the execution. Before proceedings began, George S. Yates was informed that he was to be thrown out. Indeed, some of the Impossibilists, believing it might be forcibly done, brought along a contingent of Scottish workers, who sat at the back of the hall, silent and watchful, lest the gathering turn violent.[31] Yates was accused of obstructing left unity, failing to sell *Justice*, and writing an editorial for *The Socialist* which said that within the SDF there was 'a distinct tendency to alter the centre of their former revolutionary attitude over to opportunist tactics of the worst kind.'[32] Delegates thought this conduct inadmissible. They agreed to expulsion by 56 votes to six. The resolution also empowered the executive to expel, without the right of appeal, anybody endorsing Yates' views. For good measure, the conference went on to condemn the tone and content of *The Socialist*.[33]

Faced with this new situation, the left wingers held a series of private meetings. These revealed the existence of disagreements within their ranks. Most of the London group, distrustful of their Scottish brethren, had failed to back Yates at the Shoreditch conference. They claimed that the Scots had too often acted without consulting them, had been openly provocative to the SDF leadership, and largely had themselves to blame for the expulsions. Most of the London group, active in an area where many SDFers still remained to be persuaded of the validity of their policies, favoured continuing to work inside the SDF. On the other hand, the Impossibilists in Scotland had virtually captured the entire SDF organisation, such as it was, and they could see nothing would be gained from staying within the Federation. Each side failed to understand the other. Consequently, only a tiny fraction of the London comrades left the SDF along with the group around Yates.[34]

Back in Glasgow, preparations were quickly underway to form a new party. At meetings on 15 and 31 April 1903, the Scottish divisional council voted to disaffiliate from the SDF and hold the inaugural conference of the new party on 7 June 1903. In the meantime, much spadework needed to be done, holding public meetings, persuading people to support the new venture and increasing the circulation of *The Socialist*.

Two important statements of policy were made. The first, the *Socialist Labour Party: a Manifesto to the Working Class*, was written by John Carstairs Matheson and subsequently endorsed as a statement of official policy. He endeavoured to situate the new party in the political scene as well as providing it with a perspective. The Manifesto made four central points: first, that the working class was becoming increasingly disenchanted with existing political parties; second, that this arose because of their failure to do anything effectively to repel the ruthless attacks of the ruling class upon the workers; third, that consequently there was a need for a party to represent the working class; and, fourth, that for this to be successful the party had to favour Socialism.

Matheson went on to say what he meant by Socialism, giving a definition at variance with the one customarily coming from ILP and SDF circles:

By this we do not mean what is variously called 'State Socialism',

'Public Ownership' or 'Municipalism' — that is, the ownership of
certain public utilities by a community in which capitalism is still
dominant. A worker is as much exploited by a capitalist state or
corporation as by a private employer — as post office or municipal
employees can testify. We insist upon the political overthrow of
capitalism as an absolutely necessary preliminary to the emancipation of the working class. Otherwise an industry controlled by an
individual capitalist state differs from one controlled by an individual
capitalist only in the superior powers of the former to rob and
oppress those under its thraldom.[35]

The second important pronouncement came from James Connolly. In
the autumn of 1902, he went on a speaking tour of the United States.[36]
From his experiences, he wrote an article on 'The American Socialist
Labour Party of America and the London SDF' where he compared the
two organisations to the detriment of the latter. Connolly began by up-
braiding *Justice* for racialism: it had expressed 'much satisfaction' at
the recent Shoreditch SDF conference for 'dealing effectually with
those malcontents who are bent upon following the lead of the
German-Venezuelan Jew Loeb (or De Leon) to the pit of infamy and
disgrace.' This remark, retorted Connolly, was merely a continuation of
the anti-semitism displayed by *Justice* during the Boer War. Far from
being a pit of infamy and disgrace, De Leon led a party that had
achieved many things which the SDF had failed to do. The American
SLP had its own printing press, whereas the SDF had to rely upon one
which was privately owned. The American SLP had gained 53,000 votes
in a recent election while the SDF vote was invariably minute. Yet the
SDF, purporting to be independent, solicited support from the ILP in
parliamentary elections and pandered to the radicals. Moreover, the
SDF, reluctant to attack Labour politicians, had asked its branches to
refrain from criticising the Labour Representation Committee. All told,
it was clear that for Connolly the American SLP provided the paradigm
for what needed to be built in Britain.[37]

Disappointments met him when he returned to Britain. In the course
of the summer of 1903, one of the worst summers on record, Connolly
relentlessly trekked around Scotland, addressing dozens of meetings
each week. But his efforts yielded poor results. The inaugural conference was sparsely attended. Delegates came from Kirkcaldy, Dundee,
Edinburgh, Leith, Falkirk, Dunfermline and Glasgow. The lack of
support gave grounds for disquiet. As the business manager of *The
Socialist* pointed out, the journal did not pay its way. From March

1903, it had been printed on their own press in Edinburgh. Despite the resultant cost savings, *The Socialist*'s financial position was critical. Delegates agreed to a levy of each branch according to its membership.

Controversy at conference arose over the question of whether immediate demands should be included in the party programme. One reason why the majority of London Impossibilists remained within the SDF had been that they disagreed with the majority of the Scottish comrades on this subject. To the Londoners, the struggle for better educational facilities and welfare provisions were examples of an unfortunate lapse into reformism and had no place in a fully-fledged socialist programme. The Edinburgh comrades had the same view. They tried to convince conference, but most delegates realised the importance of the new party relating itself to the needs of the working class. Immediate demands had to be included if progress was to be made.

The decision showed how false the accusation of Hyndman and other critics happened to be. They depicted the Impossibilists as mere shadows of the American SLP, slavishly repeating whatever De Leon said. In fact, right from the outset Connolly and his comrades thought for themselves and asserted their political independence. The American SLP strongly proclaimed its opposition to immediate demands; this had no effect on the inaugural conference. Deviations from the American line often happened subsequently.

Delegates at the Edinburgh conference wished to dissociate themselves from the American SLP and hoped to indicate this by the title of the new party. But, as so frequently occurs in politics, they found themselves stuck with the name given by their opponents. Tom Bell, who attended the inaugural meeting, described in his autobiography how this happened:

> The question of the name of the new party required a little thought. We were anxious not to create the impression which the official SDF was trying to encourage, that we were only the tools of the American SLP. We thought of 'Republican Socialist Party', etc., etc. It was Connolly who, with characteristic directness proposed 'The Socialist Labour Party'. 'It doesn't matter what you call yourself,' he declared, 'you'll be dubbed the SLP anyway.' And SLP we became.[38]

On reflection, the choice did not seem too bad. They came to realise that it encapsulated their aims:

Socialist because through Socialism alone can the workers be emancipated;

Labour because by the labouring classes alone can Socialism be attained;

Party because we are not merely an educational or propagandist body but stand for the political expression of our class interests, for the formation of the Socialist Republic.[39]

As one wag at the conference said: 'Every man for the SLP and the De'il tak' the Hyndman.'[40]

Notes

1. Chuchichi Tsuzuki, 'The Impossibilist Revolt in Britain', *International Review of Social History* (1956), p. 383; James Joll, *The Second International* (1955), pp. 94-8.
2. Thomas Bell, *Pioneering Days* (1941), pp. 36-7.
3. *Edinburgh Evening News*, 4 May 1903.
4. *Justice*, 13 July 1901.
5. Engels' letter to Sorge, 12 May 1894, published in *Marx and Engels on Britain*, p. 536. Also *SDF 1896 Conference Report*, p. 18.
6. *The Socialist*, October 1904.
7. Colin Cross, *Philip Snowden* (1966), pp. 36-7.
8. Marx to Sorge, 15 December 1881, published in *Marx Engels Correspondence*, p. 397; Chuchichi Tsuzuki, *Hyndman and British Socialism* (Oxford, 1961), pp. 42-4.
9. Letter from Hyndman quoted in *The Socialist*, December 1904.
10. *The Socialist*, May 1903.
11. *Justice*, 20 July 1901; C. Tsuzuki, *Hyndman and British Socialism*, pp. 128-9; Bill Baker, 'The Social Democratic Federation and the Boer War', *Our History*, Summer 1974, pp. 10-11.
12. *The Socialist*, September 1902.
13. *SDF 1900 Conference Report*, p. 13.
14. *The Socialist*, January 1903.
15. *Justice*, 21 June 1902. The SDF executive sent an illuminated address to Edward VII.
16. *The Socialist*, August 1902.
17. Daniel De Leon's letter to W. Walker, 3 February 1898, in my possession.
18. James Connolly to the secretary, Edinburgh SDF, 1 November 1901, published in *Socialist Standard*, October 1973.
19. *Justice*, 24 January 1901.
20. Ibid, 10 August 1901.
21. C. Desmond Greaves, *The Life and Times of James Connolly* (1961), pp. 108-9; Samuel Levenson, *James Connolly* (1973), pp. 77-8.
22. C. Desmond Greaves, op. cit., p. 112.
23. *SDF 1903 Conference Report*, p. 25.
24. *The Socialist*, October 1902; Robert Blatchford, *Britain for the British*, p. 42.

25. *Manchester Guardian*, 23 September 1901.
26. *The Socialist*, January 1903.
27. Labour Representation Committee, *Report of Third Annual Conference*, Newcastle upon Tyne, 19 February 1903, p. 30.
28. Quoted *The Socialist*, April 1903.
29. George Haw, *The Life Story of Will Crooks MP* (1907), p. 195.
30. *Dunfermline Press*, 28 March 1903.
31. Leonard Cotton, 'The Socialist Labour Party of Great Britain: A Historical Sketch', *Weekly People*, 29 April 1950.
32. *SDF 1903 Conference Report*.
33. Ibid.
34. W.S. Jerman, 'The London Impossibilist Movement and the men who built it up', *The Socialist*, December 1906; Jack Fitzgerald, 'The SPGB: A Statement of Difference', *Socialist Standard*, August 1906.
35. *The Socialist*, May 1903; 'The Socialist Labour Party: a Manifesto to the Working Class' was reprinted later as a leaflet.
36. Manus O'Riordan, *Connolly in America* (Belfast, n.d.) published by the Irish Communist Organisation, contains a good account of Connolly's activities in the United States.
37. *The Socialist*, May 1903.
38. Thomas Bell, op. cit., pp. 40-1.
39. *The Socialist*, May 1903.
40. Ibid., August 1903.

2 PIONEERING DAYS

The infant SLP did not have an auspicious start in life. A weak and puny thing, it had hard struggles to survive. *The Socialist*, begun with a princely capital of £11 13s, swallowed most of the scanty funds.[1] Its circulation, a mere 1,400 copies, obstinately refused to rise. In some places sales dropped because the circle of sympathisers diminished. There were people who would buy *The Socialist* when published by a group of SDFers but refused after it had become the organ of a new party. Likewise some members had difficulty in making a similar adjustment. The SLP thought it would initially have a membership of around 200. This calculation was based on the assumption that, since the left had gained control of the SDFs Scottish district council, the membership would transfer its allegiance *en bloc*. But it failed to occur. The Scottish district council reflected the more active, more articulate, section of the SDF; the less active, not well acquainted with the causes of the split, tended to keep their traditional loyalty. These people remained in the Federation and, along with some branches that had stopped attending the Scottish divisional council as long as it stayed under the sway of the left, they succeeded in partially reviving the SDF in Scotland after the split. As a result, instead of having the anticipated 200, the SLP found itself with, at most, only 80 members.[2]

The size of the membership was not the only problem. The SLP faced severe geographical and occupational limitations. Almost entirely, supporters came from engineering trades in Central Scotland. This necessarily meant reaching political conclusions on restricted experience and trying to plot the way ahead for the British working class, with whom contact was highly tenuous. A further handicap was that the SLP membership was young and inexperienced. Few of them possessed any idea of how to build a new political party. Their inexperience and lack of tactical finesse may have been responsible for them reaping such a meagre harvest from three years factional struggle in the SDF.

In addition, the SLP was weakened by the absence from its ranks of middle-class intellectuals. At first, this may appear a good thing, making it genuinely a working-class party. This, however, overlooks an important point: the stage of development reached by British socialists at the beginning of the twentieth century. They spent most of their time in propaganda activity, spreading the socialist message, rather than in direct involvement in the class struggle. The talents most required were the abilities to speak and write fluently, qualities more frequently found among middle- than working-class people. But the deficiency could have had an even more grievous effect on the SLPs theoretical progress than on its propaganda work. For workers, being compelled to use most of their time and effort on daily toil, were not well placed to study, to formulate new ideas, or to write books like *Capital*. Karl Marx devoted most of his life to developing socialist theory — a thing workers, because of their position in society, could not do. Neither Marx, originally aspiring to be a lawyer, nor Engels, a mill owner's son, was a horny-handed son of toil, and the same was true of most Socialist theoreticians. As Lenin, himself a lawyer, acknowledged in his pamphlet *What is to be done?*, the role of such middle-class intellectuals was to transmit socialist ideas to the proletariat. That the SLP did not have any individuals to perform this function was a severe handicap. It was particularly so in view of the state of the British Left at that time. Operating within the empirical tradition, socialists generally shunned theory, spending their time on so-called practical activity, which achieved little. Even those who realised the inadequacy of the prevailing attitude could do little about it: very few of the socialist classics were available in English.

The SLP sought to remedy the situation. It became the distributor for Charles Kerr & Co, of Chicago, and the New York Labor Publishing Company, which were printing, for the first time in English, large quantities of socialist material. As well as basic texts by Marx and Engels, the writings of Kautsky, Labriola, Plekhanov and many other left-wing thinkers were made available in handy-sized editions. The SLP augmented the flow by printing cheap pamphlets. Their production, given the SLPs limited resources involved much sacrifice and ingenuity. Print workers freely gave their labour while materials were begged or, to put it euphemistically, 'borrowed'. One SLP veteran describes in his memoirs how costs were reduced almost to vanishing point:

> I was assured that they really paid for the printing ink; and they went through the motions of paying for their printing-paper, or some of it. If the man in charge of despatch at the paper-warehouse made a mistake and sent 10 reams where only one was invoiced — accidents will happen, and the incident should not necessarily be attributed to the fact that the despatcher and invoice-clerk was a member of the SLP.[3]

The accessibility of theoretical work stimulated educational activity.
The SLP took this task exceedingly seriously. The aim was to create
worker-intellectuals, socialists able to state their case irrespective of
the company in which they found themselves. Through the study of
books produced by socialist thinkers elsewhere in the world, the Party
could overcome, to a large extent, the lack of theoreticians within its
own ranks. Ideas were highly mobile. They could be used in Britain
even though written in other parts. In a sense, it was international
socialists benefitting from their internationalism.

One of the thinkers who had the greatest influence upon the SLP
was the American, De Leon. Although sometimes marred by sectarian
rigidity, his works had the advantage of being highly readable and easy
to understand. He also needs to be credited, although this is often forgotten, with developing new concepts. One of these was that he understood, far better than most of his contemporaries, the role of social
democracy. In a period when socialists belonged to the Second International, De Leon saw that its parties had an essentially stabilising
effect on the social system. While they sometimes expressed workers'
grievances, they were careful to do so in a manner that did not
challenge the existing power structure; protest movements were
diverted into channels that made them harmless, not a threat to the
capitalist state. De Leon, who advanced this theory in his pamphlet,
Two Pages from Roman History, described the leaders of this kind of
organisation as 'the labour lieutenants of capitalism'. From his analysis,
a corollary necessarily followed: if social democratic parties would
never establish a socialist society and if a socialist society were to be
established, it would first require the creation of a revolutionary
party to act as capitalism's executioner.

De Leon's vision extended to the question of how the struggle for
socialism could be best furthered. He strongly advocated industrial
unionism. He saw this as a means of breaking down craft and sectional
barriers, which divided worker from worker, and exerting the maximum
united pressure upon the capitalists. At the same time, De Leon
envisaged industrial unions playing a vital role in the creation of a
socialist society. He thought they would be used as the instruments
whereby workers not only controlled and ran industry but also saw the
political system operated in their interests. When eventually, in 1919,
Lenin read De Leon's writings for the first time he expressed himself
'amazed to see how far and how early De Leon pursued the same train
of thought as the Russians. His theory that representation should be by
industries, not by areas, was already the germ of the Soviet system.'[4]

The startling percipience of De Leon largely went unrecognised by his contemporaries. The reason was that he remained cut off from the mainstream of socialist politics. The American SLP, to which he belonged, was dominated by émigrés, many of whom did not speak English and therefore had no influence on the average US worker. But De Leon's ideas had a much greater impact when they were expounded in a different context. What had been of little or no consequence when set forth by German émigrés in America had entirely different consequences when Clydeside engineers proclaimed them in Scotland.

But the British SLP did not learn De Leon's writings by rote and apply them mechanically; rather they were used as a tool of analysis, to be improved and developed wherever possible. On his first point, the role of the Labour Leadership, the SLP found little difficulty in furnishing British examples to illustrate De Leon's argument. *The Socialist* inveighed against Arthur Henderson, the opponent of the eight-hour day, Will Thorne, the advocate of using soldiers against strikers in Ireland, David Shackleton, the supporter of child labour, and countless others. These were easy targets for the SLP because of the ideological weakness of the Labour Party. What was more difficult was to expose the apostasy of other social democratic parties, which tried to conceal their backslidings beneath a fog of socialist rhetoric. The SLP had no inhibitions about attacking the inadequacies of the leaders of the French Socialist Party in general and adding a caustic comment about Jean Longuet in particular.

> Mr. Longuet is a thoroughly self-satisfied gentleman, who evidently has some vague notion in his cerebellum that he is entitled to rank as Caliph of the International Socialist Movement in virtue of his descent from Karl Marx. The descent is tremendously precipitous, in fact.[5]

Nor did the German Social Democratic Party emerge unscathed. The SLP remained unimpressed when it secured three million votes in the 1903 general election. 'Their mere mass of constantly increasing support at the polls,' *The Socialist* declared, 'is the most dangerous ground that a revolutionary party can accept: the lumping of opinion and diversity of interest is, to our mind, the beginning of the undoing of German Socialism.' Observing the presence at SDP congresses of 'a large and seemingly growing section who have declared in favour of the most moderate and bourgeois-like minds amongst them', the journal reached the conclusion that 'the party has become a ghost of its former

self . . . the German socialist party has ceased to be revolutionary and
has become reformatory.'[6]

Interestingly, *The Socialist*'s criticism aroused a response from Dr
Robert Michels, who wrote:

> The need for a revolutionary spirit in the German Party is great. I
> and others are striving to create that spirit; the parliamentarianism
> of the party and the tactics of the past have so tied its hands that
> one feels its energy is being to a great extent run to earth and
> wasted.[7]

Of course, Dr Michels ultimately despaired of transforming the German
SDP into a revolutionary party. He expressed his demoralisation in his
famous book on political parties, where he enunciated the iron law of
oligarchy.[8]

The overwhelming majority of socialists in the world, blinded by
the high prestige in which the German Social Democratic Party was
held, failed to accept the diagnosis of the SLP and Dr Michels. This was
not surprising. Frederick Engels had written in glowing terms about the
German Social Democratic Party's progress; Rosa Luxemburg had
described 'the organisational jewel of the class-conscious proletariat';
Lenin said it had been the foremost party of the Second International,
the organisation that socialist parties in other countries attempted to
model themselves on.[9] The traumatic moment of truth came on 4
August 1914, when German Social Democratic deputies voted in the
Reichstag for War Credits. So distressed by this was Rosa Luxemburg
that for a while she contemplated committing suicide. Such was Lenin's
confidence in the SDP that he thought the issue of the party journal,
Vorwarts, was a forgery, produced by the German general staff.

By contrast, the SLPs understanding was superior. It would have
thought *Vorwarts* a forgery had it *not* reported the Social Democrats
supporting the German ruling class in the conflict. Likewise, when the
less well-publicised event occurred in the British Parliament on 6
August 1914, where pacifist Members of Parliament and Will Thorne,
the solitary MP claiming to be a Marxist, did nothing to oppose the
Government's legislation for war expenditure, again it came as no surprise to the SLP:

> The failure of the International Socialist Movement is the direct out-
> come of its leaders and thinkers having forsaken the revolutionary
> traditions of Socialism. Revisionism has eaten out the heart and

softened the brain of the Movement. Men of the type of Hardie and
MacDonald had gained a controlling influence.[10]

Clearly, the SLP was among the first to see the need for an organisational and ideological split from social democracy. Of course, once the
various sections of the Second International had supported their respective capitalist classes, Lenin too saw the bankruptcy of social democracy
and called for the building of a new international.

Although there were obvious differences, the British SLP and the
Bolsheviks shared many characteristics in common. Both of them had
an avowedly revolutionary outlook, believing that socialism could only
come after the capitalist state had been smashed. And both realised
that this could only be done once a revolutionary party had been
created. Although the SLP did not use the term 'the vanguard party',
it envisaged this as being the role the party would play. Spokesmen
emphasised the need for members to gain the experience and knowledge
so they could lead, when the time came, workers in the class struggle:

> In all revolutionary movements, as in the storming of fortresses,
> the thing depends upon the head of the column – upon the
> minority that is so intense in its convictions, so soundly based on its
> principles, so determined in its action, that it carries the masses with
> it, storms the breastwork and captures the fort.[11]

Likening itself to a crack fighting unit, the SLP saw there would be
dangers in accumulating large numbers of members, people with scanty
knowledge who only partially agreed with the party's principle. To
adopt that path might lead in the short run to more influence; at the
same time, it would make the party fat and flabby, incapable of functioning as the vanguard. As one SLPer put it, milk does not improve
by dilution. So, frankly, the SLP did not attempt to hide its minuteness:

> The SLP has never sought to exaggerate its numbers. Numerically,
> it is probably the smallest political organisation in Great Britain. In
> point of principle, tactics, knowledge of goal, and the way to reach
> it, it is the strongest.[12]

Other left organisations, like the ILP and SDF, might have more members, yet, lacking firm theoretical foundations, they offered 'a spectacle
of internal bickering in comparison with which Donnybrook Fair and
the Kilkenny cats would be a picture of sweet harmony and concord.'

But the Socialist Labour Party, as it stated in its declaration, *The SLP:
Its Aims and Method*, understood that nothing of lasting significance
could be accomplished by groups torn with internal strife:

> A party which has undertaken the work of revolutionising society
> must be dominated not only by a common purpose but also a
> common plan of action. Artemus Ward, writing at the time of the
> American Civil War, talked about organising a regiment for the field
> of conflict in which every soldier was a Brigadier General. A revo-
> lutionary socialist party, which is engaged in a much more serious
> conflict, must present not only the appearance but the reality of an
> intelligent disciplined unity.[13]

How did the SLP seek to attain this objective? It maintained that
decisions had to be reached by the normal democratic processes, so
power ultimately rested with the membership. However, once a
decision had been reached, every party member's duty was to see to it
being carried out. Anybody who did not do this, irrespective of the
position he might hold, was certain to be expelled. Membership, regarded as an honour and a privilege, could easily be lost through failure
to keep the exacting standards expected. The SLPs history is strewn
with instances of discipline being imposed: Douall, the Edinburgh
engineer, although responsible for first establishing links with De Leon,
was not permitted to join the SLP because he was a drunkard; Neil
Maclean, the general secretary, was expelled in 1908 when he failed to
abide by the party policy on unemployment; and George Yates, despite
playing such an important part in forming the SLP, was expelled when
he fell behind with his subscriptions. (Actually, this was caused by his
moving from Glasgow to Teesside, and he rejoined once he had settled
down in Middlesbrough.[14]) Nevertheless, these examples reveal that the
rules were applied with strict impartiality to all members.

In many respects, the SLP employed methods similar to the
Bolsheviks. Both were striving to build groups of professional revolutionaries. Like Lenin, the SLP insisted it carried no passengers: everyone, as a condition of membership, had to be active with the organisation. When, for example, one of the founder-members, William Walker,
took a job where he would be unable to participate in SLP activities, he
was immediately thrown out. High subscription rates, plus frequent
levies, also tended to drive away those who did not have a 100 per cent
commitment.

To outsiders, not understanding the rigorous requirements involved in building a revolutionary party, the conduct of the SLP — expelling members right, left and centre when it had so few already — appeared the height of stupidity. Equally wrong seemed the SLP expectation of such a considerable intellectual grasp of socialist principles before it would permit a person to join, and cynics suggested that as a consequence the party adopted the attitude expressed in the Calvinist Hymn:

> We are the pure, selected few,
> And all the rest are damned!
> There's room enough in Hell for you —
> We don't want heaven crammed!

But the SLP would defend itself by turning to history:

> In previous revolutions the party which engineered the transition, which carried through the revolution at its crucial state, was often, though not always, the smallest of the revolutionary parties in its origin. In no case do we find the faction that effected the transformation of society to have predominated in numbers until the very eve of the revolution.[15]

A subsidiary reason was that the Party had the concept of the long haul. Not believing that socialism would come overnight, introduced by parliamentary legislation or some miraculous change of heart, the SLP envisaged a lengthy preparatory period. James Connolly sometimes compared its position to that of John the Baptist, who prepared the way for the Messiah he never expected to see.[16] Anticipating a slow tempo of development, the SLP realised it would be some time before there was much hope of influencing events; what was required in this initial stage was to make the preliminary preparations, laying the basis upon which the struggle for socialism could be successfully carried out at some future date.

In the SLPs opinion, the immediate need was for educational and propaganda work. It was to these ends that the Party directed its energy. The typical branch, consisting of a handful of dedicated individuals, would spend its time on the three Ss of socialist campaigning — studying, selling the paper and soapbox oratory. Let us examine how these were done:

Studying

Education took a number of forms. James Connolly used to like to give students newspaper cuttings. They had to comment on them, analysing them from a socialist viewpoint without having much time for thought. This, it was hoped, promoted the ability in arguments with political opponents to deal, off the cuff, with any new points that were introduced. The same knack might also be encouraged by another technique of Connolly's — getting members to make mock-speeches in front of other members, who would be expected to heckle.[17]

Besides these, classes of a much more theoretical kind would take place as well. In a series of weekly meetings, a subject would be studied in a serious and systematic manner, differing from the average university course only in the general outlook adopted. A detailed account of how the classes were run is contained in Chapter Five, where Tom Bell's description of the SLPs educational activities in Glasgow is quoted.[18] Clearly students took their studies seriously. Attendance registers reveal remarkably few absences. Students purchased impressive quantities of literature, as surviving records of class literature secretaries show, so that they could continue their studies at home.[19] Frequently, at the end of a course students were expected to sit a written examination, which could contain formidable questions.

But however esoteric the concepts learnt, the SLP tried to relate them to practice. Every effort was made to translate them into language understandable to other workers. Knowledge was not acquired for its own sake; it was for use as a weapon in the class struggle. The Glasgow class applied this principle by holding regular open-air public meetings after it had finished its studies.[20]

Soapbox oratory

Before the First World War was the Golden Age of Soapbox Oratory. Workers normally had little money to spend. The tub-thumping orator provided light relief in Britain before the mass entertainment industry developed.

Recognising that this situation gave the Party an opportunity to put its message to large numbers of people, the SLP encouraged all its branches to hold regular outdoor meetings. It issued advice, some of which now seems rather comical, on how they should be organised. First, the branch should form a propaganda committee. Then it should find a site 'wherever wage slaves congregate', although the proviso was added that 'it was useless going to slum districts as the people there seem to be hopeless.' The meeting could be opened by a song, but it hastened to add, somewhat ominously, that 'unless the singers have a knowledge of harmony, it is not good.' Then the chairman should open the meeting, give the name of the branch, call upon the speaker, and then draw attention to the literature available. Next should come the collection, followed by questions, which should be answered courteously. 'But should any "fakir, freak or fool" dare to cast ridicule on our Party or our principles, then the speaker should wade in and annihilate him, as a street crowd always like to see a "smart" chap get taken down.'[21]

Street-corner oratory could have its problems. Sometimes difficulties were experienced in getting the initial crowd to stop and listen. One speaker in Liverpool used to overcome this by shouting, at the top of his voice: 'I've been robbed! I've been robbed!' Quickly, an inquisitive audience would assemble, and he would explain how the thieves were the capitalists.[22] But, even after acquiring a crowd, there was still the question of holding it, particularly if an amateur comedian decided to set up in competition. In his organiser's report, William Paul cited an instance where this happened:

At Accrington on Wednesday, I addressed an audience of about 800 for about 40 minutes. This splendid meeting was broken up by the opening of another meeting under the auspices of an individual known as Peter Pan. By dint of continuing speaking, we gradually won our audience back by question-time.[23]

The secret of street-corner oratory was to speak in an attractive, clear and simple manner. An old campaigner explained this to Frank Budgen after he had made his first faltering attempt on a soapbox:

For Christ sake,' he said, 'next time you give 'em the blood and the shot of the working class, lay off all that stuff about emancipation, and alienation. Any word ending in —ation (unless it's fornication) makes 'em glassy-eyed and very sad. Make a joke about Joe Chamberlain's orchid or Chaplin's three acres and a cow for every-body.'[24]

Public speaking could be a hazardous occupation. At any moment, violent interruptions could come from the police, rival political groups or from hecklers. Knowing how to deal with these threats, learning how to express political opinions with forceful clarity, was a hard, but never-theless necessary, process in the development of revolutionary leaders.

Many of those who led the revolt on the Clyde graduated through this tough university of the streets. Whatever the opposition, they remained cool and effective.

In dealing with such people, the authorities frequently discovered they had taken on more than they had bargained for. Take, for example, the case of Muir and Mitchell, charged with holding an illegal meeting at Bridgeton Cross. The prosecutor, expecting it to be an easy case to win, called no witnesses except policemen. But he had not reckoned with Johnny Muir who, as *The Socialist* said, wished to prove the truth of W.S. Gilbert's assertion that a policeman's lot is not a happy one:

> Comrade Muir opened the defence for the SLP by asking to be permitted to examine the fiscal. This demand scandalised the legal gentlemen in court, who informed the audacious requester that such a preposterous proceeding would be illegal. Unabashed, Comrade Muir addressed the court in a speech as logical as it was eloquent, which admitted that the SLP caused their opponents some annoyance. 'Hundreds of meetings were held there. Why had the promoters of these meetings not been arrested for obstruction? Why during the election times were men who perchance were now seated on the magistrates' benches allowed to hold large public meetings and, aye, with police protection?'
>
> The case was dismissed.[25]

On another occasion in Glasgow, the Conservatives unwisely held a meeting on 'The Fallacies of Socialism', but did not permit any questions. An SLPer mounted the rostrum:

> After having failed to throw the SLPer off the platform, they put the lights out, thus compelling the large audience to leave the hall. Outside the hall, a large and enthusiastic audience, numbering about a thousand, was addressed by the SLPer who had been refused discussion.[26]

Customarily, however, the disruption of meetings was the other way round — it was socialist meetings that were attacked by people who disagreed with them. In 1901, James Connolly was unable to continue speaking in Oxford, when assailed by a band of undergraduates and unemployed. Then they pursued Connolly through the town, throwing stones at him while he retaliated by laying four of them out with the flagpole to which the red flag had been attached. The police intervened.[27] One consequence was that Leonard Cotton, Connolly's main supporter, lost his job as a gardener. He had already served a month's

imprisonment because he broke Manchester Corporation's bye-law
relating to public meetings, and his employer, Oxford Botanical
Gardens, refused to tolerate the new bout of unwelcome publicity.[28]

The Oxford incident was far from being isolated. According to T.A.
Jackson, whose political activities were largely centred on London,
meetings were frequently disrupted. He claimed, perhaps with some
exaggeration, that 'it was often necessary for the "chairman" to silence
rowdy interrupters by laying-out one or two per meeting.'[29] But most
of the trouble was caused by left-wingers belonging to rival groups. Of
these Moses Baritz, for a long time a member – indeed, the only
member – of the Manchester Branch of the Socialist Party of Great
Britain, could undoubtedly claim to be the supreme genius at the art of
wrecking meetings. Although his appearance resembled that of a dirty,
disreputable tramp, fallen upon hard times, he was actually the distinguished music critic of the *Manchester Guardian*. His technique was
disconcertingly simple. Placing himself near the rostrum, Moses waited
for the speaker to make a point. Then, as if talking to himself, he would
shout, 'Tripe! Rotten Tripe! Bloody awful stinking tripe!' And then he
would spit on the floor. 'A few repetitions of this,' according to
Jackson, 'would shake the nerve of all but the very stoutest; and in the
discussion which followed Moses would say it all over again with a
volubility matched only by his dogmatism and his total disregard for
the feelings of everybody.'

Moses Baritz's greatest triumph was the wrecking of a meeting of
H.M. Hyndman. The Manchester and Salford SDF had hoped it would
be a splendid occasion. The Federation's new hall, to be known as the
Hyndman Hall, was to be officially opened by the great man himself
and, to prevent unseemly incidents, undesirables were barred from the
proceedings. But the SDF had not calculated for the resourcefulness of
Moses:

> There was a ventilating shaft which opened just above the platform,
> where the speaker stood. Unperceived Moses climbed to the roof,
> and to the ventilator, so that when Old Man Hyndman – who had
> been rapturously received – rose to speak, Moses put his clarinet
> to his lips and provided an obligato-accompaniment to the oratory.
>
> 'Mr. Chairman!' said Hyndman – and 'Squark, squark!' came
> down the ventilator.
>
> The old man was puzzled, but tried to get going. Moses responded
> with a succession of the most obscenely bestial noises ever emitted
> by a musical instrument. And, in short, in two minutes a deputation
> was offering Moses a front seat, if only he'd shut up and come down![30]

There may have been only one Moses Baritz, but many others possessed similar qualities of dogmatism, crankiness and intolerance. Abuse was liberally sprinkled around on the left. Keir Hardie was called 'Queer Hardie', H.M. Hyndman became 'Hairy M. Hyndman', and Philip Snowden was 'the self-styled Saint Paul of the Labour Movement'. Occasionally, mutual animosity spilled over into violence.[31]

Hostility arose because the various parties were competing fiercely with each other. In that period, very few workers were attracted by left-wing ideas. When one group made a member, it robbed the rest of a potential recruit. As a consequence, the rivals tended to emphasise their differences, extolling their own virtues while degenerating the efforts of the others.

Selling

The sale of the various socialist journals, which took up such a large amount of the time of left-wingers in those days, simply served to reinforce divisive tendencies. Each group had its own periodical. Production often involved members in considerable personal sacrifices, and so it was important to believe that your particular journal was making a unique contribution. The SLP required from its members a levy of 18 shillings in the year 1907 to cover the deficit arising from the Press fund.[32] When it is remembered that many unskilled workers then only received 16 shillings a week, and SLP members were expected to pay the levy on top of a hefty monthly subscription of one shilling and sixpence, the size of the expected commitment can be judged. It is an indication of the great store placed upon maintaining the journal because it functioned as an organiser. Neil Maclean, in one sales drive, declared: 'Everyone who purchases *The Socialist* is a prospective member of the SLP.' The average branch would be out selling on a door-to-door basis at least once a week, as well as at work and in trade unions. One of the main places where they could be sold was at public meetings, both of the SLP and of other parties. In this manner, *The Socialist*'s circulation rose slowly and with expenditure of much effort. By 1907 it had reached 3,000 copies a month and two years later had gone up to 4,000.[33]

These figures may appear unimpressive, but it should be remembered that other literature was sold as well. The American *Weekly People*, bigger and appearing more frequently then *The Socialist*, devoted much space to British affairs. Most SLP members and supporters read it regularly. Then there was the SLPs production of pamphlets, which had a big impact on the political scene. For the first time, Marxist ideas reached a sizeable section of the British working class. Usually produced in editions of 10,000 copies and sold for a penny, these pamphlets had considerable influence. In his chairman's address to the 1916 SLP conference, Tom Bell rightly told delegates:

> There had been a change in the attitude of the movement towards scientific socialism and its founders. The name of Karl Marx was no longer derided nor his teaching despised. The terms 'class consciousness', 'class struggle', 'price of labour power', etc., were no longer treated with contempt . . . The SLP was entitled to credit for this.[34]

In a country with a strong empirical tradition, where people were prone to eschew theoretical questions, this was no mean achievement. It was accomplished against tremendous odds.

From the outset, the SLP possessed inadequate resources, making it impossible to function effectively. Lack of funds compelled the Party to dispense with its full-time organiser. This was a grievous loss. In an organisation composed almost entirely of youngsters, James Connolly provided valuable knowledge and experience. Indeed, as Tom Bell explained in his memoirs, it was built by him and around him:

> Connolly never demurred to speak anywhere or at any time. In this connection, I think he was shamelessly exploited by us. We had not yet trained many speakers — that was to come — and I have known him to do as many as twelve meetings in one week apart from his literary work.[35]

For many weeks, Connolly failed to receive his full wage. Party members would have a whip round, collecting coppers and sixpenny bits to hand to him. But he could not hope to keep his wife and six children on what he received. He decided, therefore, to emigrate to the United States.

In the same month as Connolly sailed from Glasgow — September 1904 — the SLP suffered a second setback. George S. Yates resigned from the editorship of *The Socialist*. He had found the job quite a strain for some time, since he had been doing it on top of his full-time professional job as a designer, which frequently involved him working well into the night. Combining the two tasks, however, became an impossibility when the Glasgow contract was completed and his firm moved him to Teesside. Unable to keep in close, regular contact with what was happening nationally inside the SLP, he necessarily dropped out of the leadership.[36]

As a result of Connolly and Yates leaving Glasgow, control of the
organisation devolved upon younger, more inexperienced members,
also working in their spare time. The most important of these were
Neil Maclean, an engineer at Singer's Clydebank factory, who became
general secretary, and John Carstairs Matheson, the Falkirk school-
teacher, who edited *The Socialist*. They were helped by an Executive
Committee selected from members of the Edinburgh and Leith
branches in order to save travelling expenses. When the SLP membership grew, this body was augmented by a National Executive Committee, which had four members and met quarterly. In theory, the EC was
supposed to deal with day-to-day matters and to be subordinate to the
NEC, which determined broad, general issues of policy. These arrangements proved to be unsatisfactory. At criticial times, the Party lacked
firm leadership. The Edinburgh branch, probably the most sectarian
and least representative, was liable to come into conflict with the
National Executive Committee, particularly as the roles of the EC and
and NEC had not been clearly defined. Problems arose from having to
operate on a shoe-string.

In those early days, the SLP continued propaganda work — the three
Ss of speaking, studying and selling — which brought in small, modest
returns. Rarely did anything happen to enliven the routine. In 1904, a
speaking tour of Daniel De Leon heightened interest. He addressed
three well attended meetings in Scotland, at Falkirk, Edinburgh and
Glasgow. His London meeting was marred by an unpleasant incident.
When De Leon criticised 'the Labour lieutenants of capitalism', Jim
Connell, author of the 'Red Flag', charged the platform and had to be
restrained by Cotton, Geis, Jerman and Pope. [37] Notwithstanding this
interruption, the audience was generally impressed by De Leon's 'rare
talent of being able to expound Marxist doctrine in the language of
the market-place.'[38]

De Leon's visit came as he was returning from the Second International Congress at Amsterdam, where the main issue remained the
controversy over the Kautsky resolution passed by the Paris Congress
four years earlier. Backed by Rosa Luxemburg, Plekhanov and others,
De Leon attempted to get delegates to rescind their previous decision.
The German Social Democrats, the most influential delegation, pro-
pounded a formula that combined verbal opposition to joining coalition
governments with the underlying principles of acceptance. De Leon
likened the Germans' attitude to that of a priest who, confronted by a
wife, badly beaten by her husband, agreed that the husband has a right

to hit his wife but thought he had taken it too far.[39] Despite his reservations, once his own resolution had been defeated, De Leon voted for the German resolution. He argued that this was the lesser evil: the alternative to the German resolution of verbal condemnation of Millerandism was no criticism at all.

The British SLP sent a delegation to the Amsterdam Congress consisting of Thomas Drummond, Charles Geddes, Andrew Ferrier, J.C. Matheson and Charles Haddow. They operated within the conference until the third day. Then the International Bureau introduced a new method of verifying credentials: each national group had to determine precisely who would be its representatives, entitled to cast its two votes, which were given to each national group regardless of size. As the new ruling would have meant the British SLP being submerged within the much larger British delegation, it decided not to submit to the new procedure. Instead, it issued a public statement to gain maximum publicity for its own policies. The SLP declared that it was farcical for the British delegation to have men like Shackleton, an advocate of child labour and avowedly anti-socialist, sitting as accredited delegates. For Congress to permit this to happen was a sign of the lack of serious socialist commitment: non-socialists were determining socialist policy.

Also at the Amsterdam Congress, and taking the same attitude as the SLP, were representatives of the other wing of the Impossibilist Movement. Although resolving to remain in the SDF and fight the Hyndmanite leadership, they had discovered that the Federation's leadership would not tolerate such conduct. After two leading members of the tendency — J. Fitzgerald and H. Hawkins — had been expelled, it was decided that the other critics should leave the SDF to form their own party. The Socialist Party of Great Britain held its inaugural meeting at the Printers' Hall, Fetter Lane, London, on 12 June 1904. It denounced the SDF as undemocratic and riddled with reformism.[40]

Many of the criticisms levelled at the SDF by the SPGB were the same as those of the SLP, and it may appear strange that this other wing of the Impossibilists felt the need to create their own independent organisation. There were, however, disagreements. Personal feuds, which in small groups sometimes assume disproportionate importance, had embittered relations. As we have already seen in Chapter One, most of the London groups were angered by the Scottish group's failure to keep them fully informed during the factional dispute inside the SDF in 1902-3. But the Scottish group also had criticisms of leading personalities in the London group. According to Matheson, before Alex

Anderson absconded from Edinburgh with all the funds of *The Socialist*,
he put the 'poor, little Pearson girl' in the maternity hospital.[41]
Connolly had been equally scathing about Con Lehane, who was
appointed general secretary of the SPGB. According to Connolly, he
left Ireland after the Bishop of Cork had denounced him. When Connolly
accused him of being a deserter, Lehane replied that he could change
his residence whenever he liked. 'I answered,' Connolly told Matheson,
'that he had, but when a man at the head of a regiment made up his
mind to change his residence at the moment the enemy attacked, he
was usually called by a very ugly name.'[42]

Underlying this personal animosity lay disagreements about fundamental principles. The SPGB was not attracted by the ideas of James
Connolly or Daniel De Leon. It believed that greater attention should
be paid to electoral activity, whereas the SLP related itself primarily to
the industrial struggle. Also, the SPGB thought a socialist programme
should contain no immediate demands: rather than try to improve
conditions under the existing system, all energies should be devoted to
its overthrow.

Among the SLPs ranks, there were those who supported the SPGB
line on immediate demands. At the inaugural conference, the
Edinburgh branch tried unsuccessfully to move the deletion of all
immediate demands from the programme. It tried again at the next
conference, only to be beaten by eight votes to four. The majority of
members believed in making a distinction between reforms and palliatives. Palliatives were defined as legislative measures introduced by the
government to give greater stability to capitalism, and therefore should
be opposed. Reforms, on the other hand, helped to improve the lot for
workers under capitalism, and therefore should be supported:

> Reforms are like patching a worn out boot. Nevertheless, the SLP
> recognises and always makes clear that by whatever measures the
> workers may be able, even temporarily and in a small degree, to
> resist the inevitably increasing powers of exploitation of their
> masters, such measures have the full and wholehearted support of
> the SLP.[43]

Encapsulated within the SLP attitude was confusion that subsequently
led to theoretical dispute. The distinction between palliatives and
reforms frequently cannot be made. Legislation may be introduced
which not only improves the workers' lot but also gives greater stability
to the existing system.

But there is no doubt that the SLPs attitude to reforms gave it a relevance, as well as a socialist content, that other parties lacked. In local government elections, SPGB candidates monotonously intoned that the answer to each and every problem was the introduction of socialism. The SLP candidates, while arguing for socialism, still put forward demands with immediate relevance. The 1903 election manifesto began by stating the limitations of local councils:

> Fellow workers, we do not expect to be able, within the limits of a single municipality, to stamp out the cause of your poverty and toilsome life; all we can expect to do is to ease the pressure of wage-slavery, pending the entire overthrow of capitalism. Our candidate, therefore, if elected, would press forward in the teeth of all opposition such measures as would tend to brighten the existence of the army of toilers.[44]

It went on to give the SLPs policy: Council houses 'to be let at the cost of construction and maintenance'; a minimum wage for council employees of 30 shillings; the right of all council employees to an eight-hour day and to appoint their immediate superiors; the provision of free school meals; public works programme to relieve local unemployment; and the provision of relief for workers involved in industrial disputes.

These are the kinds of demands the SLP advanced annually at local elections. It provided a platform from which to express the Party's programme, an opportunity to show that its policies were different from those of other political organisations. The SLP measured its success not by the number of votes for its candidates but in terms of members made and increased circulation for *The Socialist*.

While the SLPs aim was to raise class consciousness, the vast majority of Labour and socialist councillors saw their role in an entirely different light. They acted with propriety, doing nothing to stir up discontent, but showing that they could be relied upon to behave responsibly when administering a small segment of capitalism. To the SLP, this approach was anathema. It denounced George Lansbury when, at London East End Board of Guardians, he moved that a trade union delegation be not received because it was trying to intimidate the Board. Similarly, the SLP attacked A.T. Wrampliney, another SDF London councillor, for opposing the suggestion that all council workmen should have a minimum wage of 30 shillings a week on the grounds that it would send the local authorities' estimates awry. It also criticised

ILPers on Musselburgh council, who did not support a strike by council workmen for higher pay. Corporation employees, they argued, should not have 25 shillings but make do with 21. One ILP councillor went so far as to argue that twopence an hour was the right rate for scavengers.[45]

Involvement in local politics loomed larger while the SLP was in its initial phase. The tempo of the class struggle remained slow, and there was little else to do. So long as industrial peace prevailed, the SLP could have no impact within factories. Even so, two events happened in 1905 that confirmed the correctness of emphasising industrial work. Although neither occurred in Britain, they still served as guidelines for British socialists. The first was the founding of the Industrial Workers of the World in America; the other was the 1905 Russian Revolution.

From the Russian experience, the SLP gained two lessons. First, it confirmed its views on the vital necessity of having strong cadres, capable of giving a lead at the decisive moment. *The Socialist* declared: 'Revolutionaries must be the greatest self-sacrificers – witness Russia.'[46] And, second, the profound difficulty encountered by Tsarism in re-capturing control showed what an important part industrial organisation could play in the conquest of power.

The formation of the Industrial Workers of the World, 'the Wobblies', showed how a new type of organisation could liberate dormant class forces, unleashing a new form of struggle against the capitalists and for a new society. The IWW broke down craft barriers, recruiting workers from any and every industry, regardless of skill, sex or race, into one big industrial union. It was, to a large extent, a reaction to the long-established American Federation of Labour, which only organised the better paid and more highly skilled. Besides rebelling against the AF of L's aristocratic exclusiveness, the Wobblies disagreed with its deeply-ingrained conservatism: to the Wobblies, the fight for better conditions was inextricably linked to the fight for revolution. At its inaugural conference, 200 delegates adopted a constitution which began with the declaration: 'There can be no peace so long as hunger and want are found among the millions of working people and the few, who make up the employing class, have the good things of life. The working class and the employing class have nothing in common.' Among the well-known figures attending the conference were Big Bill Haywood, the miners' leader; Lucy Parsons, widow of the Haymarket martyr; Mother Jones, the militant feminist; and socialists like Debs and De Leon. They represented about 150,000 workers. This included the powerful Western Federation of Miners which, in the great strike of 1902, had demonstrated what a deadly weapon industrial unionism could be.

To many British SLPers, weak and isolated from the working class, the formation of the IWW was viewed with envy. What had been accomplished in America today, they wanted to do tomorrow. But it would have to remain a dream. As *The Socialist*'s editorial observed, the stage of development reached in Britain was less advanced than in the United States:

> In this country we stand in a more unfortunate position. Politically and economically Great Britain, if not so far advanced as America, is far ahead of the Continent. And yet the day when the British counterpart of the Chicago Convention will be summoned is in the indefinite future.

So the executive committee of the British SLP contented itself with sending congratulations on the formation of the IWW and expressing the wish that, at some time in the future, a similar organisation might be created in this country.

Such a statement represented a shift in SLP policy, however, and aroused hostility in the ranks. Richard Dalgleish, of Glasgow SLP, published a pamphlet, *The Decadence of the Socialist Labour Party*.[47] This pointed out, correctly, that policy had been changed without reference to the membership. Up till then, it had been SLP policy to advocate socialist industrial unions. But the IWW was not a genuine socialist union because members did not have to accept a given set of political principles before being enrolled into membership. This meant that non-socialists could belong to it. The pamphlet went on to complain about the American SLP supporting a non-member — Big Bill Haywood — standing for the governorship of Colorado. This infringed the rule contained in both the British and American SLPs constitutions saying that candidates at elections would only be endorsed if they belonged to the SLP and stood on the Party's platform. If the IWW were truly socialist, the pamphlet claimed, then it would affiliate to the SLP instead of having no declared political affiliation.

The Dalgleish pamphlet, essentially a reaction from those favouring the *status quo*, gained considerable support. Six members of the Glasgow branch, including Tom Bell, agreed with its conclusions, as well as leading English SLPers, like Budgen and Cotton. The magnitude of the dissent merely served to underline the charge that the decision had been taken by a small, unrepresentative group: the Executive at that time contained only members of the Edinburgh branch.

Faced with the crisis, the Party resolved to encourage full and frank discussion. Everyone was at liberty to express his views on *The Socialist*. This was done without acrimony. And, by power of persuasion, the critics were eventually won round. Most of them re-joined the Party after little over a year; the last to be re-admitted was Tom Bell, by the Newcastle conference in 1908.[48] The breach was healed and a new policy emerged.

But once SLPers were convinced that the IWW was a good thing, another issue arose — the question of to what degree the same type of organisation could (and should) be built in Britain. This became the major debate at the SLPs fourth annual conference, held in Edinburgh 14-15 April 1906. For the executive, Neil Maclean argued that a propaganda body, the Advocates of Industrial Unionism, should be formed to spread the ideas that would ultimately make it possible for a socialist industrial union to be built. Tom Clarke, a Glasgow engineer and later AEU executive member, thought this would dissipate resources: 'It would be a waste of energy to endeavour to form industrial union clubs'. He pointed out that the SLP remained weak; all efforts should be devoted to strengthening it. Moreover, Clarke maintained that even without an Advocates of Industrial Unionism exerting pressure from without, many trade unions were already becoming less craft conscious as a result of internal pressures. T. Drummond, of the executive, replied to this last point. He said that nobody objected to members working within existing unions to expose the treachery of union leaders, but something more was required. The majority of delegates agreed with him. Conference felt that discontent with union leaders needed to be backed by organised expression. The Glasgow and Edinburgh branches' opposition to the proposal — namely, that it would impose too great a strain on limited resources and distract members from other activities — was outweighed by the conviction that, once an industrial organisation had been started, the SLP would tap fresh seams of support. By ten votes to four, conference agreed to take the preliminary steps necessary to form the Advocates of Industrial Unionism.

Heightened activity followed the Edinburgh conference. Wherever it had members or contact, the SLP held meetings and distributed leaflets, explaining the inadequacies of existing unions. Party propaganda argued that something akin to the IWW was needed. This could be built, the SLP claimed, if all workers who wanted militant policies would unit. For this to happen, the Advocates of Industrial Unionism would have to be entirely independent of the SLP and accept members irrespective of their political affiliations. The criteria for belonging to the AIU would be agreement with a set of industrial, not political, principles. Only in this way could the widest possible unity be achieved in the fight against Capital.

The call for industrial unity came at an opportune time. Disenchantment among the working class with existing organisations was growing. In April 1906 *The Socialist* carried the headline 'Dundee Labour War — Biggest Strike in Ten Years a Women's Strike'. Dundee, known as a 'she town', had a labour force predominantly composed of women. Pay and conditions were bad. Employers sought to make it even worse by imposing a wage cut and threatened that unless the workers accepted, they would be locked out. The Factory Operatives' Union, led by the Rev. Henry Williamson, advised its members to go to work while the union continued negotiations. But tempers flared and the women, in no mood to compromise, demanded an increase and stayed out until they secured a 5 per cent rise.

Dundee presaged the pattern of things to come, an industrial storm where timorous trade union officials confronted an irate rank-and-file, where the lack of fight at the top was paralleled by a combative eagerness on the shop floor. Spontaneously, workers, many of whom had never held a union card, seized the initiative. Into the Dundee dispute, the SLP flung all available resources. It held as many as seven crowded meetings a week, where speakers like William Paul sought to draw the political lessons from the strike as well as helping to secure victory. By the end of the dispute, the SLP had formed a Dundee branch. This showed that socialists could not only participate meaningfully in an industrial dispute but also make converts at the same time.

But none of the other left-wing organisations were prepared to join the fray. The SDF persisted in its belief that strikes were an extravagance, a waste of resources involving unnecessary suffering because the same ends could more easily be attained through legislation. For the ILP and Labour Representation Committee, involvement in industrial disputes would damage that image of respectability they were sedulously trying to cultivate. It would alienate their Liberal colleagues, making cooperation more difficult. Significantly, journals like the *Labour Leader* and *Clarion* did not dwell on the poor wages and bad conditions prevailing in Dundee.

Naturally, some socialists disagreed with this approach, of turning one's back on workers involved in the class struggle. Yet, their opposition did not stop the official attitude becoming more pronounced. The success of the Labour Representation Committee at the 1906 general election — it changed its name to the Labour Party immediately afterwards — simply served to reinforce the trend towards opportunism because 25 out of the 29 constituencies won by Labour had been secured with tacit Liberal support. Typically, at Ince in Lancashire, the reactionary local paper, the *Wigan Observer*, had backed the Labour candidate, Stephen Walsh; Liberals had spoken from his election platforms; Winston Churchill had sent him a letter of encouragement.[49] Likewise when Ramsay MacDonald, the secretary of the Labour Party, was returned as MP for Leicester, the complete identity of his views with those of the Liberals led G.K. Chesterton to remark:

> It would not have made the slightest difference for good or ill, to the future of anything or anybody, if a tiger had eaten him. There would have been a Liberal Member for Leicester instead, who would have made the same speeches, given exactly the same votes; and, if he were the usual successful soapboiler, would have eclipsed Mr. MacDonald in everything except good looks.[50]

Even Keir Hardie, who did occasionally make the odd socialist remark, still felt the need to extol the virtues of the Liberal Prime Minister: 'Sir Henry Campbell-Bannerman has earned and fully deserves all the praise that is being heaped upon him.'[51]

But the bestowing of compliments was a two-way process. Liberals felt constrained to utter a few flattering phrases about their junior partner, the Labour Party. Winston Churchill declared that the Parliamentary Labour Party was 'a stable and not an unstable element', which had 'added greatly to the wisdom and the earnestness and consequently the dignity of the House.'[52] Government ministers sought to assuage any lingering doubts their supporters might have about the Liberal alliance with the Labour Party. Lloyd George remarked:

> Even the socialists, though some of them might make very wild speeches outside, in the House of Commons were thoroughly tame. He had never heard them propose a resolution in favour of upsetting society; he had never heard a revolutionary statement emerging from them.[53]

Harmony between Labour and Liberal politicians inevitably created some anger among working people as industrial strife began to grow. For instance, in the Belfast strike of 1907, when troops fired on the workers, killing three and injuring many others, the Parliamentary

Labour Party had to choose between supporting the government or siding with the strikers. As *The Socialist* pointed out, Labour MPs did not utter a word of protest:

> Beyond asking a couple of questions, they did nothing. Like the other capitalist members, they accepted the butchery of a few workers as a trifling incident, not worthy of special comment. From Shackleton to Will Thorne, they have become silent accomplices of capitalist murder.[54]

Such conduct obviously could not escape notice or criticism from some rank-and-file socialists. Yet, even had they wanted to, the official socialist journals were inhibited from denouncing the Belfast shooting. Had the SDF denounced the Parliamentary Labour Party's silence, then by implication they would also be denouncing Will Thorne, an MP who belonged to the SDF. Likewise, were the ILP to be critical of the Parliamentary Labour Party, then it would find itself at odds with some of its most influential leaders. Philip Snowden MP had come out strongly in favour of the government over Belfast, saying 'every sensible person would agree that the employment of the military to quell disorder was not only defensible but necessary.'[55]

In these circumstances, it is not surprising that there were some misgivings among socialists in the ILP and SDF. This largely expressed itself within these organisations, although a few did leave to join the Socialist Labour Party. Among these were a group in Wigan which included W.R. Stoker, sen., and Jim Cannon, the father of Les Cannon (Electrical Trades Union president, 1963-70). They objected to the SDF supporting the anti-socialist candidates, Thornley Smith and Stephen Walsh, at the 1906 general election. But even in Wigan, most of the critics stayed inside, hoping to change the organisation to which they belonged from within. Among the criticisms frequently made was that undue emphasis was placed on electoral activity, that greater importance should be attached to industrial work, and efforts to co-ordinate militant activity in the unions. It was primarily to people making such comments, particularly as the strike wave grew in dimension, that the Advocates of Industrial Unionism appealed.

While larger socialist groups succeeded in withstanding the strain of internal dissension, the issue of industrial unionism plunged the SPGB into a severe crisis. Probably the Party's bleak prospects aggravated the situation: while the SPGB placed overriding emphasis on parliamentary politics, its chance of securing a seat remained non-existent. Opponents

of official policy, led by E.J.B. Allen, argued that industry provided a
more fruitful field for activity. He attacked the SPGBs equivocal attitude towards trade unions, claiming that the party did little or nothing
inside trade unions to attack the class collaborationist line of the
leaders. Allen was a powerful, persuasive speaker, and for four evenings
the SPGB 1906 conference debated his views of industrial unionism
before eventually turning them down by 110 votes to 81. By the end
of the year, Allen and his supporters had either left the SPGB or been
expelled, most of them drifting into the SLP.

At first, the Social Democratic Federation tried to adopt the same
tactics. When one of its members, J.E. Clark, became general secretary
of the Advocates of Industrial Unionism at its inaugural conference, he
was promptly expelled. His branch, Marylebone SDF, did not even permit him to speak in his defence. In the opinion of the SDF, as Quelch
said: 'Industrial unionism was a ridiculous attempt to enter into rivalry
with existing unions.'[56] Yet, however much Quelch may have wanted
to expel others who accepted Clark's views, the numbers rapidly grew
so the task became too formidable. Blood-letting on such a colossal
scale could easily have endangered the SDFs existence. Similarly with
the ILP: support within its ranks for industrial unionism grew and, in a
Party not famous for its discipline, the leadership learned to live with it.
This does not mean that politicians like Ramsay MacDonald and
Snowden did not criticise or even write books against it, but they were
too preoccupied with Parliamentary manoeuvrings to spend time on the
unpleasant task of expelling those who disagreed with their industrial
policy. To belong to the Advocates of Industrial Unionism and be a
member of the ILP was not a hanging matter.

The thought of working alongside ILPers and SDFers did not dismay
the Socialist Labour Party so long as it was on the basis of a militant
policy. Unity had to be forged through struggle. It had to come not by
discarding principles, or forgetting they existed, but by mutual activity
to translate them into practice. The SLP thought the Advocates of
Industrial Unionism could provide the means in the short-run for
breaking down sectarian barriers that divided socialist from socialist and
in the long-run could play a vital role in the attainment of socialism:

> The industrial unionism will constitute a body of men and women
> at once intensely practical and uncomprisingly revolutionary. It
> can never degenerate into a sect, which is the danger to which politi-
> cal organisations representing a revolutionary position had hitherto
> been exposed, but will palpitate with the daily and hourly

pulsations of the class struggle as it manifests itself in the workshop. And when it forms its own political party and moves into the political field as it surely will, in that act superceding or absorbing the Socialist Labour Party and all other socialist or labour parties, its campaign will indeed be the expression of the needs, the hopes, the aspirations, and the will of the working classes, and not the dreams and theories of a few unselfish enthusiasts or the ambitions of political schemers . . . Finally, having overthrown the class state, the united Industrial Unions will furnish the administrative machinery for directing industry in the Socialist Commonwealth.[57]

The Advocates of Industrial Unionism held its inaugural conference at Birmingham on 3-4 August 1907. An indication that the SLP had been the prime force behind its creation was that W.F. Holliday and Johnny Muir, both party members, acted as chairman and secretary respectively. It is significant that they were replaced by J.E. Clark and W.O. Anguilly. Although the SLP had a majority of conference delegates, they took neither of the leading positions. Since it was intended that the AIU would be broadly based, the Socialist Labour Party did not want to be accused of dominating it.

The Advocates of Industrial Unionism represented a fresh departure, a journey into uncharted seas. Never before in Britain had a movement been formed to challenge the union leaders. Without historical experience as guidance, the Birmingham conference naturally expressed many confused and contradictory points of view. Some delegates wanted the AIU to confine itself to propaganda work. Others thought it should strive to become a socialist trade union, competing with existing unions. Still others saw its role as a militant rival to the TUC, a body to which militant unions could affiliate and which, ultimately, would replace the TUC as British workers moved leftwards.

These disagreements, while important, were not disastrous. Whatever vision of the future delegates possessed, they were reasonably agreed at the next step forward. The first requirement was to spread the ideas of industrial unionism. It was therefore decided to publish a monthly, *The Industrial Unionist*, as well as leaflets and pamphlets. A small band of zealous workers, scattered in many different industries, quickly began to distribute its literature. By March 1908, E.J.B. Allen boasted: 'Without exaggeration, we can safely say there is hardly a body of class-conscious workers in Great Britain who have not heard of industrial unionism.'[58] While Allen, despite his assurance, may well have been overstating the position, a great deal of progress had undoubtedly been made.

Indirectly, this had a considerable influence on the fortunes of the SLP. As it justifiably claimed in its report to the Stuttgart Congress of the Second International (August 1907), the SLP 'has been the pioneer of revolutionary unionism in Great Britain.' Playing that role, its circle of contacts and the influence of its publications had greatly extended. For the first time, it had gained significance in terms of the class struggle. What was more, it had developed a small, hard group of cadres, capable of playing a leading part in the struggle ahead as well as developing a firmer theoretical grasp of reality. From being in 1903 a weak and puny babe, after four years' growth the SLP had grown into a small, but nevertheless healthy and robust, child with considerable potentiality.

Notes

1. *The Socialist*, July 1906.
2. Interview with Archie Henry, 9 August 1972. Walter Kendall, *The Revolutionary Movement in Britain 1900-21* (1969) p. 314, gives the same estimate.
3. T.A. Jackson, *Solo Trumpet* (1953) pp. 147-8.
4. Reports of Lenin's flattering references to De Leon can be found in the *New York World*, 2 January 1919; Arthur Ransome, *Six Weeks in Russia in 1919* (1919) p. 147; John Reed's report, *Weekly People*, 11 May 1919; and William Paul's article, *The Worker*, 26 March 1921.
5. *The Socialist*, March 1906.
6. Ibid, July 1903.
7. Ibid, July 1905.
8. Robert Michels, *Political Parties, a Sociological Study of the Oligarchical Tendencies of Modern Democracy*, first published 1911.
   It was translated into English by Eden and Cedar Paul, two British socialists, who also translated the Everyman Edition of Karl Marx's *Capital*.
9. Rosa Luxemburg, 'The Junius Pamphlet', published in *Rosa Luxemburg Speaks* (New York 1970) pp. 263-4; V.I. Lenin, 'Dead Chauvinism and Living Socialism', December 1914; Engels' introduction to *The Class Struggles in France* in Marx-Engels, Selected Works (Moscow 1951) vol. 1, pp. 124-5.
10. *The Socialist*, September 1914.
11. Daniel De Leon, *Reform or Revolution* (New York, 1961 ed.) pp. 22-3.
12. *The Socialist*, August 1905.
13. Ibid, April 1908.
14. Ibid, September 1903; letter from John Carstairs Matheson to James Connolly, 9 November 1905. (The Connolly-Matheson correspondence is deposited in the National Library of Ireland.)
15. *The Socialist*, April 1908.
16. J.T. Murphy, *New Horizons* (1941) p. 42.
17. Samuel Levenson, *James Connolly* (1973) p. 105.
18. Thomas Bell, *Pioneering Days*, p. 36.
19. Ibid, p. 55. In my possession are the Glasgow branch Educational Classes

book for the 1910-11 session and the Bridgeton Class Literature Account Book.

20. Thomas Bell, op. cit., pp. 38-9.
21. *The Socialist*, October 1904.
22. Wilf Braddock's reminiscences, *Socialist Review*, October 1958.
23. *The Socialist*, August 1911.
24. Frank Budgen, *Myselves when Young* (Oxford, 1970) p. 84.
25. *The Socialist*, July 1908.
26. Ibid, April 1908.
27. Desmond Greaves, *The Life and Times of James Connolly* p. 109.
28. Interview with Miss Jean Budgen, 11 October 1973.
29. T.A. Jackson, op. cit., p. 55.
30. Ibid, p. 84-5.
31. *The Socialist*, May 1905, describes a fight between N. Maclean (SLP) and T. Kennedy (SDF).
32. SLP Executive Committee, 8 September 1907. (The Socialist Labour Party Executive Committee minutes 1903-1907 are deposited in the British Museum.)
33. *The Socialist*, October 1909 and the SLP Executive Committee 13 January 1907.
34. *The Socialist*, May 1916.
35. Thomas Bell, *Pioneering Days,* pp. 48-9.
36. Letter from J.C. Matheson to James Connolly on 12 March 1906, mentioning George Yates, claimed that 'He is sadly changed . . . Another good man gone stale!'
37. *The Socialist*, October 1904.
38. Frank Budgen, *Myselves when Young* (Oxford, 1970) p. 86. Also, J.C. Matheson's letter to James Connolly, 7 October 1904, described De Leon's tour as 'first rate'.
39. Daniel De Leon, *Flashlights of the Amsterdam Congress* (New York 1929) pp. 64-5.
40. Socialist Party of Great Britain, *Questions of the Day* (1932 ed.) pp. 11-14; Robert Barltrop, *The Monument* (1975) is a history of the SPGB.
41. J.C. Matheson's letter to J. Connolly, 7 June 1904.
42. J. Connolly's letter to J.C. Matheson, March 1903.
43 *The Socialist*, April 1906.
44. Thomas Bell, op. cit., pp. 53-5, reprints in full Thomas Clark's election address when he stood as an SLP candidate in Glasgow in 1903.
45. *The Socialist*, March 1906.
46. Ibid, November 1907.
47. Besides Richard Dalgleish and the other members of Glasgow SLP, Mitchell and Robertson of Edinburgh also resigned.
48. In his autobiography, *Pioneering Days,* Bell made no mention of the fact that he was for a time expelled from the SLP.
49. *Wigan Observer,* 15 December 1905 and 13 January 1906.
50. G.K. Chesterton quoted by G.D.H. Cole and R. Postgate, *The Common People* (1968 ed.) p. 486.
51. *Labour Leader,* 4 January 1907.
52. Quoted by Donald Read, *Edwardian England* (1972) pp. 77-8.
53. Lloyd George's speech at Madeley, Staffordshire, on 1 November 1907.
54. *The Socialist*, September 1907.
55. *Sheffield Guardian,* 23 August 1907.
56. T. Quelch's letter to A.J. Hibbert, 13 March 1907.
57. *The Socialist*, April 1908.
58. Ibid, March 1908.

3 INDUSTRIAL UNREST

Just before the First World War, Britain experienced industrial conflict on a level rarely, if ever, previously known. The underlying cause was the condition of capitalism in this country: encountering ever-increasing difficulties, employers tried to solve their problems by placing the burden on the shoulders of the working class. Confronted by this challenge, the trade unions failed, abjectly. Small, fragmented, led by cautious and conservative-minded officials, they proved incapable of repulsing the employers' offensive, and initiative passed to the shop floor. It remained for the rank-and-file to develop its own ideas and forms of struggle. Respectable union leaders were brushed aside and, under the banners of industrial unionism and syndicalism, workers conducted struggles of great militancy. All this happened in a political climate unfavourable to the ruling class: it was a time when wealthy women, wanting the vote, smashed windows and encouraged lawlessness; when die-hard Tories, incensed at the thought of Home Rule for Ireland, encouraged the Orangemen of Ulster to take up arms seditiously; and when the constitution itself — in particular, the place of the House of Lords — was brought into question. The cumulative effect of these crises was to lessen the cohesion of the upper echelons of society and their ability to cope with the discontent emanating from the lower depths. It also weakened the power of authority: with Acts of Parliament being flouted by those of exalted rank, persons who should set an example, how could a plausible law-and-order appeal be made to workers?

The problems of the British economy arose from its relative decline. Other countries were developing more rapidly and beginning to out-strip Britain's industrial production. Britain's share of world manufacturing output dropped from 31.8 per cent in 1885 to 14.1 per cent in 1913.[1] It is impossible to dwell here on the reasons for the country's poor performance. Economic historians attribute it, among other things, to a lack of enterprise by British businessmen; to an over-reliance on old staple industries, like textiles and coal; to a failure to play a leading role in new, rapidly expanding industries, like chemicals and electrical goods; to an absence of large home markets, permitting full advantage to be gained from economies of scale; to an inadequate provision for scientific and technical education, resulting in Britain having a smaller

pool of skilled labour than its main rivals; and to an unwillingness by
manufacturers to adapt goods to the special needs of overseas customers.

Whatever the actual configuration of causes, one effect of Britain's
decline remains indisputable. Instead of ploughing back profits into
home industries, capitalists found it more lucrative to invest abroad. In
the period 1901-5, an average of under £50 million a year went in
foreign investment; by 1907-10, the figure had shot up to £150 million
a year; and in 1911-13, the figure reached a colossal £200 million. This
meant the ownership of overseas assets by British citizens rose from
£2.4 milliard at the turn of the century to £4 milliard by the outbreak
of the First World War. From 1907 onwards, annual investment abroad
exceeded net investment at home.[2] This was quite satisfactory to the
capitalists. They did not mind where their income came from, home or
abroad, so long as it grew! But for the British worker the picture was
rather different: new equipment was being installed in other countries
and, although he did not possess modern machinery, he was supposed
to compete with the foreigners' output. Extra effort was expected to
compensate for lower investment.

Squeezed profit margins pushed employers in the same direction. As
the yield of capital invested in Britain dropped, they sought to offset
this by lowering labour costs and increasing productivity. The capitalists
mounted a three-pronged assault: first, they used their superior
bargaining position *vis-à-vis* the workers; second, they introduced new
techniques that helped to lower the wage bill; and, third, they
tightened up laws that could be employed against trade unionists.

Capitalists derived their superior bargaining position from the natural
development of economic forces. Larger concerns tended to grow at a
faster rate than smaller ones, which were more liable to go bankrupt or
be taken over. Hence, there was a tendency for a few giants, perhaps
even one, to dominate a given industry. Augmenting this process, firms
joined each other to form trade associations. These reached agreement
on pricing policies and often had a common attitude towards trade
unions. The consequence was that capital arrayed itself with vast
strength and unity. In contrast, working class forces were weak and disunited. There were 1,302 trade unions in 1900, squabbling among themselves, not possessing sufficient financial resources for a real battle with
the employers.[3] Functioning unsatisfactorily, providing an inadequate
service, unions recruited a small proportion of the working class — only
one worker in eight held a card.[4]

In any trial of strength between the giants of Capital and the
Lilliputians of Labour, the outcome could easily be predicted. Even one

of the most powerful unions, the Amalgamated Society of Engineers,
failed to repel an attack: the 1897 lock-out ended after 30 weeks, with
the Society compelled to accept humiliating terms as a condition for a
return to work.[5] In his presidential address to the TUC in 1898, James
O'Grady described the Engineering Employers' Federation as 'a
mammoth combination of military-led capital, whose object, as openly
stated by its leader, was to cripple, if not crush, the forces of trade
unionism.' What made matters worse for organised labour was the
continuing deterioration of the situation. E.J.B. Allen, a talented
socialist and advocate of industrial unionism, acknowledged this fact:
quoting Board of Trade figures, he showed that there was a tendency
for employers to win a greater proportion of industrial disputes.
Workers had been successful in 40 per cent of the struggles in 1893; by
1904 the figure had slumped to 17 per cent.[6]

Defeats naturally served to reinforce the caution and timidity of
the trade union leaders, and high in their list of priorities was the need
to avoid class conflict. So when employers sought to introduce new
production methods — greater specialisation and standardisation — they
could usually rely upon pliant union officials, ready to smooth over any
problems that might arise. Similarly, as the principles of scientific
management came into use, union leaders counselled their members to
accept the new arrangements.

A highly-paid craftsman might find his job had been broken down
into a number of simple operations that could be speedily accomplished
by women or young people — at much lower rates. Professor Phelps
Brown explains what happened:

> The new high speed steels in cutting tools, the wind hammer or the
> electric drill in the shipyard, the sheer r.p.m. of the new and
> rackety machines built to be run to death, threatened 'technological
> unemployment'. With the pneumatic chisel, it was reported from the
> Clyde in 1902, a boy could do in a few hours the day's work of a
> man; and boys had never been so plentiful.[7]

The rate of exploitation increased. In their history of the foundry
workers, Fyrth and Collins state that employers pushed up work-
norms, abolished breakfast breaks, and expected men to do jobs
previously done by other types of workers. One of the results of speed-
up was to increase the accident rate: in 1898 22.5 per thousand
foundry workers were injured; by 1907 the figure had risen to 48 per
thousand. The tempo of production became too great for many older

men and the cry of 'too old at forty' began to be heard. To get jobs, men with grey streaks began to dye their hair and tell foremen they were still in their thirties.[8] With variations, what happened in the foundries also occurred elsewhere in industry.

The impact of new production methods and speed-ups naturally aroused opposition, and employers usually had enough strength to deal with it. But where their resources were stretched, or when they wished to administer a salutary punishment on the workers, they could always rely on the Law. Friends in Parliament and the judiciary were determined to preserve the rights of property, and during the engineers' lock-out of 1897, chief constables and magistrates were asked to adopt a more stringent line towards picketing. 'Imprisonment with hard labour soon became the rule,' as a Royal Commission on Trades Disputes in 1906 was informed.[9]

A spate of court cases also whittled away the workers' rights to strike. The most well known was the Taff Vale judgement, which arose when South Wales railwaymen struck without the approval of their union, the Amalgamated Society of Railway Servants. A prominent local member had been victimised. The railway company, which did not recognise the men's union, took a determined stand. It set about recruiting blacklegs, and sued the union for losses incurred through industrial action. In December 1902, the High Court awarded the Taff Vale Railway Company £23,000 in damages. When its own legal expenses were added, the litigation cost the ASRS a total of £42,000, a considerable amount for those days.[10]

The significance of the Taff Vale judgement was that it provided employers with a legal weapon for nullifying the effect of strikes. When workers downed tools, they merely damaged themselves; employers could recoup their losses by suing the unions. What was more, no limits were placed upon the amount of damages: union coffers could be drained. Awareness of this danger served to reinforce the already strong influences within union leaderships to renounce militancy and strive for industrial peace.

It is common knowledge that, as a result of the Taff Vale judgement, railway workers were fined £42,000 for breaking the law; what is perhaps less clearly recognised is that the rest of the working class was 'fined' an immeasurably bigger amount for obeying the law. In its desire to avoid litigation, the trade union movement failed to seize opportunities, provided by an upswing of the business cycle, to win wage increases. As Cole and Postgate pointed out: 'The Taff Vale judgement had so paralysed trade union action that, despite the high profits which were being made, they were powerless to strike for higher wages.' Sidney and Beatrice Webb endorse the same conclusion. In their *History*, they say that, with the Taff Vale judgement, 'trade unionism had to a great extent lost its sting.'[11]

In these circumstances, it may seem amazing that many union leaders actually welcomed the Taff Vale decision. They saw it as a powerful weapon in their fight to curb militancy and assert their authority. James Sexton, general secretary of the Dock Labourers, thought 'that the decision in the Taff Vale case will be a blessing in disguise, and will tend to strengthen executive control and minimise, if not entirely kill, irresponsible action in the localities.'[12] Likewise, W.E. Harvey, the Derbyshire miners' leader, thought that the judgement

> would never have been given but for the harum scarum action on the part of the ILP and socialistic men. It brought before them many object lessons, and they ought to see how it applied from their side. It behoved them to exercise the greatest care in the selection of representatives and officials.

Subsequently, Harvey used the fear that union funds would be jeopardised to thwart a strike threat.[13] Richard Bell, general secretary of the Amalgamated Society of Railway Servants, the union that was £42,000 poorer (or wiser) as a consequence of Taff Vale, wrote in the *Railway Review* that the judgement may have 'a useful influence in solidifying the forces of trade unionism and in subjecting them to wholesome discipline.' He went on to declare: 'Rules, executive committees and responsible officials have been ignored.' In his opinion, the court decision would have a beneficial effect in bringing 'some of the rank and file and the young bloods of our trade unions' to act with more responsibility.[14]

It is important to place the reaction of trade union leaders to Taff Vale in historical perspective. They were the second or third generation of officials who had grown accustomed to establishing close working relations with the employers. Class collaboration had become a way of life. Long ago they had come to regard the existing economic system as natural, inevitable and beneficial. Fifty years of experience lay behind this attitude. Professor Royden Harrison described how it emerged in the 1850s:

> Just as the Professor of Political Economy at Oxford thought 'it might be convenient in times of trouble, which are perhaps not so

far off as many think, that we should be able to work upon the mind of the working classes through teachers and advisers whom they trust', so the New Model employers themselves cultivated the trade union leaders. Lord Elcho would have the miners' leader to a champagne breakfast and A.J. Mundella would congratulate himself on the good effects of wining and dining delegates to the TUC. Special relationships grew up between particular employer politicians and trade union politicians. For example, such relationships existed between A.J. Mundella and Robert Applegarth; Lord Elcho and Alexander MacDonald; Samuel Morley and George Howell; Crawshay, the ironmaster, and John Kane. Just as Samuel Plimsoll concerned himself with the welfare of the merchant seamen, so his fellow employers, Bass and Morley, actively aided trade union organisation among the railwaymen and agricultural workers.[15]

Trade Unionism was no threat to capitalism so long as it did not try to increase wages through industrial strength. The provision of friendly society benefits, helping members when sick or unemployed, could be positively beneficial to the employer. Instead of having to engage men who were too thin and emaciated to do a good day's work, a boss could hire men who, despite the misfortunes they had suffered, were nevertheless in fine fettle and capable of hard work. Friendly society arrangements were a collective form of self help: they combined the capitalist virtue of thrift with that of prudence.

Moreover, many trade unionists had another important capitalist attitude. Far from wanting to unite the working class and overthrow the existing economic system, they sought to differentiate themselves from the rest of the working class, to rise up the social ladder. They aspired to become an aristocracy of labour, as interested in keeping less skilled workers at arms' length as they were to remain on amicable terms with their employers. It would be wrong to think that such trade unionists begrudged their leaders a much higher standard of living: rather than being taken as a sign of selling out to the bosses, their affluence was the symbol of a success story from which many union members gained vicarious satisfaction.

Capitalists derived considerable benefit from arrangements with unions of this kind. As industry grew in size, the need increased for established channels of communication between management and men. The dangers of misunderstandings and strikes were lessened when the men's spokesmen were respectable, responsible individuals. Such officials acted as a shock absorber, minimising conflict and transmitting ideas, especially those of the capitalists, to the workers. But the benefit was not entirely one way: real wages rose throughout the fifty years 1850 to 1900. People accustomed themselves to slowly improving conditions. The comforting theory of the inevitability of progress, an expression of the prevailing mood of capitalist optimism, pervaded all sections of society by the turn of the century. So when adversity hit wage-earners, workers' leaders were inclined to see it as a temporary setback, not the beginning of a new trend. Instead of attempting to organise resistance, union officials tried further to strengthen existing links with the employers.

An interesting move in this direction was the formation of the National Industrial Association in 1900. It sought to organise both sides of industry, being 'a National Association of Employers' Associations and Trade Unions'. Its literature emphasised the underlying common interests of all classes and the need to cultivate goodwill. Created in the same year as the Labour Representation Committee, the National Industrial Association had some significant people among its leadership. On the employers' side, these included G.B. Hunter, the Tyneside ship-builder, who fought the 1900 General Election as a Liberal candidate. His running-mate, Alexander Wilkie of the Labour Representation Committee, in the two-member constituency of Sunderland was also prominent in the National Industrial Association. Richard Bell, of the Railway Servants, remained active in both organisations. As one of the two Labour MPs returned at the 1900 General Election, he was well placed to influence LRC policy. An avowed anti-socialist and elected to Parliament with active Liberal support, he visualised the Labour Representation Committee playing the same role politically as the National Industrial Association did industrially. To gentlemen like Richard Bell, class collaboration was all-encompassing.

Capitalism had nothing to fear from trade unionism so long as officials of the Richard Bell-type stayed in control. Such leaders some-times actually went out of their way to point out to employers their peaceful intent. David Shackleton MP, leader of the Weavers' union, proudly declared that unions were spending very little money in strike pay. Quoting Government returns, he showed that total expenditure of 100 trade unions in the ten years ending 1904 was £16 million, of which only £2 million was spent on dispute pay. The tendency, more-over, was for the amount to dwindle: by 1904 the number of disputes had fallen to less than half the 1899 figure.[16] Unions were well on the road to operating merely as friendly societies, steering clear of industrial confrontation.

While this strategy created a feeling of self-satisfaction among union leaders, it produced mounting discontent in the rank and file. To many workers, the *raison d'être* of trade unionism was the fight for higher wages and better conditions. When it ceased doing this, then it stopped being of much use to workers. In 1904, Will Thorne reported to the Gasworkers' union annual conference that 'members have threatened to leave the union if the EC did not allow them to come out on strike.' Four years earlier, the Gasworkers' union quarterly report quoted an aggrieved member as asking: 'What is the use of men being in a union if the employers are to act as though no union was in existence?'[17] The answer to the question, which must have been asked in many parts of the movement, sometimes appears to have been 'None'. After 1900, union membership began to drop. By 1904, there were 60,000 fewer workers holding union cards than four years previously. This trend must have been as disturbing to the union hierarchies as the growing restiveness displayed by those who remained members.

There were deep and powerful reasons why the traditional policy of class collaboration was being challenged. First, there was the fact that real wages declined from 1900 to 1913 somewhere between 3 and 5 per cent. Professor Pollard has suggested that these figures underestimate the decline for most of the period: 1913 was an exceptionally good year for wages: if 1909-11 had been taken, then workers were receiving in real terms only 90 per cent of what they had done ten years before.[18] Second, while workers received less, they produced more: between 1900 and 1913 productivity per man rose by 7 per cent.[19] And, third, at the same time as workers experienced growing impoverishment, they saw other sections of society becoming richer. Real national income per head rose by 8.5 per cent between 1900 and 1913.[20] All this went to create a situation in which inequality became greater and more difficult to bear. Explosions of working-class anger were the inevitable consequence.

A strike wave of unprecedented dimensions hit the country. The number of days lost through industrial disputes quadrupled in 1908. In the years 1910 to 1913, the figure never dropped below 10 million per annum, while in 1912, due largely to the coal dispute, it reached the hitherto unheard of total of 38 million. It was not, however, merely a question of magnitude. Industrial strife at times verged on civil war.

Sir George Askwith, a conciliation officer of the Board of Trade, drew vivid descriptions of the more important struggles. This is what he witnessed in the 1907 Belfast lock-out:

The city of Belfast held up by a state of civil turmoil, with guards at
the railway station, double sentries with loaded rifles at alternative
lamp-posts of the Royal Avenue, a very few lorries with constabu-
lary sitting on bales and soldiers on either side, proceeding to guard
congested but lifeless docks, and ten thousand soldiers in and about
the city. There had been fights in the streets, charges of the cavalry,
the Riot Act read, shooting to disperse wrecking mobs, a few men
and women killed and scores wounded, and the whole business of
the city at a standstill.[21]

A similar scene greeted Sir George when he visited Hull during the 1911
seamen's strike: 'One shipowner came to me and discussed the matter;
he spoke of it as a revolution, and so it was.'

Sir George discovered that Goole and Hull workers had new leaders,
men hitherto unheard of, and that the employers did not know how to
deal with them. As he attempted to get both sides to reach agreement,
news reached him that fires, looting and rioting had broken out:

I heard one town councillor remark that he had been in Paris during
the Commune and had never seen anything like this, and he had
known that there were such people in Hull — women with hair
streaming and half nude, reeling through the streets smashing and
destroying.

Ultimately, when agreement had been reached, a mass meeting was held
to tell workers the terms of settlement:

It was estimated that there were 15,000 people there when the
leaders began their statement. They announced their statement:
and before my turn came an angry roar of 'No!' rang out; 'Let's
fire the docks!' from the outskirts, where men ran off.[22]

Meanwhile, a general strike gripped Liverpool. Winston Churchill, as
Home Secretary, sent two warships to the Mersey, and they trained
their guns on the rebellious city. The police, wielding truncheons like
flails, broke up a peaceful demonstration. In its account, the *Manchester
Guardian* declared that 'even when the crowd was separated into groups,
the police continued the onslaught . . . It was a display of violence that
horrified those who saw it.'[23] Later, troops with loaded rifles and fixed
bayonets were brought to Liverpool. They fired on the crowd, killing
one man and wounding others. But the strike committee remained

defiant:

> Let Churchill do his utmost, his best or his worst, let him order ten
> times more military to Liverpool, and let every street be paraded
> by them. Not all the King's horses nor all the King's men can take
> the vessels out of the docks to sea. The workers decide the ships
> shall not go. What government can say they shall go and make the
> carters take the freight and the dockers load same, and the seamen
> man the steamers? Tell us that, gentlemen?[24]

Equally bitter was the Cambrian Combine strike of 1910-11, which
spread until it involved 26,000 South Wales miners. After pitched
battles between police and strikers, who were trying to stop the colliery
pumps, the authorities telegraphed for military reinforcements. These
were promptly despatched by Churchill, along with contingents of
Metropolitan Police. From this time forward, reported Ness Edwards,
'the "specially imported police" sought any and every excuse to attack
strikers, and were aided in their atrocious work by detachments of the
Hussars and the Lancashire Infantry.'[25]

The most serious incident happened at Llanelly. This was described,
from the official viewpoint, in a telegraphic report from the Chief Constable of Carmarthenshire to the Home Secretary:

> Attack made on train which passed through Llanelly station, under
> military protection, at railway cutting sloping on either side to con-
> siderable height near station. Troops under Major Stuart quickly on
> scene, followed by three magistrates. Troops attacked on both sides
> by crowd on embankment hurling stones and other missiles. One
> soldier carried away wounded in head and others struck. Riot act
> read. Major Stuart mounted embankment and endeavoured to pacify
> mob. Stone throwing continued, crowd yelling defiance at troops.
> Shots fired as warning. [This, as the inquest later proved, was
> untrue. RC] No effect. Attitude of crowd threatening and deter-
> mined. Other shots fired. Two men killed, one wounded. Crowd
> fled.[26]

The ferocity with which industrial struggles were fought can be attributed to a number of factors. First, there was the pent-up anger of the
strikers — men who for years had endured intolerable conditions and
who were prepared to fight, desperately if need be, for their cause.
Second, there were in all towns the poorest of the poor, the most

oppressed and the most helpless, who would gladly seize the opportunity to go on the rampage, smashing shop-windows and looting. Third, and most important, was the provocative conduct of the authorities, who used violence whenever they felt it would serve their purpose — to cower, to intimidate, to destroy the workers' will to struggle.

But the extensive use of troops did have its problems. The young men who volunteered for the army were of the working class and might resent being used against their own kith and kin. Militants made a number of attempts to make soldiers realise that they were acting as tools of the capitalists, helping the employers to depress even further workers' living standards.

The most famous 'Open Letter to British Soldiers', written by a Liverpool worker named Bower, began:

> Men! Comrades! Brothers!
> You are in the Army.
> So are we. You, in the army Destruction. We, in the Industrial, or army of Construction.
> We work at the mine, mill, forge, factory or dock, etc.,
> producing and transporting all the goods, clothing, stuffs, etc.,
> which makes it possible for people to live.
> You are Workingmen's Sons.
> When we go on Strike to better our lot, which is the lot also of your Fathers, Mothers, Brothers and Sisters, YOU are called upon by your officers to MURDER US.
> Don't do it.

This 'Don't Shoot' leaflet, first published in Connolly's *Irish Worker*, was reprinted in January 1912 in the *Industrial Syndicalist* and three months later in *The Socialist*. A railwayman, Fred Crowsley, had 3,000 copies printed, at his own expense, which he distributed among soldiers at Aldershot. A series of arrests quickly followed. Crowsley received a four-month jail sentence, the printers of the *Industrial Syndicalist* six months, and its editor, Guy Bowman, nine months.

To show solidarity with his imprisoned comrades, Tom Mann courted arrest by reading the 'Don't Shoot' at the beginning of the 1912 coal strike, when troops were deployed around the coalfields. In his memoirs, he described what happened:

> In Manchester, where I then was, the authorities were having premises prepared as temporary barracks, and were concentrating

military forces a few miles out of the city. At public meetings, I
drew attention to this, and asked what the temporary barracks were
for. I described what had happened the previous year at Liverpool,
when everything was orderly until those responsible for Law and
Order caused disturbances. I also directed attention to the imprisonment of my comrades in connection with the 'Don't Shoot' letter,
read the letter to the audience, and declared I believed in every
sentence of it.[27]

Tom Mann was arrested on his return to London, and sentenced to six
months' imprisonment for incitement to mutiny. The attendant trial
aroused widespread interest, particularly among working people. Tom
Mann was regarded as a proletarian hero, a victim of class injustice.
Syndicalism became well known as the creed of militancy. Its typical
supporter may not have been aware of the subtleties of syndicalist
doctrine, but he wholeheartedly identified himself with Tom Mann's
declared aim, 'to fight the employer, to fight him, to fight him, to
fight him.'[28] And in this struggle between the two great clashes, many
battles did take place, each developing its own characteristics according
to the grievances of the workers in that particular sector of industry.
    The railways were one of the most trouble-torn sectors of the
economy before the First World War. This was partly due to an Act of
Parliament, passed in 1894, which deprived railway companies of the
right to raise fares and freight rates. As this was a period of rising costs,
the companies found this restriction especially irksome. Working
expenses as a percentage of total receipts rose from 55 per cent in 1880
to 62 per cent in 1900. Dividends tended to fall.
    Managers strived to counteract this trend with improved efficiency.
They introduced bigger trains and wagons, abolished unnecessary dupli-
cation, and economised generally. But these moves had a detrimental
effect on railwaymen. What was involved was a lessening of labour costs
through a reduction in the number of men employed and simultaneously a reduction in the wages of those still employed relative to
those workers in other industries. In the 1880s railwaymen were among
the most highly paid; in the next twenty years the wages of industrial
workers as a whole rose by 25 per cent whereas theirs crept up by only
5 per cent.[29] Moreover, railwaymen's hours were longer than those of
many other workers: most worked a 60-hour week, and some even 72
hours, whereas engineers and building workers were on a 54-hour week.
Another advantage of the railwaymen, that of security of employment,
vanished as companies cut staff, and promotion prospects dwindled as

fewer well-paid jobs were available. As a result, talented young railwaymen who, a generation before, would have had their eyes fixed on the
promotion ladder, now realised that the only way to better themselves
was along with their fellow workers. Instead of becoming foremen, they
became trade union militants.

All railway companies, with one exception, failed to recognise the
unions. A general manager, H.A. Walker, expressed the employers'
argument in the following manner:

> There is no doubt that the most serious effect of the recognition of
> the trade unions from the point of view of the railway companies
> would be the lowering of the standard of discipline throughout the
> railway service. Without a high standard of discipline, the safe
> working of the line would be jeopardised. The entire responsibility
> for the maintenance must rest with the railway companies.[30]

George Findlay, general manager of the London and North Western
Railway, expressed the same idea more bluntly. He told a Parliamentary
enquiry in 1893: 'You might as well have a trade union or an amalgamated society in the army, where discipline has to be kept at a very
high standard, as have it on the railways.'[31] Lord Claud Hamilton, chairman of the Great Eastern Railway, said they wished to maintain cordial
relations with their servants, 'untrammelled by the coercion and
tyranny of an outside irresponsible body.'[32]

The policy of non-recognition was subjected to growing pressure as
trade unions recruited more members and could be seen to be speaking
for the labour force. The All-Grades Movement, started in 1906, was
highly successful. Within twelve months, unions had almost twice the
membership they possessed two years previously in 1905. Simultaneously, the Campaign, a genuine expression of the rank and file,
sought to unify the unions as well as to break down the divisions
between various grades, deliberately fostered by the railway companies
to prevent united action.

In October 1907, members of the Amalgamated Society of Railway
Servants voted, by a large majority, to withdraw their labour until
recognition had been achieved. This move, which could have caused
considerable damage to the entire economy, led to the rapid intervention of the government. A series of meetings were held, and a compromise agreement reached. This provided for the setting up of a conciliation board to which the men could elect their representatives, who
could be union members or not. What this meant was that the unions

had not achieved their aim: they had not clearly established the right to negotiate with the employers on their members' behalf.

Many rank-and-filers, disgruntled at the sell-out of Richard Bell and the rest of the leaders, echoed the question asked by *The Socialist*: 'Why were the terms accepted by the officials without the men being asked to vote upon them, especially when the men had voted in favour of striking to gain that which the terms of the agreement deny them?'[33] The answer, blunt but true, came from one of the officials, who pointed to the powerlessness of the protestors because 'we control the purse-strings.' All most railwaymen could do was fulminate against the union leaders. One of the rare opportunities to demonstrate their feelings came with the South Leeds bye-election early in 1908. A. Fox, the general secretary of the engine-drivers' union, was the Labour candidate. Five branches of the ASRS in Leeds asked members to withhold their votes as a protest against the 1907 sell-out. This boycott gained extensive support, and Fox secured only a little over half the votes he won at the General Election a few months earlier.

For railwaymen, the 1907 settlement had disastrous consequences. The newly-created Conciliation Boards, operating on a sectional basis, had the effect of dividing the men. United action became more difficult, and the union officials stifled any militancy. In this way, by showing their respectability and their power to control the men, they hoped to secure eventual union recognition by the companies.

Naturally, these tactics did not have the blessing of the militants. One of them, Charles Watkins, noted that the 1907 settlement, which had placed railwaymen 'more completely in the grip of the capitalists' than ever before, had 'the warm approval of their own trade union leaders.' He went on to describe the impact of the new arrangements at grass-roots level:

> The immediate result of the 'settlement' was the dispersion of the men's forces, the dissipation of all energy generated by the National Movement, and the indefinite postponement of the consideration of the men's grievances.[34]

The quiescence of railwaymen was merely temporary. As unrest spread throughout the working class generally, they would not remain unaffected. The spark that ignited their smouldering discontent came in 1911, with the big strike in Liverpool. Initially involving dockers and seamen, railwaymen became implicated when they refused to handle goods. Ultimately the strikers emerged victorious: the Shipping

Federation conceded almost all the men's demands. Clearly this demonstrated to railwaymen that militancy paid. A wave of unofficial strikes quickly spread. With a quarter of the labour force away from work, and more coming out daily, union officials had to take a drastic step to regain control of their members, and of non-members who were showing remarkable solidarity in the struggle. The general secretaries of the four railway unions called a joint meeting of their executive committees, which unanimously agreed to call a national stoppage to secure official union recognition. As the official history of the railwaymen said: 'The leaders had to race to get up level with the men'.[35]

The widespread dislocation occasioned by the strike led to rapid Government intervention. Again, a settlement was soon reached, but this time it was more favourable to the unions. To a large extent, *de facto* recognition was gained. In the flush of victory, the National Union of Railwaymen was formed – a closer approximation to industrial unionism.

While the 1911 dispute, the first national strike on the railway, changed the class relationship of forces, it did not change economic reality. The railway companies, still saddled by the 1894 Act, continued to try to keep wages down, and the men's discontent was unabated. In the period 1911, more unofficial strikes occurred on the railways than in any other place. Rank-and-file opposition to union officialdom grew and, for a time, a journal called the *Syndicalist Railwaymen* was published.

As the militants realised, the underlying cause of conflict on the railways lay in the very structure of the industry. As long as it stayed in private hands, the companies, with the meagre profit margins, would not be able to pay a decent wage. But this did not mean that nationalisation was the simple answer. For, as the *Syndicalist Railwaymen* declared, workers

> have little reason for placing any great degree of confidence in the State as an employer. As the conflict 'twixt capital and labour becomes keener, the workers are having impressed on them the real character and functions of the existing State . . . the State is essentially a ruling class organisation and its functions are chiefly coercive.[36]

The answer was public ownership with workers' control. Only when the workers themselves democratically controlled the railways, as well as the rest of the economy, could they be sure that the industry would be run in their interests. If the railways were merely placed in the hands of the State, then they would still be run in the interests of the capitalists. The level of wages, as an article in *The Socialist* pointed out, was determined by the forces of supply and demand. If the railways were nationalised, there was likely to be a more efficient utilisation of Labour. Hence demand for labour would lessen, and wages would accordingly fall.[37]

The clamour for workers' control proved to be so strong that in 1912 the annual conference of the ASRS passed a resolution demanding that complete control of the industry be put in the workers' hands. Dr Pribicevic states that it became the first union to declare in favour of workers' control.[38] But it had been done against the advice of the union leaders, to whom such notions were an anathema. Once the ASRS had been involved in the merger that resulted in the creation of the National Union of Railwaymen, the leaders seized the opportunity to water down the policy. The resolution passed by the NUR conference in 1914 simply asked for 'a due measure of control and responsibility'. Notwithstanding this setback, a powerful section still advocated workers' control.

Like railwaymen, militant miners reached the conclusion that industrial democracy was required. But they arrived at this answer along a different route. In contrast to the railways, where the fight had been concentrated on the need for union recognition, employers in the coal industry had realised, ever since the 1893 lock-out, that clear gains could be made by recognising the union. Periodically both sides met on a conciliation board to regulate wages for the industry. Criticism of this arrangement grew, particularly after 1902, when a series of pay cuts were introduced.

The basic reason for the employers' offensive was the economic position of the coal industry. Those seams nearest the surface, easiest and cheapest to mine, were mostly exhausted. Coalowners sent their miners deeper and deeper, with the consequences that more men had to be employed on haulage and the maintenance of road-ways — essentially unproductive tasks. As a result, output per man fell and the cost per ton of coal rose. To make matters worse, coalowners had to contend with mounting competition in the lucrative export trade from other countries, where collieries had been constructed relatively recently. Their coal tended to be easier and cheaper to mine, and foreigners had the further benefit of greater technological sophistication. In Britain, only 8 per cent of output was mechanically cut by 1913, and an even smaller percentage was mechanically conveyed underground. British pits also seemed backward in the use of electricity, steel and modern production methods, although geological conditions may have been partly to blame.

In this economic context, coalowners sought to put the full burden of the industry's problems on the shoulders of the miners. Conciliation boards helped towards this end: there was equal representation of masters and men on the board, with an 'independent' chairman, usually a superannuated Tory peer, who could be relied upon to side with the owners on any crucial issue. Faced with this challenge, the unions failed to use their bargaining position to the full. Steeped in the ideology of class collaboration, they restricted their activities to the conciliation board, not mobilising the strength of the union at coal-face level.

In 1908, the British economy suffered a trade depression. As demand for coal is derivative, fluctuating with the level of industrial production, the recession had a serious effect in the mining industry. Output, prices and employment all fell. In the course of a year, the owners secured two wage reductions of 5 per cent each through the conciliation board, and they put in for a third. Having the awkward task of making their members accept a reduction in their standard of living, union officials had difficulty in persuading a recalcitrant rank-and-file. The Miners' Federation president, Enoch Edwards, argued forcefully for maintaining existing procedures:

> The system of conciliation is better, after all, than the rough and tumble methods of strife with all its drawbacks, and there is always the solid advantage that you do keep the continuity of peace generally.[39]

But the men who worked underground did not necessarily regard peace, bought for such a high price, as an advantage. George Harvey, a Durham collier, declared:

> The leaders must resort to compromise because the waging of a conflict endangers not only the existence of their unions but their own soft jobs also. Compromise is the union official's god.

Harvey went on to suggest that this attitude vitiated the organisations themselves, as well as the leaders:

> They have developed into dues collecting concerns pure and simple. Their salaried officials have everything to lose and nothing to gain in a struggle, and they prefer to obtain such tit-bits from the masters as

will satisfy their dues supporters without attempting in any way the
fighting of the class struggle. In fact, the trade union movement is
tending to create a sort of organ of oppression within the masters'
organ of oppression – the State – and an army of despotic union
chiefs who are interested in reconciling, as far as possible, the
interests of masters and men.[40]

When conflict flared, union officials fought the blaze. No word of
protest came from them when some of their members were sent to jail.
In County Durham, miners of Swalwell and Washington 'absented
themselves from work without notice'. Prison sentences were imposed
on the leading militants. They had broken the law, said the union
officials, and therefore did not deserve the protection of the union. The
militants' reply was: if the union was so concerned about what the law
thinks, why did it not prosecute the many coalowners guilty of
infringements of the Mines Acts?
   In 1909, some Northumbrian miners struck. At Ashington, the
putters – not falling into the trap of their brothers at Swalwell and
Washington – gave due notice of their strike. This did not help them so
far as gaining union support was concerned. Their dispute involved
other workers who, unable to continue their employment as a consequence of the strike, applied locally for poor relief. But the Guardians,
led by the Right Honourable Thomas Burt, refused, arguing that they
should do the work of the men on strike rather than apply for relief.[41]
   Burt and other union officials signed an agreement in 1910, and as
this was done without the mandate of the membership, a hundred
thousand miners downed tools. The agreement increased the hours that
the colliery would operate and gave the manager greater labour flexibility. But the strikers pointed out that, among other things, the new
arrangements would mean that hewers sometimes would be called upon
to do the work of shifters. Since shifters were generally older men, it
was feared that some aged miners might be thrown on the scrap-heap
– as did, in fact, happen.[42]
   The leader of the Northumbrian miners' union, Thomas Burt, was
one of the two first working men to be elected to Parliament, at the
1874 General Election. After that date, he combined his industrial and
political duties, sitting in Parliament as a Liberal MP. True, he was
venerated by the press and his fellow politicians, especially when he
became 'Father of the House', but many North-Eastern miners,
responsible for paying his salary, took a different attitude. Mutterings
increased when Liberal coalowner, Lord Joicey, presented him with a

cheque for £260. A leaflet, published by some rank-and-file Durham miners, commented: 'If £260 is the "price", then miners' leaders are cheap and worth getting hold of.' Similarly, *The Socialist* remarked on Burt's role:

> By appearing on platforms and paying tributes to capitalists, by taking the Presidency of the National Liberal Federation, by trotting around to all kinds of capitalist ceremonies, he has fulfilled a mission for the capitalists and helped to rivet still tighter the chains of the working class.[43]

Union leaders like Thomas Burt, ageing and conservative, increasingly grew out of touch with the mood of the miners. A gulf developed between the officials and the rank-and-file throughout the country, and in no place was this more true than in the biggest coalfield, South Wales. There, ever since 1875, in the demoralisation that followed the defeat of the great strike of that year, whatever miners' organisation existed was dominated by one man – W.A. Abraham, known as Mabon. Destroying militant opposition, he secured acceptance of the notion of a sliding scale, where wages automatically fluctuated with the price of coal. This obviated the need for industrial action. Wages went up – or, more usually, down – irrespective of the stage of the men's union. Membership became pointless: by 1908 it had dropped from two-thirds to only half the labour force. South Wales miners felt defenceless. Not only was the sliding scale manipulated against them, but coal-owners used the miners' lack of organisational strength to whittle away fringe benefits and traditional rights.

Sullen resentment turned to active opposition in 1910, when miners at the Ely pit in the Rhondda Valley were sent home by the management because of a quarrel about working in abnormal places. Two other pits, Nantgwyn and Pandy, stopped in sympathy with their locked-out brothers. This brought the principal union official, William Abraham MP, into action begging them to reconsider their decision – in the interests of the coalowner!

'My friend D.A. Thomas,' he said, 'has been suffering from poor health; and I feel sure that on his holiday in France he will not benefit in health if he were to hear of such a strike as this. I beg you, I beg you to hold your hand.' W.H. Mainwaring, one of the spokesmen for the Cambrian Combine lodge, tersely replied: 'Mr D.A. Thomas may be your friend, Mr Abraham; he is not our friend.'[44]

Efforts to avert the stoppage proved to be futile. Elsewhere in the coalfield, tempers were beginning to rise. The management of the Lower Duffryn colliery, Mountain Ash, suddenly decided to stop employees taking home waste wood; in future, it had to be paid for. Angry at the discontinuation of an old custom, men thought it the final straw when policemen searched them for timber, and they came out on strike. By the autumn of 1910, all 12,000 miners at the Cambrian Combine had stopped, as had about 18,000 men who worked for other companies.

The coalminers felt confident of victory. They planned to import large numbers of strikebreakers, and the authorities intended rigorously to enforce law and order. A few tough sentences, it was hoped, would set an example; strikers would see the futility of further resistance. Then, Mabon and the rest of the moderates would regain control.

But the coalowners, backed by the Government, miscalculated. Far from cowering the men into submission, each time they escalated the struggle the strike spread and became more ferocious. They came to realise that they were fighting workers who had a new type of leadership. These were young miners — men like Noah Ablett, Noah Rees, W.F. Hay and W.H. Mainwaring — who were articulate, educated and Marxist. Many of them had studied at Ruskin College and participated in the strike there against the non-socialist curriculum.

These new leaders believed in industrial democracy. This was not merely their ultimate aim: it governed their day-to-day practice. As one of them later explained, all important questions had to be placed before mass meetings that would reach the final decision. Once this had been reached, then it was everybody's duty to carry out the decision in a loyal and disciplined manner.[45] By these means, a remarkable enthusiasm and solidarity was generated in the mining villages. Officials of the National Union of Mineworkers attest to this fact.

The Miners' Federation of Great Britain, alarmed at events in South Wales and afraid of trouble spreading to other parts of the country, had adopted an attitude of nominally supporting the strikers. Each week £3,000 was despatched to them. In this way, the MFGB hoped to gain popularity among the strikers, and influence to secure acceptance of a settlement with the employers. Essentially, the role of Mabon & Co., now discredited, would be performed by officials of the MFGB.

But when two national officials, vice-president W.E. Harvey and general secretary Thomas Ashton, journeyed to South Wales, they discovered their task was very much more difficult than they had imagined. Thomas Ashton described the scene: 'When we arrived at Tonypandy, the streets were full of men and youths who, to our

surprise, shouted out: "'No ballot", "Go back to England", "Keep your
£3,000", "Give us the twentieth rule" ' — a reference to the rule em-
powering the MFGB to call a general strike.[46] In the meeting, delegates
displayed hostility to Ashton and Harvey. Afterwards, on the way back
to the station, the two union officials, who received police protection,
were roundly abused by the general crowd. Later, W.E. Harvey
exclaimed:

> Anything is better than the state of the anarchy and red riot such as
> prevails in Tonypandy today. I have been a trade union leader for
> thirty years and have never witnessed anything equal to it.[47]

Despite the vehemence with which they fought, the South Wales miners
succumbed to the united might of employers and Government, secretly
abetted by the national officials of their own union. But their ten-
month battle did not end in barren defeat. In other coalfields, miners
were stirred by the Welshmen's tremendous struggle. A radicalisation
occurred among pitmen throughout the country. The issue of abnormal
places became translated into a demand for a minimum wage for all
miners. The 1912 strike, the first nationwide strike of pitmen, came
directly from the spark that was first struck in the Rhondda Valley.
Equally important, 1911 gave a pointer to the ideological way forward.
Probably no pamphlet published in Britain has had a greater impact on
any industry than *The Miners' Next Step* had in the coal industry. Every
page was imbued with the idea of the potential power of the working
class. For this power to be properly utilised, the pamphlet argued, two
conditions were necessary: the democratisation of decision-making and
centralisation for fighting. The old notion of Mabon & Co. that an
identity of interest existed between employer and employed was swept
aside; class war must replace reliance on conciliation. For this to
happen, conservative union officials had to be cast aside, and control
vested in the hands of the rank-and-file. To attain this aim, the South
Wales Miners' Unofficial Reform Committee was formed, and similar
groups sprung up elsewhere. Significantly, it was from this committee
that many of the men who played a prominent part in the industrial
struggles of the First World War came, and who were later to form the
left-wing leadership of the South Wales miners' union.

Developments closely resembling these took place in the engineering
industry, where patterns and personalities that had emerged in the pre-
1914 period were to dominate the later period. The trend away from
craft unionism and towards industrial unionism, the emergence of shop

stewards and the rise of unofficial rank-and-file movements — all have their origins in the years before the First World War.

Engineering workers suffered a grave setback in the 1897 lock-out. It took years for them to recover. Employers compelled them to accept humiliating conditions as a settlement. They arrogated to themselves almost unlimited managerial rights: freedom to introduce non-union labour, unrestricted overtime, piece-work, and any number of apprentices. Also, they overhauled the disputes procedure, providing themselves with devices to prolong, virtually indefinitely, consideration of victimisation and similar issues. With the 1897 settlement, engineering employers thought militancy in its coffin, and union leaders, seeking to avoid strikes, had no desire to prove them wrong.

An important reason for the weakness of trade unionism in engineering was the proliferation of small organisations. Two hundred and five unions vegetated within the industry; militants like W.F. Watson, advocating amalgamation, thought there should be one.[48] Undoubtedly, the majority were too tiny to function effectively. A typical example is the United Patternmakers' Association, formed in 1872. By January 1909, it had a mere 6,963 members, 1,395 of whom were unemployed. As a result of protracted unemployment, many craftsmen who were members drifted into unskilled jobs. The union was too weak to protect its members' jobs, wages — or anything else.[49] But it did exert a negative influence: its members worked during the 1897 lock-out and again in the 1908 dispute. Such unions as the United Patternmakers, ordering their members to remain at work, could always have a baleful effect on any campaign for improvements. As Guy Aldred remarked: 'The trade unionist blackleg proves a more effectual opponent of his class than either the professional or amateur blackleg.'[50]

Many of these small unions failed to survive. Criticism of their effectiveness as well as their failure, in many instances, to provide a minimum service, led to their merger or demise. In the years 1900 to 1915, 196 trade unions vanished — in other words, well over the number affiliated to the TUC at the present time. The death of these organisations in the pre-First World War period was celebrated in a journal called *Voice of Labour* with a poem:

Ten Little Craft Unions

Ten little craft unions, working in a mine;
One of them went on strike, then there were nine.
Nine little craft unions, all digging slate;

One made a contract, then there were eight.
Eight little craft unions, working hours eleven;
One struck for shorter hours, and then there were seven.
Seven little craft unions, all making bricks;
One got blacklisted, then there were six.
Six little craft unions, trying to keep alive;
One scabbed on all the rest, then there were five.
Five little craft unions, working in a store;
One wasn't recognised, then there were four.
Four little craft unions, good as could be;
One wasn't good enough, then there were three.
Three little craft unions, working in a crew;
One committed mutiny, then there were two.
Two little craft unions, both on the run;
One lost its treasury, then there was one.
One little craft union, fighting all alone;
The business bought it, then there was none.

Despite the fatalities, the welter of unions that continued to exist made
it impossible to formulate any common strategy. They proved to be
incapable of coping adequately with the major problems of the time —
namely, low wages, the cutting of piece-work rates, and the issues
arising as a result of the rapid introduction of machinery of increasing
magnitude and complexity.

Frequently, compounding the difficulties, trade unions' own internal
organisation precluded efficiency. In the case of the Associated Society
of Engineers, the biggest union in the engineering industry, the most
important body was the executive committee. This was too small, and
was not supplied with sufficient information, to deal properly with the
myriad of problems that cropped up in factories throughout the land.
Besides the executive committee, the ASE held delegate meetings.
These were convened irregularly. Usually the period between delegate
meetings was much longer than a year, and they could exercise little
control over the executive committee nor play a big part in the formulation of union policy. By default, much of the power within the ASE
rested with the various district committees. The general picture was one
of confusion, with no clearly defined decision-making procedures. One
effect of this failure to delineate responsibilities within the union was
that it helped, unwittingly, to encourage the growth of initiative at
grass-roots level. But, to a large extent, the creation of shop stewards
was a natural and inevitable development, a necessary concomitant of

changes within the engineering industry. Messrs Clegg, Fox and
Thompson, in their history of trade unions, make this point in the
following way:

> Changes in products, in tools and machines, and in workshop
> practice and organisation added further complexities. To cope with
> them district committees were revising their by-laws and port rules,
> either unilaterally or by agreement with local employers' associations
> — some of which were reached after reference to Central Conference.
> But they could not cover the finer points of machine-manning and
> piece rates, or the growing number of disputes over discipline,
> clocking in and out, and job cards. On these matters the decisions
> depended on the strength and quality of union leadership in the
> shop, where the shop steward had already made his appearance.[51]

The ASEs 1892 delegate conference empowered district committees to
appoint shop stewards and direct their activities. Initially their main
function was to maintain membership, to see that all remain in benefit,
and tell any new employee that he must join the union. This last-
mentioned task obviously could result in conflict with management:
the workers' desire to preserve the closed shop versus the employers'
wish to engage whoever he chose. In some factories, shop stewards'
duties gradually grew. The Manchester District Committee permitted
its shop committee to negotiate piece rates with foremen. By 1897,
Manchester employers were grumbling about 'forms of interference . . .
surreptitiously and continuously exercised by shop stewards.'[52] Soon
similar complaints were heard from employers elsewhere.

The growth in number and power of shop stewards created tensions
inside the union as well as for management. The rise of opposition to
the ASE leadership was closely related to the emergence of this new
force. Disagreement related primarily to two issues. First, there was the
question of general strategy. The ASEs leaders, painfully aware of the
terrible drubbing the union received in the 1897 lock-out, wanted to
adopt a conciliatory approach, avoiding conflict with the employers
wherever possible. Among ordinary engineers, on the other hand, there
was a mounting sense of annoyance at low pay and poor conditions, a
desire to get even for the defeat of 1897. These contrasting attitudes
laid the basis for the second major disagreement: the conflict between
local autonomy and centralised authority. The ASE leaders, wanting
to maintain a cautious attitude, saw that this could easily be jeopardised
by precipitous action at local level. To avoid this happening, they

sought to concentrate power in their own hands.

From the turn of the century, the union hierarchy of the ASE became more and more estranged from the membership. In 1902, it signed the Premium Bonus Agreement. The executive's conduct was so unpopular, it did not dare to place the Agreement before the membership. The next year the executive committee quarrelled with the Clydeside engineers — significantly, an area where shop stewards were strong. In other parts of Britain, ASE had accepted a wage cut of a shilling, but the Clydesiders refused. Despite the executive's recommendation, they held two ballots that rejected this advice and, finally, they came out on strike. This annoyed the national leadership, who stopped benefit from being paid to the men and ordered that all monies already paid, on local initiative, be refunded. Eventually, the Clyde engineers — much to the satisfaction of the executive — returned to work and accepted the wage cut. 'The men have been saved from themselves and a useless squandering of the Society's money had been prevented,' declared G.N. Barnes, the ASE general secretary. 'A much needed lesson in trade union discipline has been taught.'[53]

In 1906, another centre of shop steward strength, Manchester, came into conflict with both the executive council and central conference. 'How long is this peace-at-any-price policy to continue?' asked the Manchester district council. 'How long are the results of the débâcle in 1898 to be with us?' When it refused to accept the recommendations of the national leaders, the Manchester district committee was suspended.

Erith district committee suffered the same fate. It was suspended when it resisted the introduction of a bonus scheme at Vickers & Son, a scheme which, at the most, would have given workers only a quarter of the wealth accruing from increased production.

Also in 1907, the ASE executive reached a general agreement with employers. Among its provisions was one which sought to introduce the single meal-break system — up till then engineers had had two. Of course, workers resented the innovation. When it became obvious that a majority would reject the agreement, the executive took the unprecedented step of stopping a ballot. Then it issued a statement to the membership:

The principle of collective bargaining through negotiation is at stake . . . We are normally pledged to the terms of the memorandum, and its rejection would weaken us not only individually, but would weaken anyone who at any future time should be called upon to negotiate on your behalf.[54]

Despite this plea, members rejected the agreement by a two-to-one majority. Employers operated it without the union's signature.

Its authority badly undermined, the ASE executive soon encountered another serious challenge. Engineers in the North-East refused to accept the executive's recommendation that they accept a wage cut. Twice it was put to the members, and both times rejected. The Tynesiders argued that there was no need for a wage reduction, since local firms were doing well. Armstrong Whitworth, for example, had just declared a higher dividend. But even had this not been true, the North-East engineers said, they would still oppose the cut: engineers should receive a living wage. Irrespective of economic fluctuations, there should be a definite figure below which wages should not be allowed to fall.

The concept of a living wage was new to wage negotiations in the engineering industry. When the North-East workers struck to defend the principle, employers were apprehensive, noting the fresh wave of militancy. One industrialist referred to the prevalence among engineers of 'the degrading doctrines of new unionism'. Local newspapers darkly hinted it was the result of a sinister socialist plot: the Tyneside engineers had 'fallen under the influence of an extremely aggressive set of leaders.'[55]

As the strike continued, North-Western industrialists became increasingly alarmed. The men remained solid, adamant in their determination to resist the wage cut, despite all the efforts of both employers and union. In desperation, the employers decided in July 1908, to refer the dispute to their national organisation, the Engineering Employers' Federation, which threatened to start a nation-wide lock-out unless the strike was quickly ended. With fears of a repetition of 1897 at the back of their minds, the ASE leaders made renewed efforts. George Barnes, the general secretary, attempted to persuade the men to return to work. He was loudly heckled and left for Glasgow, where he referred to the 'undemocratic feeling' of the Tynesiders which 'expressed itself in mistrust of officials and the transfer of power into the hands of unofficial leaders.'[56] The executive expelled four of these Tyneside militants for publishing 'an inflammatory leaflet' criticising the executive's decision to send the dispute to arbitration.[57]

After a five months' struggle, the strikers finally capitulated. They had been isolated; all other districts had accepted the wage cuts, and, moreover, during the stoppage the British economy had gone into a

depression, so that the employers' determination to impose the reduction was further stiffened. Many workers had been confused by the
proposal of arbitration, which finally ended the dispute. Even so, a
defiant 40 per cent of the men voted against the settlement.

The treatment of the North-East engineers aroused sympathy from
other areas. The union leaders found themselves most unpopular. In a
previous dispute, when they had come down firmly against the strikers,
all four executive members up for re-election had lost their seats.
Probably recalling this fact, the executive committee refused to endorse
the conduct of the ASE general secretary. This placed George Barnes,
who had held the post since 1892, in an impossible position. He had to
resign.

Notwithstanding this attempt to curry favour, opposition within the
union grew. In 1910, the ASE Reform Committee was formed, and in
the same year, a member described the executive — 'in reality an auto-
cracy' — as 'the most unpopular body' within the Society.[58]

The situation reached a climax at the thirteenth delegate meeting at
Liverpool in June 1912. Up till then, the infrequently-held delegate
meetings had generally endorsed, albeit sometimes grudgingly, executive committee decisions. On this occasion, however, the two bodies
were in direct conflict. Delegates demanded the holding of regular
annual conferences, the appointment of an independent chairman to
keep a watch on the executive committee, and the opening of the ASEs
ranks to unskilled workers. For good measure, delegates called upon the
entire executive to resign, including those members who had just been
elected.

Not prepared to accept these decisions, the executive appealed to
the branches over the head of the delegate meeting. Receiving considerable support, it resolved to recall the delegate meeting in December
1912, and make it rescind the resolutions previously passed. But delegates
refused to do this, arguing that the delegate meeting was the supreme
authority in the union and that the executive was acting unconstitu-
tionally. The delegate meeting, therefore, appointed its own provisional
executive committee. But this new body's authority was not accepted
by the old executive committee, who took ample provisions into the
union headquarters in Peckham Road and barricaded the place.

The siege of Peckham Road did not last long. Supporters of the delegate meeting gained access to the house next door and broke through
the wall into the union headquarters. Ralph Fox, who was standing outside the building, gives a vivid eye-witness account in his autobiography:

We waited expectantly. Suddenly the door was flung open. Across the inside, pieces of wood had been nailed and these had been wrenched and hammered away. A few pieces were still stuck round the door, hanging up a nail or two.

Fifteen or twenty men stood in the hall, some of them had been busy on the door. They were a robust looking group: young workmen in their prime, energetic and excited with their activity . . .

'And they call themselves engineers!' said one, holding up a piece of wood which he had wrenched from the door. 'It's a disgrace to the trade! I'd be ashamed if I couldn't fix a door better than that!'

A laugh answered this.

'Take your coat off!' said another to me — I was wearing a thick winter overcoat — 'there's two or three more upstairs that have got to be thrown out. We've got three down already!'

I looked around. At the foot of the broad flight of stairs was a sandy complexioned man with a fair moustache. He was ruffled and dishevelled. His glasses had been broken in the scuffle. His mouth was bleeding and he had lost one or two teeth. Another man, tall, pale, cadaverous, with dark hair, clung to the banisters. Several men were tugging him down.

'This is an outrage!' he cried. 'I demand the names and addresses of everyone here!'

Another voice, cold and curt, answered him from the floor:

'We don't take orders from you any more. I take full responsibility for everything that has happened!'

After a short parley the dispossessed Executive members agreed to go quietly. They were led out of the Reform Committee and stalwarts formed a chain across the foot of the wide stairs and the door was closed.

Suddenly a heavy knock came at the door. It was opened. Outside stood three Executive members. They had not been part of the all-night garrison. They were men on the further side of fifty, big, slow-moving men with expanded waist-belts. Not bad men, I should imagine, but men whose consumption of beer and beef had outweighed their mental activities. A doctor might have recommended diet and exercise. A look of consternation and bewilderment passed over their faces as they saw the determined band blocking their passage.

'You can't come in,' the leader told them coldly. 'You're trespassing!'

They gasped.[59]

Ralph Fox described the struggles as a victory for the rank-and-file. This is partly true. Many of the old agreements that had hung, like albatrosses, round the necks of engineers were swept away. The structure of the union was improved, but many of the gains were quickly lost. The main reason for this was that the opposition was heterogeneous, with no clear, alternative policy. Placed in the power-structure themselves, they quickly succumbed to the same influences that had made their predecessors so obnoxious. This transition to capitalist respectability was hastened by the First World War, when ASE leaders could submerge principles in a patriotic miasma.

To sum up on industrial relations from 1908 to 1914. The disputes were of unprecedented size and ferocity. While they were obviously very disturbing to both employers and Government, they never constituted a serious threat to the existence of capitalist society. Coming into being after fifty years of working-class quiescence, they represented the first attempts at mass militant resistance. Like a child's first efforts at walking, they were clumsy and confused, of significance primarily as a portent of future potential. This is not to denigrate the achievements of trade unionists during the period — many behaved in a bold and courageous manner — but it is to suggest that they must be seen in their historical context.

Notes

1. Quoted D.H. Aldcroft and H.W. Richardson, *The British Economy, 1870-1939* (1969) p. 65.
2. S. Pollard, *The Development of the British Economy, 1914-1950* (1962) p. 19.
3. G.D.H. Cole, *An Introduction to Trade Unions* (1918) p. 109.
4. G.S. Bain, *British Journal of Industrial Relations*, November 1966.
5. J.B. Jeffreys, *The Story of the Engineers* (n.d.) pp. 144-9.
6. E.J.B. Allen's article, *Socialist Standard*, June 1906.
7. E.H. Phelps Brown, *The Growth of British Industrial Relations* (1959) p. 92.
8. H.J. Fyrth and H. Collins, *The Foundry Workers* (Manchester, 1959) pp. 112-5.
9. Royal Commission on Trades Disputes and Trade Combinations, 1906, Q. 3208.
10. P.S. Bagwell, *The Railwaymen* (1963) p. 224.
11. S. & B. Webb, *History of Trade Unionism* (1920 ed.) p. 603; G.D.H. Cole & R. Postgate, *The Common People*, p. 458.
12. Quoted H.A. Clegg, A. Fox & A.F. Thompson, *A History of British Trade Unions since 1889* (Oxford, 1964) vol. 1, p. 319.
13. J.E. Williams, *The Derbyshire Miners* (1962) pp. 389-390.
14. F. Bealey and H. Pelling, *Labour and Politics, 1900-1906* (1958) p. 75.
15. Royden Harrison, *Before the Socialists* (1965) p. 36.

16. Clegg, Fox and Thompson, op. cit., p. 327.
17. G.D.H. Cole, op. cit., p. 112.
18. S. Pollard, op. cit., p. 25.
19. A.R. Prest, 'National Income of the United Kingdom, 1870-1946', *Economic Journal*, 58/229, 1948.
20. Ibid.
21. G.R. Askwith, *Industrial Problems & Disputes*, p. 109; Bob Holton, *British Syndicalism, 1900-1914* (1976) pp. 73-122, gives a good account of the industrial unrest.
22. Ibid, pp. 149-50.
23. *Manchester Guardian*, 14 August 1911; H.R. Hikins, 'The Liverpool General Transport Strike 1911' in *Transactions of the Historic Society of Lancashire and Cheshire*, vol. 113 (1961) pp. 169-95, and Bob Holton, 'Syndicalism and Labour on Merseyside, 1906-1914', in *Building The Union* (Liverpool, 1973) give a good account of the strike.
24. Tom Mann's *Memoirs* (1967 ed.) p. 223.
25. Ness Edwards, *History of the South Wales Miners' Federation* (1938) p. 40. It is interesting to note that, amid the mayhem and murder, Ness Edwards reports one bright spot – the King expressed his grave concern for the 'safety of the pit ponies'.
26. Quoted George Dangerfield, *The Strange Death of Liberal England* (1970 ed.) p. 241. Brian Pearce, 'Some Past Rank-and-file Movements', *Labour Review*, April-May 1959, puts the Cumbrian Combine dispute and other strikes of the time into historical perspective.
27. Tom Mann, op. cit., pp. 230-1. Commenting on the imprisonment of Tom Mann and his comrades, *The Socialist* (April 1912) said: 'We are not syndicalists, we have no sympathy with syndicalism, but we are fighters for freedom, and we are determined to uphold the right, no matter what the consequences, the right of free speech and free press.' *The Socialist* went on to reprint the 'Don't Shoot' leaflet, and was not prosecuted.
    The first journal to publish it, the *Irish Worker*, felt a deep sense of injustice because the authorities had taken no action against them.
28. *London Record*, 2 December 1910.
29. E.H. Phelps Brown, op. cit., pp. 298-9.
30. P. Bagnall, op. cit., p. 96.
31. Ibid.
32. E.H. Phelps Brown, op. cit., p. 301.
33. *The Socialist*, December 1907.
34. Quoted Eugene Burdick, 'Syndicalism and Industrial Unionism in Britain until 1918' (Oxford Ph.D. thesis, 1950) vol. 2, pp. 8-9.
35. P. Bagnall, op. cit., p. 291.
36. E. Burdick, op. cit., p. 9.
37. *The Socialist*, October 1911.
38. B. Pribicevic, *The Shop Stewards' Movement and Workers' Control* (Oxford, 1959) p. 5.
39. R. Page Arnot, *The Miners* (1949) vol. 1, p. 327.
40. George Harvey, *Industrial Unionism and the Mining Industry* (Pelaw on Tyne, 1917) p. 3.
41. Ibid. pp. 7-8, and also *The Socialist*, February 1909.
42. *The Socialist*, February 1910.
43. Ibid, August 1910.
44. R. Page Arnot, *South Wales Miners* (1967) p. 177.
45. Ibid.; David Evans, *Labour Strike in the South Wales Coalfield 1910-1911* (Cardiff, 1963) gives a detailed account of the strike.

46. T. Ashton, *Three Big Strikes in the Coal Industry* (Manchester 1927) vol. 2, p. 187. Also, R. Page Arnot, op. cit., p. 231.
47. Eugene Burdick, op. cit., vol. 2, p. 233.
48. W.F. Watson, *One Union for Metal, Engineer and Shipbuilding Workers* (n.d.)
49. *Industrial Unionist*, May 1909.
50. Guy Aldred, *The Logic and Economics of the Class Struggle* (1908) p. 7.
51. H.A. Clegg, A. Fox, A.F. Thompson, op. cit., p. 431.
52. Second Series of Examples of Restriction and Interference, given by Federated Engineering Employers, cited by H.A. Clegg, A. Fox, A.F. Thompson, ibid.
53. *A.S.E. Monthly Report*, June 1903.
54. Ibid, July 1907.
55. *Northern Mail*, 16 March 1908. Richard Croucher's article, 'The North Eastern Engineers' Strike of 1908', in the *North East Group for the Study of Labour History Bulletin*, No. 9, October 1975, gives a detailed analysis of the dispute.
56. *Newcastle Daily Chronicle*, 24 April 1908, *North Mail*, 24 April 1908.
57. *The Socialist*, August 1908, *Newcastle Daily Journal*, 23 April 1908.
58. J.T. Brownlie writing in *A.S.E. Monthly Journal*, September 1910.
59. R.M. Fox, *Smoky Crusade* (1938) pp. 102-3.

4 SOCIALISTS AND THE INDUSTRIAL STRUGGLE

From 1907 onwards, the SLP functioned in a rising tide of industrial discontent. Opportunities for growth presented themselves and, often, were taken. But the Party was conscious of its own inadequacy; its puny resources did not meet the needs of the times. When industrial disputes occurred, the SLP was liable to find itself without a branch in the affected area. Or even if a branch existed, it might have no members working in the particular industry. Therefore, the Party was frequently condemned to the role of onlooker, rather than participant. It could comment on the struggle but not influence its outcome. There were occasions, even more tantalising, when the SLP failed to establish contact with the strikers. This happened where the Party had insufficient money to send a representative to meet the workers in dispute, or when it did not even have the address of the strike committee. This meant that copies of *The Socialist* could not be sent, nor could a first-hand account of the strikers' case appear in its columns. But despite such frustrations, the SLP continued to progress. Modest, unspectacular, the expansion was nonetheless gratifying. Delegates attending the fifth annual conference, held in Edinburgh, on 30-31 March 1907, heard that the Party now had fifteen branches — in other words, three times the number reported at the inaugural meeting. What was more, most of the growth had been in England. There were branches in important centres like London, Birmingham, Sheffield and Southampton. Indeed, two-thirds of its branches were outside Scotland. At the same time, *The Socialist*'s circulation had risen in the course of the year by 447 copies.

Delegates at Edinburgh realised the importance of the Party husbanding its resources, utilising them to best advantage. They debated a motion that the SLP should suspend electoral activity and devote itself entirely to spreading the ideas of industrial unionism. Although this resolution was rejected, it was carried out in spirit. From then on, the Party's energies were primarily given over to industrial affairs. As we have seen, it was largely instrumental in creating the Advocates of Industrial Unionism, which was formed in August 1907. Then there were the pamphlets, mainly on industrial issues. These were very influential, and were of a high intellectual quality, works that required thought and were intended to be read and re-read. In 18 months, the Party published eleven pamphlets. In one month, it printed 18,000 copies. In this way, the SLPs ideas acquired an audience among the growing number of discontented workers. The Party's pamphlets helped to mould the theoretical principles of a generation of militants.

It must be remembered that this was the first attempt, at least in a concerted and nationwide sense, to build a rank-and-file movement. Obviously, in some respects, policies would necessarily be wrong and confused. A new set of tasks presented themselves, for which little or no guidance existed on methods of accomplishment. The multiplicity of unions and the widely differing conditions prevailing in various parts of the country made it difficult to co-ordinate activity, particularly on matters of detail.

The SLP confined itself largely to propounding certain basic princi-ples. It argued that the class struggle was central to the fight for socialism; that it could best be fought by the elimination of craft unions and the formation of new ones built on industrial lines; that the role of labour leaders, both political and trade union, was to sabotage the workers' struggle; and, finally, that a revolutionary party was required not only to combat these 'labour lieutenants of capitalism' but also to lay the foundations of a new society. In a leading article in *The Socialist* (June 1907), the SLP expressed its view of what was to be done:

> Let us then organise industrially as well as politically for our class emancipation. Industrially, to build up in the womb of capitalism the foundations of the future state of society, reared upon the structure of our class interests, marching shoulder to shoulder, steadying up our class in their onward march to economic freedom.
>
> Politically, to unseat the capitalist class from the power of govern-ment, to remove the legal enactments that today safeguard the rights of private property, to prevent, if possible, the capitalist class from using the physical power of the nation against the industrial workers of this or any other nation.

The SLP thought the Advocates of Industrial Unionism would play a vital role in the industrial struggle. At the AIU inaugural conference only 19 branches were represented, but it recognised its own weakness, resolving to limit itself to propaganda work and not trying to perform the function of a *bona fide* trade union. There was lack of clarity about precisely how it would develop. Should AIU members work within existing organisations, trying to convert them to industrial unionism? Or should they try to gain sufficient support to set up a separate and rival union? If it were decided to create a new union, should dual unionism be encouraged — in other words, members remaining within the old-style union to gain added protection and make new recruits? Not one of these questions was properly answered — because the AIU never grew enough to pose them seriously. Although it influenced quite large sections of the working class, it remained a weak organisation with a small membership. Insofar as the AIU had a leadership, it never acquired sufficient power to impose a definite policy on these questions. Rather members confronted them in a haphazard and piecemeal fashion. Frequently, pressure from others would have a bigger influence on their tactics than their own decisions. For example, at Woolwich engineers who sympathised with the AIU made it plain that they would not join if it meant losing the friendly society benefits of the ASE while in Glasgow and Birmingham factories workers threatened to go on strike if men left the ASE to join the AIU.[1] Such counter-moves were usually enough to dissuade Advocates of Industrial Unionism from adventurous projects. Instead they contented themselves with selling their literature in union branches and factories, getting resolutions sent to union head-quarters, and attempting to link up with like-minded militants in other areas. They acted as what we would call an unofficial movement within the trade unions.

The AIU leaders realistically appreciated that they had undertaken an immense task. E.J.B. Allen envisaged many years of hard work ahead, remaining sure of ultimate victory:

> Our ideas will establish themselves even if not through us . . .
> though the particular organisation we started is knocked, a larger
> and better one will inevitably step on its ruins and take the field; our
> efforts will not be lost.[2]

As the prospect was one of a long haul, it was important to mobilise every scrap of support. The SLP believed that the Advocates of Indus-trial Unionism should not be linked to any particular political party; it should be open to all, regardless of political persuasion. Indeed, it saw positive advantages from ILP and SDF joining: the barriers of sectarian suspicion would be broken down, and there was a fine opportunity for testing SLP principles, applying them in practice. By providing the theoretical basis for industrial unionism, as well as much of the propa-ganda material, the SLP would be doing an invaluable service, one that no other socialist group even thought of doing. Besides having socialism

as the ultimate goal, the SLP had something which made it unique —
an idea of the next step forward for the class. 'Until workers have
grasped that,' declared *The Socialist*, 'the SLP will only appeal to their
minds as one of the political sects out of the four or five claiming to
be *the* party of the working class, just as the broader-minded view with
amusement the spasms and gyrations of the Plymouth Brethren, the
Exclusive Brethren and the strict Baptists of total immersion.'[3]

At the inaugural conference of the Advocates of Industrial Unionism
the SLPers sought to carry out this policy. Although they had done
most of the work to establish the new organisation and had a majority
of the membership, they decided not to capture the leading positions.
J.E. Clark, of Marylebone SDF, was national secretary and W.O.
Angilly, a member of the SPGB, was treasurer. The AIU was to be run
from London, a place where the SLP was very weak.

But things did not go as the Party planned. Politics in the AIU
became polarised. This partly arose as a result of the antagonism of
other socialist groups: both the SDF and the SPGB expelled all
members who advocated industrial unionism. Almost everyone thrown
out gravitated to the SLP. Meanwhile, what progress the AIU was
making was not amongst workers of any political persuasion, but
among those who were decidedly anti-politics. To these new members,
politics was synonymous with parliamentary politics, the cavortings of
Ramsay MacDonald & Co., who supported the Liberal government
when it attacked the workers. Even those with reservations about
adopting a completely anti-political standpoint were inclined to feel
that the most urgent need was for industrial unions, with all energy
being thrown into the struggle on the factory-floor, not dissipated in
arid political activity.

E.J.B. Allen and most of the other leaders of the AIU were influenced by this proto-syndicalism. When the *Industrial Unionist* first
appeared in March 1908, the journal declared:

We are revolutionists, and we seek to organise all class conscious
workers. Until this is accomplished, there can be no real working
class political action.

An article entitled 'The Bankruptcy of Parliamentary Socialism'
affirmed:

The ballot by itself is sterile. As a means, however, for registering
the strength of the organised working class, as a kind of manifesto,

a declaration of rights, it may serve a useful function at a later stage
in the struggle after the industrial union has created the force to
register it.

The line of the *Industrial Unionists* annoyed members of the SLP
greatly since it denied that there was any role at all for a revolutionary
party in the struggle for socialism. In March 1908, Frank Budgen
criticised the journal's policy at an executive meeting of the AIU, but
the majority of the members backed Allen. The executive circulated
a resolution to branches, asking for their approval.[4] The membership,
being mainly SLPers, did not respond as the EC had hoped. Rather
they supported a letter sent by Budgen and C.W. Peachey, calling upon
them to repudiate the position on the executive. Chaos ensued. At its
next meeting the executive, incensed by what it regarded as the dis-
loyalty of Budgen and Peachey, moved Peachey from the chair. Meanwhile in Scotland, SLPers quickly decided to publish an issue of the
Industrial Unionist on the Party press to attack the Allen line. Although
the executive tried to suppress it, most copies seem to have been distributed. By this time, members were aligning themselves with one
camp or the other. It was quite clear that the executive was in a
minority within the organisation. So, in May 1908, Allen & Co.
resigned from the AIU and formed the Industrial League.[5]

On 27 May 1908, a newly-formed AIU executive expelled all the
'pure' industrialists, including most of the AIU membership in London, as
well as a large number of the SLP there. Entire branches were expelled,
disbanded and re-organised. But most SLP members agreed with Frank
Budgen's verdict that the purge was necessary and beneficial: 'The
party had lost weight, but its pulse beat more regularly and it was no
longer suffering from those giddy spells.'[6] This, it would seem, is too
optimistic a conclusion: later, both the SLP and AIU suffered from
numerous other bouts of dizziness. The loss of members as a result of
the 1908 faction fight does not appear to have seriously impeded
growth. The AIU, which had only 18 branches represented at its
inaugural conference in 1907, had 39 branches by June 1909. And the
SLP grew from 15 branches in 1907 to 25 branches by 1911.

Even so, the purge of Allen and Co. constituted a temporary setback,
and it was politically significant that surgery of such a drastic nature
was required. In part, many of the London SLPers expelled were
recent recruits, who had not properly assimilated the Party's principles.
But this was not the whole explanation. Encapsulated with the SLPs
notion of the way forward was an ambiguity which created the

conditions on which a large-scale split could occur. The Party had two perspectives of how the overthrow of capitalism would be accomplished. The first could be called 'the double-barrelled shot-gun' approach: the working class's industrial and political strength would grow; this would manifest itself in a greatly expanded AIU and SLP; these two organisations, representing the might of the class industrially and politically, would simultaneously deliver the fatal blow to capitalism. The second would be termed 'the mother-and-child' approach. Starting from the realistic point that the SLP was small and isolated, it saw industrial unions as the means of ending this. Once the unions were mass organisations, they would be strengthened by workers' struggles and experiences. These powerful industrial unions would be the mother of a revolutionary child:

> The industrial unions will constitute a body of men and women
> at once intensely practical and uncompromisingly revolutionary.
> It can never degenerate into a sect, which is the danger to which
> political organisations representing a revolutionary position had
> hitherto been exposed to, but will palpitate with the daily and
> hourly pulsations of the class struggle as it manifests itself in the
> workshop. And when it forms its own political party and moves
> into the political field, as it surely will, in that act superseding or
> absorbing the Socialist Labour Party and all other socialist or labour
> parties, its campaign will indeed be the expression of the needs,
> the hopes, the aspirations and the will of the working classes, and
> not the dreams and theories of a few unselfish enthusiasts or the
> ambitions of political schemers.[7]

Anyone holding this concept of future development could easily succumb to the E.J.B. Allen position. To build industrial unions seemed to be the first step forward; from them the revolutionary party would grow. It seemed, at the time, that the most pressing need – the one to which all effort should be devoted – was to this industrial task. Only after it had been accomplished could political progress be made.

But, ultimately, E.J.B. Allen went further than this. He came to the conclusion that the revolutionary party was not required; all its roles could be performed as well, if not better, by the industrial unions themselves. In taking this step, Allen was embracing syndicalism. It is not surprising that, when Tom Mann started to propagandise, Allen should be one of his main supporters.

The emergence of syndicalism as a powerful force in this period can

be attributed to a number of factors. First, in view of the bitter
industrial struggles raging, it became a pressing need for socialists to
direct their energies to work in the factories. Second, this course
seemed most likely to bring quick returns, breaking down the isolation
of revolutionaries and often giving them the leadership of big groups of
workers. Third, in contradistinction to industrial action, political
activity appeared to be unproductive and sterile. When political discussions occurred, workers tended to lose the unity essential for
industrial victory since they would support the various socialist group-
lets, each at each others' throats. Far better, it was felt, to put these
contentious issues on one side and concentrate on the industrial tasks
at hand. And, finally, there was the widespread hostility to politics,
which was thought of in purely parliamentary terms. The conduct of
the Labour Party was largely responsible for this antipathy.

In the industrial struggles, the Liberal government openly sided
with the employers. But Labour MPs, the majority of whom owed their
seats in Parliament to electoral arrangements with the Liberals, could
not bite the hand that fed them. They would remain silent in the
House — or, at best, make a few inconsequential comments — when
police and troops bludgeoned workers. In 1910, when Richard Bell,
the railwaymen's leader, decided not to stand at the next election,
Winston Churchill expressed his regret and found him a well-paid post
at the Board of Trade. Yet, within a few months of doing this, the same
Churchill was ordering warships up the Mersey. The Government pointed
guns at Liverpool strikers while it gave the railwaymen's leader a
comfortable job. Many workers saw the contrast. Could they fail to
show their disgust when, in 1911, four Labour MPs, including Arthur
Henderson, introduced a Parliamentary Bill that would make strikes
illegal unless thirty days' notice had been given?

Perhaps some idea of the sense of outrage felt by militants may be
conveyed by quoting the London dockers' leader, Ben Tillett. In a
pamphlet, 'Is the Parliamentary Labour Party a failure?', published in
1908, he wrote:

> I do not hesitate to describe the conduct of these blind leaders as
> nothing short of betrayal . . . While Shackleton took the chair for
> Winston Churchill, thousands of textile workers were suffering
> starvation through unemployment; his ability and energy could
> have been well used in Stevenson Square, in Manchester, instead of
> mouthing platitudes and piffle in Liberal meetings. The worst of the
> winter is coming on, time thrown away will never be recovered, and

thousands will perish for want of bread.'

Ben Tillett described the Labour leaders as 'These unctuous weaklings' who 'will go on prattling their nonsense while thousands are dying of starvation.'[8] Only one Member of Parliament took the kind of stand which Ben Tillett wanted. He was Victor Grayson, who won the Colne bye-election, much to the surprise of the Press and the annoyance of respectable Labour politicians. On 2 November 1908, as the Licensing Bill was making its tranquil progress through the Commons, Grayson rudely interrupted the proceedings: 'Mr Chairman, Mr Chairman, before you proceed any further. Thousands of people are dying in the streets.' Cries of order came from startled Members in all parts of the House. 'I will not give order,' Grayson shouted back, 'in a chamber that starves people wholesale.' He refused to sit down or leave. Parliamentary business could not continue. His suspension was moved and carried. As he was being escorted out, Grayson commented: 'I leave this House with pleasure – it is a House of Murderers.'[9]

Grayson believed that Socialism could only come through the organisation and self-activity of the working class. To emphasise the point that it could not be presented to people on a plate, he declared paradoxically: 'If the House of Commons voted for Socialism to-morrow, I would vote against it.' Not that he had any illusions about Parliament and its role:

> That dignified assembly is composed of 670 members, mostly capitalists . . . To them the words hunger, poverty, destitution, are abstract and academic phrases, with no real meaning . . . For myself, I have no hope for the House of Commons, constituted as it is . . . The Cabinet is an heterogeneous collection of vested interests.[10]

Grayson's importance lies in his expression of opinions that were widely held in left-wing circles. Where some workers parted company with him was in the conclusion he drew from his analysis: he wanted to see the formation of a revolutionary party; they on the other hand considered that the failure of the Labour Party and the futility of Parliament proved that political activity itself was wrong. They drew syndicalist conclusions.

But the Socialist Labour Party never succumbed to this powerful current. When, on 26 November 1910, Tom Mann held the Manchester conference which set up the Syndicalist Education League, the SLP sent along a representative – James Morton, a foundry worker – to express its opposition. Articles in *The Socialist* and *Industrial Worker* elaborated on these disagreements.

The first and most important issue was politics. Syndicalists shunned politics, believing that industrial power could accomplish all. 'With workers properly organised,' declared *The Syndicalist*, 'there is nothing they cannot successfully demand from the capitalists by means of a general strike.'[11] In the SLPs opinion, this greatly exaggerated the possibilities of a general strike, and it failed to see the importance of political power – in particular, the role of the capitalist state. Even in the preliminary period, well before the conquest of power, syndicalists were doing a disservice by turning their backs on politics. Johnny Muir said: 'To leave this important field to the capitalist politician is reactionary. The socialist must take political action to educate the masses.'[12]

Another source of disagreement was industrial sabotage. This was a period in which American and French syndicalism, which favoured sabotage, gained some influence in Britain. Mainly, this took the form of literature, but there was also a sprinkling of agitators, like G.H. Swasey, who came over from the States. Ralph Fox, in his autobiography, related how Swasey advocated sabotage at a public meeting:

'Every inch of fat on the boss's belly means another wrinkle in yours,' he cried. 'Waiters, put oil in their soup! Dish-washer, break their dishes! Stop their machines,' he yelled to the machine men, 'put sand in their bearings!'

Swasey was the spirit of the class war, of combat, of hatred of the rich, of destruction.

'Put nitric acid on their hops! Shrivel their crops!' he roared. 'That's what we did in America! Wherever the IWW got a grip of the hop fields, the Sabcat purred. They gave us what we wanted or the crops shrivelled up!'[13]

English advocates of sabotage usually used more restrained language. E.J.B. Allen, who became an organiser for the Syndicalist Education League, in his pamphlet 'Revolutionary Unionism' made a number of suggestions:

Moulders can turn out casts full of bubbles, electricians make faulty insulations or put in weak fuses, carpenters putting in windows need only slacken the sash cord instead of stretching it, and in a week or two another carpenter will have to go and put it right. Shop

assistants, by giving full weight and measure and an accurate and
truthful description of the goods supplied, can damage trade during
the excessive hours that they have to work, and make employers
realise it would be more economical to shut up at a reasonable time
than to keep open so long. Numberless devices can be adopted in
this guerilla warfare, according to the ingenuity and daring of the
individuals concerned.[14]

'The ingenuity and daring of the individuals concerned' — the phrase
pointed exactly to where the SLP critique of Allen began. Sabotage
was a protest action taken by workers as individuals, not as a class. It
was, consequently, a symptom of despair, a futile gesture taken by
those who did not recognise the real power that came from activity of
the class. George Harvey, writing in *The Socialist* from personal experience, said that where the Durham miners were well-organised, they
had no need to resort to such methods.[15] A second criticism of the SLP
was that the destruction of machinery and tools could be a self-inflicted
wound. In his pamphlet, Allen had cited the case of a gang of navvies,
faced with a wage reduction. They cut a strip, about an inch to an inch
and a half wide, off their shovels, shouting, 'Shorter pay, shorter
shovels.'[16] But, commenting on this picturesque illustration for the SLP,
W.S. Jerman said that navvies' shovels were of various sizes, owing to
constant use. As it was the custom for workers to buy their own shovels,
the behaviour Allen reported, and appeared to recommend, was sense-
less. Jerman then went on to make the point that the socialist aim was
not the destruction of the means of production but their capture.[17]

Finally, syndicalists and the SLP parted company on the whole
question of organisation, its scope and functioning. For Syndicalism
was more an attitude than a movement. Tom Mann was its originator
in Britain. He took the decisions, along with a small group of friends.
As Mrs Mann explained in an interview with the *Daily Herald*: 'The
term (Syndicalism) was adopted by my husband and Mr Guy Bowman
after due consideration to designate our plan of campaign.'[18] Tom
Mann himself remarked on the informality that surrounded the Syndicalist Education League: 'There were a few comrades who started it,
and the need for a definite constitution, rules and so forth was not felt.
We were all personal friends, and we just selected a committee of
five.'[19] To the SLP this was wrong. Perhaps its difference on this question was symptomatic of a more fundamental difference of approach:
the SLP saw a much more far-reaching change had to be made to the
trade union movement, a transformation that could only be attained

with regular and systematic work, guided and led by the Advocates for Industrial Unionism.

If the SLP won the better of the ideological conflict, it had the worst of it in practice. The lack of clarity of the syndicalists was, at least in the short-run, an advantage, helping them to gain adherents. Theirs was the articulate expression of the militancy, often confused and contradictory, of a large section of the working class. The syndicalists also had the advantage of being led by Tom Mann, a person who had been a household name in the labour movement for twenty years, while most of the SLPs industrial cadres were young and unknown. In these circumstances, it is not surprising that the masses tended to be attracted to Syndicalism and that the SLP support stayed relatively small.

Although only briefly a force of consequence, Syndicalism still had a lasting influence on the development of the British labour movement. It was a nursery school, a training ground for militants. Many of those tested in the pre-1914 period rose to prominence in the industrial struggles of the First World War and afterwards. The personal contacts established under the aegis of Syndicalism also served a purpose, often providing the basis later for formation of shop stewards' committees and other rank-and-file organisations.

Nor was Syndicalism's influence purely industrial: while an avowedly non-political movement, it nevertheless allowed people with political affiliations to join, which is what many socialists did. Syndicalism acted as an umbrella, providing the cover under which members of the various socialist groups could acquire the habit of working harmoniously together. Besides helping to break down the feelings of suspicion on the Left, Syndicalism also led Socialist parties, particularly the SDF, to adopt a more flexible attitude to industrial questions. Traditionally, the SDF leaders were suspicious of strikes, believing that the same objective could be better achieved through the ballot box. This view seemed less tenable in the industrial turmoil from 1908 on, when their own members frequently led in the struggles. When one of the SDFs leading personalities, Tom Mann, became the main exponent of Syndicalism, it must have had a big impact on the Federation's membership. Support inside the SDF for Syndicalism and industrial unionism appears to have grown too much for the SDF leaders to continue the policy of persecuting industrial dissidents, even if they wanted to. In 1907, a man like J.E. Clark could be expelled from the SDF for preaching industrial unionism; by 1911 no expulsions were made on those grounds. Both industrial unionism and Syndicalism

could be advocated by SDF members with impunity. The same applied
to the ILP.

So one of the effects of Syndicalism was that it encouraged socialist
parties to adopt a more tolerant and realistic approach to industrial
questions: paradoxically, a non-political movement had important
political consequences. But Syndicalism itself represented a dead-end.
Beyond emphasising the need for forceful protest, it gave no idea of the
way forward. One of the reasons for the drop in the number of days
lost in industrial stoppages from 40 million days in 1912 to less than
10 million days in 1913 and 1914 was that workers were beginning to
realise more and more the inadequacies of Syndicalism as a doctrine.
From 1912 onwards, Syndicalism was in decline.

There were, though, other factors contributing to the wave of
militancy's decline. First, workers had become better off and therefore
did not feel the urgency of protest action so much. Real wages rose
between 1910 and 1913: having been about 10 per cent lower than
they were in 1900, they were probably only three per cent less by
1913. Second, there was the defeat of the miners' strike (1912) and
the Dublin strike (1913), affecting the whole climate of labour relations. These were not catastrophic defeats, merely temporary setbacks,
which won for the employers a respite while workers licked their
wounds and regrouped. And, third, as part of this process of regrouping, came the spate of union amalgamations, which tended to pre-
occupy union militants. Time and energy were diverted from the class
struggle itself to the task of making these new organisations better than
those which had preceded them.

Numerically much smaller than the syndicalists, industrial unionists
also suffered from the decline in industrial activity. By 1913, their
organisation, too, was in a state of collapse. A few years previously
the prospect had appeared bright. After the split with E.J.B. Allen and
his followers, the executive committee had been moved to Manchester
and in 1909, in anticipation of rapid expansion, the name 'Advocates
of Industrial Unionism' was discarded for the more grandiose title of
'Industrial Workers of Great Britain'. Only the name changed; the
amount of support remained the same. Its journal, *Industrial Worker*,
survived a mere 14 months before being killed by falling circulation
and rising costs. By January 1913, T.L. Smith, then the IWGB general
secretary, was reporting dwindling membership. Lugubriously, he
declared: 'Even those that stuck with the IWGB have become dis-
heartened with the non-success.'[20]

So much effort expended, so little to show for it — that seems to have been the picture. But it was only partially true. The ideas of industrial unionism had been spread throughout the country and influenced many militants. Frequently, those playing a leading part in union amalgamations and strikes had been members. That they no longer remained in the IWGB was because the struggle in the wider movement took all their time.

An innovation of the IWGB was the introduction of factory branches where industrial and political matters could be discussed. These branches, including skilled and unskilled workers, contributed to the breaking down of union divisions and helped to widen the horizons of workers, who began to think of mutual problems, encompassing the factory as a whole. Conventional union branches tended to balk at this type of issue. As an IWGB leaflet, published in Glasgow, said, criticising the ASE:

A branch may be composed of members no two of whom are working in the same shop or factory, the only thing they have in common is that they are in one trade, namely, the engineering trade. Their branch bears no resemblance to their everyday working life.[21]

In most instances, IWGB factory branches remained small. About half a dozen people would meet and discuss how to relate revolutionary politics to their industrial life. Their direct influence was minimal: few people joined and, as a bargaining force, they were non-existent. Indirectly, however, they sometimes had a seminal influence: their ideas would get through to workers within the works and, via the traditional trade union structure and procedures, sweeping changes would occur. The two major battles of the IWGB took place on the Clyde, at Argyle Motors and the Singer Sewing Machine Works.

Singer's factory at Kilbowie, Clydebank, was ultra-modern. The latest techniques of mass production were applied there, and speed-ups, price cutting and sackings were common place. The 10,000 employees, mostly unskilled, were cowed into submission, poorly paid and without a trade union:

It was typical of the new machine age. The sub-division of labour was carried to a fine art, and young boys and girls were brought into the factory to operate the simple processes on ridiculous low wages. I remember Arthur MacManus describing a job he was on, pointing needles. Every morning there were millions of these needles on the table. As fast as he reduced the mountain of needles on the table, a fresh load was dumped. Day in, day out, it never grew less. One morning he came in and found the table empty. He couldn't understand it. He began telling everyone excitedly that there were no needles on the table. It suddenly flashed on him how absurdly stupid it was to be spending his life like this. Without taking his jacket off, he turned on his heel and went out, to go for a ramble over the hills to Balloch.

The dull, deadening influence of this factory, the unbridled exploitation, etc., was favourable soil for the new ideas of industrial unionism.[22]

In 1906, three or four industrial unionists went to work at Singer's. Quietly, they began to spread their ideas. Leaflets and pamphlets were published, and *The Socialist* was sold. Slowly and patiently, propaganda work continued for years. On 29 January 1910, it was thought that sufficient progress had been made to form the Sewing Machine Workers' Industrial Union Group. Eighteen people attended the inaugural meeting. From then on, the tempo of development quickened. William Paul, of the SLP, later to be one of the finest orators in the Communist Party, held factory-gate meetings. These continued throughout the summer of 1910, often attended by as many as a thousand workers. Seven dozen copies of *The Socialist* were regularly sold inside the factory; the sale outside sometimes reached 60 copies. By the end of the year, the Sewing Machine Workers had 150 members. After holding a ballot, they resolved to change their name to the Sewing Machine Group of the IWGB — and to assume the functions of a union.

In 1911, the real conflict occurred at Singer's. In February, a foreman in No. 11 department decided to re-organise a squad of workers and to cut the price for the job. As a rule, workers meekly acquiesced in such changes, but this time the squad of 16 refused. Surprised by the reaction, the foreman quickly reverted to the previous arrangement, and this victory heightened morale. Another 60 joined the IWGB in that department, as well as others elsewhere. On 18 February, a foreman introduced a wage cut of a penny per 100 pieces in department No. 10, which would have meant a wage reduction of about 1s 9d a week. The 400 workers in the department, except for about twenty foremen and fitters, immediately stopped work, and only resumed once the proposed wage cut had been withdrawn. Similar victories took place in the cabinet polishing department (No. 26) and buffing department (No. 16).

Up to then, Singer's management had generally been successful in implementing its policies. It had deliberately fragmented the labour force, dividing the factory up into 41 departments, which in turn contained sub-groups. The result of this, said a report, had been, that a worker 'does not know what is going on outside the half dozen or so immediately alongside him.'

In an effort to overcome this disunity, the IWGB adopted what was then a new, but is now a well established, procedure. In every department where it had members, it set up a 'shop committee', to whom every grievance occurring throughout the department was reported. Then, above this, 'there was the General Committee of the Industrial Union Group, comprising representatives of Industrialists throughout the whole factory.'[23] With what was in effect a 'shop stewards' committee', the IWGB continued to make progress. In his memoirs, Tom Bell describes what happened:

> The membership began to increase, and from a handful of enthusiasts it jumped to hundreds and soon touched four thousand members in Singer's alone. Shop grievances were taken up. From small successes the influence of the organisation grew and spread to every department. The slogan of 'An injury to one is an injury to all' caught on. Simple shop disputes became departmental issues. Each shop appointed its delegate to the Department Committees, and these were linked up through a Works Committee.[24]

Bell's account probably needs more qualification. According to the statement, 'The Kilbowie Strike and Its Lessons', published by the Singer Sewing Machine Group, IWGB, its membership was only 1,500 — not 4,000 as Bell suggests — when the employers' offensive began. It may be that, in the course of the struggle, the number rose to 4,000 for a short time, but these were simply transient members. Another weakness of the IWGBs organisation was that, although it did have representatives from all departments, most of its support lay in four departments. It is not surprising, therefore, that Singer's should decide to inflict a damaging blow while the IWGBs support still remained within manageable proportions.

An incident on 11 March 1911 sparked off the conflict. A foreman in No. 26 department sacked a woman for not working hard enough. This was declared by the No. 26 shop committee to be victimisation, and 37 out of the 41 departments downed tools in support. Subsequently, the IWGB admitted that this had not been anticipated:

This development had not been foreseen by the IWGB . . . and IWGB Committee could not effectively or honestly act as representatives of a body of strikers of whom only a tiny fraction were Industrial Unionists.[25]

So the IWGB proposed that a strike committee be formed, with five representatives from each department, which meant that the IWGB right away became a small minority on the committee.

The IWGB cannot, as an organisation, claim whatever credit or blame attaches to this body of delegates. While this is so, however, the IWGB is proud to have been associated with such a Strike Committee. Its whole conduct of the strike, its spirit, courage, vigour and unanimity, were in line with the best traditions, the finest qualities of the working class. Mistakes there may have been; it is easy to be wise after the event, but the general management of the strike by this Committee is beyond all praise.

But the Strike Committee, however capable, could not have done what they did had they not been supported by men and women of proper stuff. It succeeded, where it did succeed, because it was, in a true sense, representative of the strikers.[26]

The majority of those who had come out had never been in a trade union, let alone been on strike before. But they maintained complete solidarity, displaying enthusiasm and self-discipline, particularly at their public meetings:

In these demonstrations, the workers gathered on a large field near the factory, forming themselves into regiments according to their departments and marched, each department showing its number and with several bands in attendance, right into the factory and, after receiving the wages due to them, marched out again. The magnitude of such a demonstration can be imagined when we consider it took almost half an hour to pass a given point.[27]

The demonstration held on 1 April was especially memorable. Thousands of strikers, each one behind a departmental banner, marched through the cheering streets of Clydebank. The *Glasgow Evening News* declared: 'Never before in the history of this burgh have there been more stirring scenes than those that presented themselves on the streets this morning.'[28]

Confronted with this challenge, Singer's management behaved astutely. When it judged the time to be right, it decided to hold a ballot. Each employee received a card, which he had to return to the company within 24 hours, saying whether he wished to return to work or to continue the dispute. At once, this put the Strike Committee at a disadvantage. It did not have the names and addresses of all the strikers, who lived over a wide area; there was no way of contacting them.

The ballot was being taken in circumstances highly unfavourable to the Strike Committee. Local newspapers went out of their way to put Singer's case, and the threat of extensive redundancy being made, workers feared, if they filled in the papers 'the wrong way', they would be marked men. Since the management was conducting the whole thing, not only might the company keep the voting slips as a record, to be used when selecting those for the sack, but also there was no guarantee that it would add the figures up correctly. Most of the militants did not even receive ballot forms. So, in these circumstances, the Strike Committee resolved to issue an appeal asking everyone to disregard the ballot, to send their ballot papers back to the Strike Committee and not to Singers. The company said it received 6,527 votes calling for a resumption of work; the Strike Committee had 4,025 cards sent to it. The use of a ballot sent to each employee, a new procedure in British industrial relations, aroused a comment from John Maclean:

> I think this referendum is clever because it appeals to the individual in the quiet of his home, and because it enables the firm to deal with each unit separately. If all workers were class-conscious socialists, this method would fail, but as they are not it tends to succeed. And perhaps even tried socialists would yield for a time or two.[29]

Singer's management was equally cute over the resumption of work. It said there would be no victimisation, but, due to the slackness of trade, it would be some time before all could be re-employed. By singular coincidence, all the strike leaders were among those who were promised employment some time in the indefinite future. The company, being multinational, could maneouvre to keep production low at the Kilbowie plant. It deliberately increased its imports from elsewhere — it had factories in the United States, Russia and Germany — and it put workers at Elizabeth Port, New Jersey, on overtime. As the other side to this operation, Singer's management went out of its way to be kind to the workers it decided to re-engage, and even gave some wage increases. In this manner, it drove a wedge between those it intended to employ and those it was determined should stay on the streets.

The effect on people who had been prominent in the strike was devastating. Clydebank SLP, which had 27 members, 22 of whom had worked at Singer's factory, later admitted: 'They have been practically all cleared out.'[30] Many others received the same treatment. But, ironically, the company's desire to wipe out militancy had precisely the opposite effect. Regarding agitators as a deadly virus, it sought to deny them employment. But this did not mean that they would always be out of work. Eventually they found jobs elsewhere — and so the virus was spread along the Clyde.

Tom Bell, in his autobiography, recalls predicting that this would be the result:

> I remember addressing a large meeting in the Co-operative Hall after the strike, and referring to the dismissals declared: 'If the firm imagined by dismissing the active workers in the IWGB they would stop the growth of our movement, they would be deceiving them-selves. Every man dismissed would become the nucleus of a group of industrial unionists that would spring up all over the Clyde'. This forecast proved to be fulfilled to an even greater degree than I had anticipated, for soon afterwards the war was to reveal in the Clyde Workers' Committee movement shop stewards in factory after factory who had once been at Singer's.[31]

In her life on John MacLean, Nan Milton makes the same point:

> This Strike (Singer's) had one very important result. The leaders of the strike, most of them SLPers, were distributed throughout various shops in the Clyde area. Instead of their influence being diminished, as had been hoped, it was spread over a much wider area. Much more significant, however, was that when industrial revolts of wartime grew, these revolutionary socialists occupied strategic positions throughout the whole Clyde district.[32]

Perhaps even Nan Milton and Tom Bell fail fully to grasp the signifi-cance of the Singer strike. True, men of the calibre of Arthur MacManus had been scattered throughout Clydeside. But much more important than this was that they carried with them the ideas and methods of activity that they had developed at Kilbowie. From Singer's, there came vital lessons on organisational questions which were applied in the industrial battles of the First World War. It may be no accident

that the Clyde Workers' Committee was the first Committee of its
type to be formed in the whole of Britain. It also appears to have been
the industrial area with the greatest number of shop stewards, and
where probably they exerted the most influence.

Contrasts tend to be instructive. In a single Glasgow factory —
Parkhead Forge — there were 60 shop stewards functioning by 1915,
whereas, according to J.T. Murphy, in Sheffield there were only the
same number by 1916. In other words, one factory had as many shop
stewards as did an entire city.[33] Nor did it end there. In many respects,
Clydeside and Tyneside were similar — centres of heavy engineering and
shipbuilding, greatly expanded during the 1914-18 War — and it might
be reasonable to expect developments along similar lines. But this was
not so: on the Tyne shop stewards' organisation remained at a very
elementary level. In 1919, Lyall J. Watson, writing in *The Worker*,
bemoaned this fact:

> True, there are a number of sectional Shop Stewards Committee,
> confined to their respective trade unions, but committees of the
> type of the Clyde Workers' Committee do not exist, and it is due
> to this lack of co-ordination that the present unfortunate impasse
> on the Tyne has occurred.[34]

Watson went on to say that there was no central shop stewards' committee, linking up with the workers elsewhere, and that union officials had
sought to exploit sectionalism. In the following issue of *The Worker*,
A. Bartram confirmed this point, attributing the defeat that the Tyne
boilermakers had just suffered to divisions within the working class.

Perhaps one of the factors that influenced some of the Clydeside
militants, making them wish to break down the sectional barriers, was
their experience at Kilbowie — as well as at Argyle Motors, Alexandria,
and Scotstoun — where they gained some inkling of how powerful
workers can be when they are really united. The Singer's strike may
have been a short-term catastrophe; in the long-term it looked more
like a victory. The cruel sackings of 1911 appear, at least to some
degree, to have contributed to the creation of the Clyde Workers'
Committee of 1915.

Notes

1. *The Socialist*, March 1908 and *Industrial Unionist*, December 1908.

2. *The Socialist*, March 1908.
3. Ibid.
4. New Report to Second Conference of the British Advocates of Industrial Unionism.
5. E. Burdick, 'Syndicalism and Industrial Unionism', op. cit., pp. 81-4, and D.M. Chewter, op. cit., pp. 70-86.
6. F. Budgen, *Myselves When Young* pp. 92-3.
7. *The Socialist*, April 1908.
8. Ben Tillett, 'Is the Parliamentary Labour Party a failure?' p. 8.
9. Reg Groves, *The Strange Case of Victor Grayson* (1975) p. 65, and *Hansard*, 2 November 1908.
10. W. Thompson, *The Life of Victor Grayson* (1911) p. 145.
11. *The Syndicalist*, March-April 1912.
12. *The Socialist*, May 1912.
13. R. Fox, *Smoky Crusade*, p. 136.
14. E.J.B. Allen, *Revolutionary Unionism* (1908) pp. 13-14.
15. *The Socialist*, April 1912.
16. E.J.B. Allen, op. cit., p. 13.
17. *The Socialist*, January 1911.
18. *Daily Herald*, 30 May 1912.
19. *The Syndicalist*, February 1913.
20. *The Socialist*, January 1913.
21. Glasgow IWGB, Leaflet, 'What's the best form of Organisation?' (1912).
22. T. Bell, *Pioneering Days*, pp. 72-3.
23. Singer Sewing Machine Group, IWGB, 'The Kilbowie Strike and Its Lessons', published 1911.
24. T. Bell, op. cit., p. 73.
25. Singer Sewing Machine Group, op. cit., p. 2.
26. Ibid.
27. Ibid.
28. *Glasgow Evening News*, 1 April 1910.
29. *Justice*, 7 April 1911.
30. *The Socialist*, June 1911.
31. T. Bell, op. cit., p. 75.
32. Nan Milton, *John Maclean*, p. 53.
33. J.T. Murphy's article in *The Socialist*, 5 July 1919, and Report of Labour Party Committee investigating Clyde Deportations, p. 11.
34. *The Worker*, 8 March 1919.

SLP INTERNAL DEVELOPMENTS, 1907-1914

Very, Very True

Those wanting a quiet life should never join a revolutionary organisation. It makes tremendous demands upon its members, leaving them with little time to pursue their private lives. Complete dedication, wholehearted commitment, ability to withstand pressure — these are the qualities required. Operating as it does in a hostile environment, it must be able to swim against the current. Also, it has to allocate its resources in the most effective manner. Professor Robbins' definition of Economics, 'human behaviour as a relationship between ends and scarce means which have alternative uses', can, more aptly, be applied to the situation facing a revolutionary organisation. Inevitably, within it, the various pressures build up tension. Capitalist development poses new problems for the organisation, problems that must be solved if new ideas are to be created and the struggle fought effectively. This results in members indulging in intense, often acrimonious, internal discussion. On the road to greater theoretical clarity, expulsions and splits often occur. This is not something uniquely British: the Bolsheviks in Russia had a tortuous history of battles within the ranks. Referring to these, Lenin used to quote Tolstoy, who once saw a man squatting in a door-way, making strange and seemingly idiotic gestures with his arms. On closer inspection, it turned out that he was doing a perfectly sensible thing — sharpening a knife on a stone. The revolutionary party, Lenin tersely remarked, is the knife that has to kill capitalism.

The Socialist Labour Party's development from 1907 to 1914 was hardly tranquil. This period saw the expulsion of its general secretary, Neil Maclean; the parting of the ways with its founder and most influential member, James Connolly; an expulsion of the majority of the Edinburgh branch, which set up its own party; and the mass resignation of members, particularly in Lancashire, who disagreed with its electoral policy. Yet, despite these setbacks — or, rather, because of them — the SLP survived and increased its ability to be a fighting proletarian organisation.

The expulsion of Neil Maclean came as a result of the SLPs campaign on unemployment. From 1907 onwards, the number out of work increased. As the State made no provision to pay unemployment benefit, there was widespread suffering and hardship. In desperation, some of the unemployed approached the SLP for help. 'They had received a

deputation from the unemployed asking what they could do,' reported
T.H. Nelson, of the Bury branch. 'They were face to face with starving
men.' In this situation, the temptation was merely to point out that
unemployment was a product of capitalism, that the ruling class could
not impose its industrial discipline without a reserve army of labour:

> The danger of losing touch with the working class, of erecting our-
> selves into a sect of self-righteous scholastics, speaking a language
> foreign to the average worker, and handing out chunks of undigested
> Marxism to the starving unemployed, is a very real and very near
> calamity.[1]

Instead, the SLP saw that the unemployed had to be organised and, in
this way, like other sections of the working class, fight to improve
their own lot. As one Lancashire comrade pointed out: 'Organised
demonstrations of the unemployed is a necessary work of Socialism
if only to acquaint the Belshazzars at the feast of the writing on the
wall.' The usual procedure was to parade the unemployed through the
most affluent districts. As the rich beheld the poor gazing over the walls
into their stately homes, it created a feeling of unease. Abrasive
confrontations were prone to happen. If only to protect their property,
the well-to-do were likely to show some concern about the out-of-work.
As long ago as 1887, when the unemployed had rioted in Mayfair and
other wealthy parts of London, these disturbances had been followed
by large sums of money being sent to the Lord Mayor's relief fund. This
tactic was essentially a way of gaining money by menaces.

A variation of the theme came from John McClure, of the Glasgow
branch, who told delegates to the SLP 1909 conference how a deputation to the Town Council had 'paraded the most destitute cases before
the members, creatures that were once men and women, fainting from
starvation, contaminating the atmosphere in those beautiful Municipal
Chambers.'[2] The Lord Provost burst into tears. A fund was immediately started, and 80 investigators appointed to find out the most
deserving cases.

Such incidents as this could be regarded triumphantly, but they were
of short duration. They did little or nothing to alter the long-term
position. Furthermore, the SLP learnt from bitter experience that
there was a world of difference between organising a demonstration and
organising the unemployed. The former required a few days' preparation;
the latter called for more resources than the Party possessed. Yet, there
were some SLP members who thought an attempt should be made to

form a trade union for the unemployed. This was opposed by John Carstairs Matheson on grounds of priority; they had so far failed to create an industrial union and this should remain number one task. After much heart-searching, delegates adopted Matheson's line. It was tantamount to turning one's back on the problems of unemployment — regretfully, because of insufficient resources — except for holding the occasional protest demonstration.

To Neil Maclean, this decision was not satisfactory. A large and amorphous group of political characters — Labour politicians, union leaders and middle-class do-gooders — had formed Right to Work committees up and down the country. The SLP never belonged to this body. It disagreed with the Right to Work committees' tendency not to see the problem of unemployment as an inevitable consequence of capitalism. It regarded these committees, moreover, as elitist: their aim was to do something *for* the unemployed, not to get the unemployed to do something *for themselves.* And then the SLP had a cynical feeling that electoral considerations were behind the Right to Work campaign: its leaders were less concerned about finding jobs for the out-of-work than they were in securing jobs for themselves in Parliament and on local councils.

However, Neil Maclean thought something shoud be done about the unemployed, and anything was better than nothing. Despite the party line, he joined a Right to Work committee and was on its delegation that met Edinburgh council officials. His action caused a constitutional crisis within the SLP. The national executive committee was prepared to overlook his indiscretion. He had worked extremely hard for the SLP addressing public meetings all over Scotland and conscientiously doing the unpaid job of general secretary for six years. But it was precisely because Neil Maclean was the most prominent person the SLP had that the sub-national executive committee thought strong action against him had to be taken. The sub-NEC, made up of members from the Edinburgh and Leith branches, was responsible for the day-to-day running of the organisation. No member should be allowed to break the party's rule, thought the sub-NEC. If discipline was to be enforced in the SLP, then it had to apply to every member, including those in high offices. So the sub-NEC took over the party's headquarters in Edinburgh and, countermanding the decision of the NEC, expelled Neil Maclean from the SLP for reformist deviations.

A tangled mess confronted delegates who attended the SLPs seventh annual conference in April 1909. There had been a scene at the party HQ when 'traitor' Neil Maclean had been ejected. The NEC, a committee of four members, supposed to be the supreme body within the party, were angry that the sub-NEC had usurped its power and authority. Conference resolved to reinstate the NEC. This decision was merely the assertion of the constitutional principle of the primacy of annual conference and of the NEC as the most important body in the party between conferences. It did not mean, however, that delegates endorsed Neil Maclean's conduct, or the lenient view taken of it by the NEC. After electing a new NEC, conference allowed Maclean to appeal against his expulsion, and this was turned down. The whole affair did not have any lasting effect on the SLPs expansion: by 1910 it had 20 branches, four times the number it started with in 1903.

In the same way, the break with James Connolly had no lasting effect, though it must have been a most unpleasant experience for veteran members, who could remember the tireless work of Connolly in creating the party. Dire necessity forced Connolly to emigrate to America in September 1903. In the United States, he flung himself into the political activities of the American SLP, while continuing his contacts with the British SLP and writing occasional articles for its journals.

Over the years, Connolly's views on a number of issues became increasingly at variance with those of De Leon and the American SLP. The first of these questions was religion. Connolly, a Roman Catholic, did not accept the traditional Marxian attitude that religion was 'the opium of the people'. At the inaugural meeting of the British SLP, he prevailed upon delegates not to commit the party to an anti-religious stance. After leaving for America, he contributed an article entitled 'Socialism and Other Things' in which he argued that socialists should remain neutral about religion; socialism was about life in this world, religion about life in the next.[3] Connolly's attitude could not be reconciled with that of De Leon, who accepted the traditional materialist stand on the question of God and went out of his way to attack the machinations of the Church of Rome.

Connolly's Catholicism led to another area of disagreement. When De Leon translated a book by the veteran Austrian socialist, August Bebel, called *Women under Socialism*, Connolly described the book as 'lewd' as it was 'opposed to monogamy'. All, in fact, Bebel's work did was to re-state and amplify the thesis of Engels' *Origin of the Family*. By present-day standards, it would not lift an eye-brow. But to Connolly the book was heresy. The religious issue, in Connolly's mind, was connected to the question of the whole approach of the Socialism Movement. He thought that it should confine its approach to strictly political and industrial issues, not adopting a line on the more general issues of life:

> I have long been of the opinion that the socialist movement else-
> where was to a great extent hampered by the presence in its ranks
> of faddists and cranks, who were in the movement not for the cause
> of socialism but because they thought they saw in it a means of
> ventilating their theories on such questions as sex, religion, vaccina-
> tion, vegetarianism, etc., and I believe that such ideas had, or ought
> to have, no place in our programme or our party . . . We were as a
> body concerned only with the question of political and economic
> freedom for our class. We could not claim to have a mission to
> emancipate the human mind from all errors, for the simple reason
> that we were not and are not the repositories of all truth.[4]

On a practical level, there can be little doubt that Connolly was right when he said that socialist parties tended to attract eccentrics and faddists. In 1906, for example, W.R. Stoker, senior, who believed him-self to be the rightful heir to the estates and fortunes of the Earl of Derby, joined the Wigan SLP. An alcoholic, in between spells in Prestwick lunatic asylum where he went to dry out, Stoker stood for the local council. Nobody expected him to win a ward that usually returned a Conservative candidate. But to everyone's surprise, Stoker topped the poll. An attempt was made to stop him taking his seat on the council because he was an atheist. To which he replied: 'Have you ever heard of a stoker in heaven?'[5] A person with a similar flair for the strange and peculiar was Frank Budgen, a member of the SLP virtually from its inception. After working for a time for the Post Office, when he took over from the expelled Neil Maclean as the Party's general secretary, he earned his living as an artist's model. Subsequently, he became a distinguished literary critic and personal friend of the Irish novelist James Joyce, who wrote a poem in his honour, which began 'Oh Budgen, boozer, bard and canvas dauber'.[6] A more dangerous departure from the norm was John S. Clarke, the editor of *The Socialist* from 1913 to 1914 and again during part of the First World War. Besides having periods as a secretary and seaman, he worked in the circus as a lion-tamer, being badly mauled by lions on more than one occasion.[7]

It would be wrong to think of men like Budgen and Clarke simply as eccentrics. They lived in a time when to be a socialist meant being continually in danger of losing one's job. It gave a certain independence, an ability to order one's life and find time for politics, if one could fall

back on unconventional occupations as a means of earning a livelihood.
This does not alter the force of Connolly's criticism, that the ordinary
worker is liable to think such men rather odd and may not give serious
consideration to the ideas they express. But Connolly was fundamentally wrong in his endeavour to limit and narrow the force of the
socialist critique. Essentially, the theories expounded by Marx constituted a critique of society in its entirety: not a vestige would remain
unchanged once the socialist revolution had occurred. The role of the
family and the place of women in society were, among many others,
legitimate subjects for debate, whatever Connolly might think.

Yet it was not because of his Catholicism or his narrow outlook
that Connolly fell foul of the American SLP. Although it disagreed,
the party was prepared to tolerate these quirks of Connolly. Indeed, he
held for a time leading positions within its ranks. Where the trouble
came was on emphasis placed on industrial and political activity. In
1908, the IWW split. One section took an anarcho-syndicalist position,
while those around the SLP still maintained that in the fight against
capitalism there had to be political as well as industrial action. Yet
the latter line, which was advanced with clarity by De Leon in a series
of articles, later published in pamphlet-form under the title *As to
Politics*, did not gain universal support within the American SLP. At
one stage, De Leon nearly lost his majority on the National Executive
— it was three-three with a vacillating member having the final say.

In the course of this faction fight, in which Connolly led the
opposition to De Leon, the question of his attitude to other issues, like
religion and sex, were brought in. But they were not central to the case
against Connolly. In essence, this stemmed from his failure to see the
full import of the political struggle in the fight for socialism. By giving
this a secondary, subordinate role, Connolly, it was claimed, had made
an inexcusable concession to anarcho-syndicalism and undervalued the
role to be played by the revolutionary party. Typical of Connolly's line
is the following:

> The fight for the conquest of the political state is not the battle, it
> is only the echo of the battle. The real battle is the battle being
> fought out every day for the power to control industry and the
> gauge of the progress of the battle is not to be found in the number
> of voters making a cross beneath the symbol of the political party,
> but in the number of workers who enrol themselves in an industrial
> organisation with the definite purpose of making themselves masters
> of the industrial equipment of society in general.[8]

The break between Connolly and the American SLP placed the British SLP in a difficult position. It had published one of Connolly's articles, arguing that the need for industrial organisation was paramount, without making any comment.[9] Initially, it was hoped to maintain neutrality in the Connolly-De Leon dispute. Indeed, no directly critical piece was ever written about Connolly, and the British SLP succeeded in maintaining friendly co-operation with him right up to the Easter Uprising of 1916. But this should not conceal the fact that the British SLP had a rather different view of the role of politics. Its struggle with E.J.B. Allen and his supporters in the Advocates of Industrial Unionism attested, quite clearly, to its belief that a revolutionary party was required for capitalism's overthrowal.

In one vital respect, however, the influence of Connolly and Neil Maclean persisted even after they had severed their links with the party: the importance the SLP attached to political education. From the party's inception, it treated the question of inculcating socialist ideas with great seriousness. Tom Bell described in his autobiography how they began:

These classes, I believe, were the first of their kind in Great Britain. The leader of these classes was an exceptionally clever worker – George Yates by name. By trade an engineer, while in Edinburgh Yates got employment with some professor at the University, attending to scientific instruments. He utilised his opportunities to study and became an expert mathematician, draughtsman and designer. He worked in Glasgow as a draughtsman and designer for the Central Station and railway bridge that spans the Trongate, and it was then that he conducted these classes and addressed public meetings in his spare time. A fluent speaker, he was well informed on Marxism, economics, history, philosophy, logic and literature.[10]

From Yates's classes, a new crop of lectures grew up:

These SLP classes, apart from the social and economic conditions, played an important part in gaining the Clydeside its reputation for being 'Red'. Every year produced new worker-tutors. Classes sprang up in a number of the shipyards and engineering shops. In the great majority of these classes the tutors had come through the SLP parent groups. Among the most outstanding in the West of Scotland were William Paul, T. Clark, J.W. Muir, J. McClure, Arthur MacManus, John Wilson and John McBain.[11]

Tom Bell went on to describe how the classes were run:

> Our method in the classes was to open with an inaugural survey of
> the whole field we proposed to traverse, and make the workers
> familiar with the subject as a whole; the textbooks, etc., which
> included *Wage Labour and Capital*; *Value, Price and Profit*; *Capital*
> and H. de B. Gibbins' *Industry in England* and Buckle's *History of
> Civilisation*.
>   Each student was given a series of definitions of terms used by
> Marx. These had to be studied, memorised and discussed thoroughly,
> for perhaps the first four weeks. The student would study *Wage
> Labour and Capital* at home. At the class we would read it over para-
> graph by paragraph. This practice aimed at helping students to speak
> fluently and grammatically. At the following class meetings
> questions would be put and answered, and the points raised
> thoroughly understood by everyone, the results of each lesson being
> summarised by the leader. This method was applied in the same way
> to industrial history. Later on, simple lessons in historical materialism
> and formal logic were added.[12]

These education courses were taken with earnest dedication. While
there would be slight variations from class to class — and, obviously,
those held inside factories would be much shorter — it is interesting to
note what happened at a typical Sunday afternoon class:

> We had two and a half hours' tuition; reading out aloud; questions
> and answers to last week's lessons; short discussions and examina-
> tion of homework; after which tea was made and for another hour
> we talked and discussed freely on all manner of political and edu-
> cational subjects. An hour's respite and we would repair to
> Buchanan Street, corner of Argyle Street, or to Glasgow Green, to
> hold forth on socialist propaganda to large audiences who collected
> there every Sunday night.[13]

For those who could not attend classes, correspondence courses were
available. The examination paper of the SLPs Advanced Economics
courses had questions such as: 'What is the fetishism of commodities?'
and 'Describe the development of exchange'.
    It was not long before these efforts began to bear fruit. In 1906,
John Maclean, a teacher in the SDF from Pollockshaw, began lecturing
on economics to large audiences. While he did not go into the subject

to the same depth as SLP tutors, he brought the message to a much greater number of people. Marxist ideas were becoming widely known and accepted around industrial Scotland. As it was a time of rising industrial unrest, this was especially valuable. The cadres who could lead the future struggles were being trained.

But ferment spread south of the border. As the strike wave grew, new problems arose. Old concepts seemed inadequate to solve them. A fresh generation of young militants was emerging, thirsting for knowledge and prepared to discard the dogmas of capitalist orthodoxy. The conflict turned out to be as much an ideological battle as an economic one. In 1909, Ruskin College, Oxford, became the storm-centre in this struggle. Students went on strike, complaining that courses were deliberately biased in favour of the *status quo*. Most of the young men who took part in the rebellion came from areas and occupations where there was mounting discontent. Instead of helping them to discover what was wrong with society, the Ruskin establishment sought to destroy the socialist heresy. Greater emphasis was placed on the traditional approach to Economics and Sociology, in the hope it would finally gain acceptance. Then students would go back into the outside world as a stabilising influence, perhaps taking trade union posts to counteract the influence of militancy. The student strike showed this was not to be.[14]

What happened at Ruskin College in 1909 played a vital part in helping to spread Marxist ideas in Britain. In February of that year, the students established their own journal, *Plebs*, whose contributors discussed socialist theory in a serious way. But the journal was not only a vehicle for increasing proletarian clarity and understanding; it sought to organise education nationally. One of the reasons why capitalist society continued to exist, perpetuating itself from generation to generation, was because it possessed the means of indoctrination — schools and universities that taught their victims to accept the basic tenets of capitalism. In order to combat these insidious influences, a new force had to be developed — Independent Working-Class Education, and the Plebs League was formed to encourage workers to get down to serious study. This appeal, on the whole, received an encouraging response. Thousands began systematic study of society's problems. Historians Edward and Ruth Frow, who have analysed the early days of the Plebs League in Lancashire, show how popular these classes were: for example, in Rochdale there were classes held seven times a week, from October to April 1911, which were attended by a total of 150 students. Elsewhere numbers were smaller, but classes existed in

almost every town in the country. Besides these local groups, the Plebs
League established a Central Labour College. There, students, usually
with union scholarships, could attend year or two-year courses. Many
later took classes themselves in their own localities. Others used the
skill and knowledge they had acquired to take a more prominent part
in the big industrial battles that raged in the pre-1914 period.

In an article entitled 'Brains Behind the Labour Revolt', Rowland
Kenny said in the *English Review* (March 1912): 'During the railway
strike of 1911, the chief agitators in the most militant districts were
ex-Ruskin students, who are now Central Labour College propagandists.'
The same applied to the coal industry. One of the leading and most
talented figures in the Ruskin strike was Noah Ablett, who was one of
the editors of *Plebs*. A talented writer, he not only produced a readable
outline of Marxist economics but was also part-author of the famous
pamphlet *The Miners' Next Step*. Helping him write this work, which
had a big influence in spreading militancy throughout the coal industry,
was Noah Rees, another ex-Ruskin student. And then the South Wales
Unofficial Reform Committee, the organisation that led the miners in
the bitter battle against the Cambrian Combine in 1911, was dominated
by supporters of the Plebs League. Besides Ablett and Rees, there were
W.F. Hay, Will Mainwaring, George Daggar and A.J. Cook, who later
became general secretary of the Miners' Federation of Great Britain.
To a slightly lesser degree, the same picture was true of the North-East
coalfields. Will Lawther, who was then a militant and personal friend
of John Maclean, had been to the Central Labour College in 1911-12.
He was the leading figure in the Durham 'red' mining village of
Chopwell, while George Harvey, an outstanding worker-intellectual, and
also ex-Ruskin, was checkweighman at Follonsby colliery, a few miles
away.

The movement for independent working-class education provided the
Socialist Labour Party with an excellent opportunity. A new and
expanding market existed for its literature. Comparatively large numbers
of workers suddenly appeared to be receptive to its ideas. The possibility
of recruiting some of them, or of influencing them, seemed promising.
Even from the outset in the Ruskin strike, the SLPs role was quite disproportionate to its strength. A small branch of the Party operated in
Oxford. George Harvey joined it in June 1908. Before going to Ruskin,
he had been a not particularly left-wing member of the ILP, and in
February 1907 had written an article for its North-Eastern organ, *The
Northern Democrat*, advocating conciliation boards. However, under
pressure from his fellow students, with W.W. Craik and Ablett being

probably the most influential, his views swung dramatically to the left. Although a small man, and not an impressive speaker, Harvey was able to convince people by the strength of his arguments. He wrote a number of well-researched and documented studies: *Industrial Unionism and The Mining Industry* (1911), *Does Dr. John Wilson serve the Working Class?* (1912) and *The Mighty Coal Kings of Northern England* (1918), which he employed as weapons in his struggle to build a rank-and-file movement in the coal industry.[15]

Undoubtedly, George Harvey sought to push the Ruskin strikers in an SLP direction, exerting a sway much greater than his solitary voice might suggest. Many of the students had already read SLP pamphlets and had been favourably impressed. Perhaps they were not prepared to join the SLP, but they were convinced of the need for industrial unionism and militancy. They were, moreover, largely in agreement with the SLPs idea that the union leaders acted as 'the labour lieutenants of capitalism'. Significantly, and it may be taken as a sign of the SLPs influence, the Ruskin strikers decided to adopt the term 'Plebs' for their journal and educational body.[16] It is taken from De Leon's pamphlet *Two Pages from Roman History*, which draws an analogy between antiquity and contemporary capitalism: the tribunes, while articulating some of the grievances of the Plebian masses, continued to accept the basic principles on which Roman society was founded and saw to it that any protests were kept within limits that did not endanger the system. In the same way, argued De Leon, Labour politicians and union leaders today serve merely as a safety-valve, permitting workers' grievances against capitalism to gain expression in a manner not threatening the existence of capitalism.

That so many activists accepted this cornerstone of SLP theory could not fail to come as an encouragement. A milieu existed within the working class movement that would listen sympathetically to the Party's ideas. In was, moreover, a two-way process: animosity that had prevailed for so long on the Left, the sectarian bitchiness that marred so many socialist journals in the first few years of this century, began to wane. This was, in part, due to the growing movement for Independent Working-Class Education. When socialists belonging to rival groups attended a Plebs League class, they would study together and exchange ideas. This lessened suspicion, creating the conditions on which future co-operation could be based.

In these favourable conditions, the SLP sought to modify its approach, making it more receptive to working class needs. The 1910 conference cut the high subscription rate from ninepence to fourpence.

An influx of members followed. From twenty branches in 1910, it grew to twenty-five in 1911 and twenty-eight in 1912. While increased membership only partially compensated financially for the reduction in dues, the Party tried to raise the difference by appealing to the goodwill of its expanding circle of sympathisers. In many towns, groups of socialists met and, although not formally committed to the SLP, generally followed its line. On the whole, the new financial arrangements functioned successfully. Still the SLP was unable to afford a full-time organiser or increase the frequency of *The Socialist*. But it was able to publish a stream of pamphlets, many of them Marxist classics. Sold very cheaply, these provided the intellectual nourishment of the new militants.

A further way in which the SLP changed was in shedding many of its sectarian practices. The siege mentality gradually vanished. Members were no longer forbidden to address outside bodies or to hold trade union office. How this latter change of policy was reached is instructive: it reveals how life itself pushed the Party in the direction of modification. In the north-east coalfields, where the SLP had considerable influence, contacts would have had to relinquish their offices in miners' lodges to join the Party. This they refused to do. Yet, when it came to selling socialist literature, it was precisely those lodges where officials were sympathetic that had the greatest sales. It seemed that holding a union post provided an opportunity to spread propaganda and increased one's influence in the struggle against the union leadership. As George Harvey, a supporter of the change in policy, argued: 'I ask why should not the SLP fight for points of vantage and spread the light? Why should not the SLP fight for every inch of ground both within and without?'[17] But it was not always a question of fighting for position; the force of argument may sometimes convince others who already held union positions of the correctness of the SLPs line. In the same issue of *The Socialist* that printed Harvey's remark, a letter appeared from George Barker, of Abertillery, stating that he and two other members of the executive committee of the Miners' Federation of Great Britain agreed with SLP policy.

What this constituted was a major change of orientation, a turn to the class, on the part of the SLP, and obviously it could not be accomplished without difficulties arising. Some members, inured to the old routines, unable or unwilling to adapt themselves, began to grumble. This led to two large-scale revolts: the first by those who favoured sectarianism, the other by people who strayed in a more anarcho-syndicalist direction.

The first sign of trouble came in 1910. Critics did not go so far as to challenge the general policies of the Party, they simply chafed at the move towards democratic centralism. They asserted the need for local autonomy, which would allow time to pick and choose which conference decisions to apply. What they objected to was the Party's attempt to build up its own leadership, which they described as 'bossism', and the fact that so much of the SLPs resources went into the industrial struggle. In a pamphlet, putting forward the dissidents' views, R. McCraig described the changes with which they disagreed, especially with those who had gained leading positions within the Party:

> This was the element that had captured the S.L.P. Their cry was 'Let us have a big Party as soon as possible!' At first the S.L.P. bid fair to develop into a sound working-class movement but, alas, the Party had allowed itself to be dominated by an official gang. A large number of members had only a dim conception of what the Party stood for. Suffice it to say that fully three-fourths of the Party consisted of members who were connected with shop stewardism.[18]

To have so many shop stewards among the membership was a bad thing, in these critics' opinion. It was a sign that 'the Party had been well-diluted ideologically by kowtowing to trade unionism.' They only wanted those who were doctrinally pure, who had mastered the intricacies of Marxist theory, to have the privilege of belonging to a party.

Clearly, two different conceptions of the way forward existed within the SLP, and the issue was resolved at the NEC meeting on 17 December 1911, which expelled Robert Gillespie and the Edinburgh branch. Initially, Edinburgh sought to reverse the decision. It wrote to other branches, appealing to them to support a referendum of the membership to decide whether the NEC had majority support. But Edinburgh gained only limited backing. In June 1912, it decided to set up its own organisation, the British Section of the International Socialist Labour Party, which issued its own journal, *The Proletariat*, and came to hold the view that strikers were inherently bad and anti-revolutionary.[19]

The second split, of a more serious and damaging character, arose out of the ambiguous policy the SLP had towards its members securing seats on local councils and in Parliament. Originally, the question arose as a result of a query from a Liverpool reader named Murphy, who asked what the SLPs representatives would do if ever they were elected. Frank Budgen was then general secretary, and he replied:

The Party's attitude has been that in the event of a candidate being returned and any measure of a repressive character being proposed, he should not only criticise it but should try to force a division on it and logically register his vote against it.

In the event of any measure of a constructive nature, which makes for the social well-being, such as improvements in the postal, telegraph and telephone services — lines of development which will continue in socialist as well as capitalist society — being introduced, and containing more advantages than disadvantages, either to society or the working class, he should be free to record his vote for it.

This letter, which became known as the Budgen-Murphy letter, aroused objections from readers of *The Socialist*. In March 1912, the editor, George Harvey, replied to some of these critics. He freely admitted that attempting to reform capitalism was a futile task, 'like trying to get the wrinkles out of the tripe', but nevertheless they should try to improve the lot of the working class. This could be best done by Labour politicians, who adopted a 'modest, beggar-like attitude' that only got them despised: 'The revolutionary party is the best way to get reforms.'

Harvey's line was far from gaining universal acceptance within the Party. At the 1912 Manchester conference, Ashton branch moved a resolution saying that 'to support reforms . . . is inconsistent with the revolutionary character of the S.L.P.' Birmingham, Croydon and Sheffield branches supported Ashton's stand — 'to vote is to participate in capitalist legislation and administration.' Before long, claimed Walmsley of Croydon, this would lead to the party sliding down the slippery slope of compromise, ending up like the ILP, with Parliamentary seats but no principles. In reply, Symington (Glasgow) argued that it would be ludicrous for an SLP councillor not to vote when, as had recently happened in Glasgow, the local council was debating whether to give extra money to the unemployed. Another Scotsman, Johnny Muir, also thought it important that the Party have a line on immediate issues. When a strike of corporation employees occurred, it was vital that an SLP Councillor should both speak and vote. He did not claim it was possible for them to control the capitalist state but they could have a say in it.

Supporters of the Ashton position, on the other hand, made it clear that they did not want to have 'a say' in capitalist decision-making, since it compromised the Party's principles without gaining it extra power. They also doubted the value placed by the Glasgow comrades on casting one's vote. Important issues, those which were vital to capitalism's existence, would not be decided by majority votes. Ultimately, the determining factor was the relationship of class forces.

At the end of the debate, conference supported the Glasgow position by a narrow 16 votes to 14. The Ashton branch and four other Lancashire branches, the majority of the membership in the country, resigned on the grounds that the Party had become reformist. The consequence was debilitating. The issue had not truly been settled, and differences were expressed right up to the outbreak of war.

In fact, the period immediately before the First World War was very depressing. First, there was the ebbing of the tide of industrial discontent, giving militants less opportunity for meaningful activity. Syndicalism as a movement faded out of existence. The defeat of the Dublin strike of 1913 spread temporary disillusionment. And the Industrial Workers of Great Britain, having been crushed at Singers and Argyle Motors, prudently decided not to attempt to form active branches inside factories but merely to do propaganda work. Second, there was a fall in the membership of all socialist organisations. In 1912, the Social Democratic Federation had merged with a few ILP branches and changed its name to the British Socialist Party. In 1912, it claimed its membership was 40,000; by 1914 it was down to 13,755, with the majority merely card-holders.[20] Similarly with the SLP: its branches dropped from 28 in 1912 to 15 in 1914, probably representing a total membership of around 300.[21] And, of course, a third source of depression was the approaching war — a force socialists were powerless to prevent.

Notes

1. *The Socialist,* May 1909.
2. Ibid.
3. Ibid, May 1904.
4. Ibid.
5. Information from Lester Hutchinson, 8 May 1972. W.R. Stoker, a small businessman, helped the SLP financially and, along with Richard Hutchinson and George Yates, helped to keep the Party solvent.
6. James Joyce's verse is entitled 'To Budgen Raughty Tinker' — a reference to a randy sailor's ballad Budgen once sung to the delight of Joyce and his friends.
7. John S. Clarke's experiences as a lion-tamer are re-told in his book, *Circus Parade* (Batsford, 1936).
8. *The Socialist*, June 1908. It is interesting to note that J.T. Murphy wrongly takes Connolly's line to be the official position of the SLP (See *Preparing for Power* (1934) p. 65). It would seem that Murphy only joined the SLP in 1913 after visiting Connolly during the Dublin strike of that year. He was

not fully conversant with the Party's history, and many of his statements about it are suspect.

9. Ibid.
10. Tom Bell, *Pioneering Days*, p. 36.
11. Ibid, p. 55.
12. Ibid, p. 38.
13. Ibid, pp. 38-9.
14. For accounts of the Ruskin strike see W.W. Craik, *The Central Labour College* (Lawrence & Wishart, 1964) pp. 72-83; J.F. & Winifred Horrabin, *Working-Class Education* (Labour Publishing Company, 1924) pp. 44-7. Also I.W. Hamilton, 'The Plebs League and the Labour College Movement' (Warwick, MA thesis, 1972), passim.
15. John Wilson was a Lib-Lab MP and leader of the Durham miners. He prosecuted George Harvey for publishing the pamphlet about him. He won £200 damages but had his reputation tarnished by admissions made under cross-examination. Harvey used the court case to further expose the right-wing leadership.
16. W.W. Craik, op. cit., p. 62.
17. *The Socialist*, December 1911.
18. R. McCaig, *Report on the Decline and Fall of the S.L.P.* (Airdrie, n.d.) p. 5.
19. D.M. Chewter, op. cit., p. 114.
20. W. Kendall, *Revolutionary Movement in Britain*, p. 310.
21. Helen R. Vernon, 'The Socialist Labour Party and the Working Class Movement on the Clyde 1903-1921' (Leeds University, M.Phil, 1967) also makes the same estimate.

6 THE FIRST WORLD WAR

The declaration of war in August 1914 was greeted with widespread jubilation. Crowds thronged the streets, cheering and dancing; a carnival atmosphere prevailed. *Rule Britannia* and the National Anthem were heard on every street corner, and men flocked to the recruiting-centres. Enthusiasm for war — so difficult for the present-day mind to comprehend — can, at least in part, be attributed to the drabness and monotony of workers' lives. They had little conception of what was meant by modern war. They imagined a few glorious battles, replete with heroic deeds, and a quick return home. By the Christmas fireside, they would be able to regale families and friends with stories of their exciting exploits.

Another influence stimulated this chauvinistic dance of death: capitalist ideology possessed a very much greater hold over the working class than it does today. Many people passionately believed in King and Country. Told the war was being fought to safeguard civilisation, they accepted every word that came from politicians' lips. A fever gripped young men, irrespective of class or political view. Of the Oxford University Socialist Society's 125 members, all but 15 volunteered.[1] In the coal industry 191,170 trade unionists, almost a fifth of the total labour force, had joined the armed forces by February 1915.[2] Altogether, by 1916 a total of two and a half million men had answered Lord Kitchener's call: 'Your Country Needs You'. That such a large number behaved in this way is without historical precedent: it is a testimony to the power and pervasiveness of patriotism.

Labour and trade union politicians, accustomed to accommodating themselves to the prevailing capitalist ideology, swam with the tide. They backed the war by speaking at recruitment rallies and urged workers to rise to the national crisis. They told trade unionists to forget demands for higher wages, to buckle down to the task of increasing production. Their appeals met wide success. Before the outbreak of hostilities, it had seemed likely that the second half of 1914 would have witnessed many major industrial disputes. As it was, these vanished: in the last month before the war began, July 1914, nearly 100,000 days had been lost in industrial disputes; by December 1914 the figure had dropped to a mere 3,000 days.[3] The cooperation of the workers made the Government exceedingly pleased. Sir Walter

Rundiman, president of the Board of Trade, expressed satisfaction:
'They are working longer hours and more regularly than ever before,
and it is all done of their own free will — no conscription or compul-
sion.'[4]

In attaining this object, the Government had the active support
of many avowed socialists. Men who had previously preached internationalism, albeit in a soggy and sentimental fashion, were
transformed overnight into raving jingoists. Ramsay MacDonald, MP
for Leicester, wrote to the Mayor of Leicester six days after the outbreak of war expressing his fervent desire to help in every way possible:

> Should an opportunity arise to enable me to appeal to the pure love
> of country — which I know is a precious sentiment in all our hearts,
> keeping it clear of thoughts which I believe to be alien to real
> patriotism — I shall gladly take that opportunity. If need be I shall
> make it for myself. I want the serious men of the Trade Union, the
> Brotherhood, and similar movements to face their duty. To such
> men it is enough to say 'England has need of you.'[5]

Keir Hardie took the same line in his constituency of Merthyr:

> A nation at war must be united . . . With the boom of the enemy's
> guns within earshot the lads who have gone forth to fight their
> country's battles must not be disheartened by any discordant note
> at home.[6]

Like Keir Hardie, George Lansbury, the editor of the *Daily Herald*, was
a well known pacifist —until war actually broke out. Then he even
refused to print resolutions opposing the war in the paper.[7]

A tiny minority took an anti-war stand. Most of the individuals who
did so, based their objections on pacifist or religious grounds. Some of
them was members of the ILP. But there was also a handful of
socialists, small groups like those led by John Maclean in Glasgow and
Sylvia Pankhurst in London. And the Socialist Labour Party never
wavered from its stand of proletarian internationalism. Issue after
issue of its journal attacked the warmongers. A leading article in
September 1914 ridiculed the notion that it was necessary to fight
to preserve civilisation:

> No explanation is offered as to what civilisation has done for the
> workers that they should fight for it. To the majority, civilisation

means 10 or 12 hours a day in a factory or on a railway, or 8 hours
in a coal mine, with a hovel to sleep in and the prospect of being
clubbed by the police or shot down by the military if they make
too much fuss about it. We had some 'civilisation' recently in
Dublin; we experienced it at Featherstone and elsewhere.

The same article ended:

A class that can contemplate unmoved the sufferings of the workers,
their wretched conditions and pauper deaths, is not civilised. A class
that can callously consign millions of their fellow creatures to
mutilation and death for the furtherance of their own ends is not
civilised. The world will never be civilised so long as capitalism
endures.

The SLP saw the First World War as a consequence of mounting rivalry
between the big powers. Imperialist wars were a necessary and inevitable result of the functioning of capitalism. Unlike the ILP, which
thought that greater tolerance and understanding could lead to a
negotiated peace, the SLP considered that no peace could be properly
secured within the framework of the present system and drew revolutionary conclusions from its analysis.

Our attitude is neither pro-German nor pro-British, but anti-
capitalist and all that it stands for in every country of the world.
The capitalist class of all nations are our real enemies, and it is
against them that we direct all our attacks.[8]

Unwittingly, the editor of *The Socialist* was using almost the same
words as Karl Liebknecht, the German socialist, who told German
workers that their real enemies were not British workers but the
German capitalist class – 'the real enemy is at home'.
In the first few weeks of the hostilities, the British Press carried
reports that Liebknecht and Luxemburg had been killed. When
subsequently these were proved to be false rumours, newspapers praised
them for their courageous opposition to Prussian militarism. They
presumably thought that, by sowing the seeds of dissension inside
Germany, Liebknecht and his comrades helped the allied cause.
Support of German international socialists did not mean supporting
their principles: the Press combined applause for German Liebknechts
with detestation of their British equivalents.

The Socialist Labour Party displayed greater consistency. It rejoiced 'to see that Dr. Liebknecht had given his powerful support to the "Stop the War" movement.' His bravery should spur British socialists to similar action in this country:

> If Karl Liebknecht, Rosa Luxemburg and others have the courage, at such a time and in a country, that is said to be under the heel of militarism and tyrannically governed, to demand in the name of humanity that the slaughter shall cease, can we do less than meet him half way?

The example of Liebknecht and others vindicated the SLPs belief in international solidarity. Beneath the seemingly hopeless situation, *The Socialist* saw tremendous opportunities were developing:

> That a revolutionary element exists in the French,German and Russian armies, there is no reason to doubt ... I believe there is a large revolutionary element in the British army also, particularly the new army under training. The widespread industrial unrest in Great Britain during the last few years was symptomatic of deep-seated dissatisfaction ... As revolutionary socialists, we are bound to make the most of whatever opportunities present themselves for carrying our revolutionary principles into effect, and this war, involving as it does the working class of the leading countries in Europe in common disaster, may prove a blessing in disguise by providing them with the opportunity of throwing off the yoke of their common oppressor.[9]

The need, in the SLPs opinion, was to turn a capitalist war into a socialist revolution:

> For this reason, and because every member of the working class should be in possession of arms and trained in their use, the workers should enrol themselves ... that they may be in a position to play a part in the great task that is before them — their own emancipation — should the opportunity present itself. Remember the war of 1870 gave birth to the Paris Commune; who knows what the future holds in its womb.[10]

But difficulties did arise in applying this tactic. With a small number of branches and members, the SLPs top priority remained to keep the

Party alive. Often, in many towns, a handful of men were all there was to spread socialist ideas: take a few key men away and vital industrial work would go by default. Where, as often occurred, a militant had secured for himself a position of influence within a factory, it would be foolish to discard this and volunteer for the army. Trained and experienced cadres were more precious than gold – future development depended upon them. Of particular importance was the small group who, despite colossal pressures, kept the Party's central organisation functioning.

It is hard to imagine how great the strain upon certain individuals must have been. For example, Arthur MacManus was editor of *The Socialist*, and in 1915, when the Clyde Workers' Committee was formed, he became its chairman. As spokesman for this rank-and-file organisation, the most powerful of its kind in the country, he played a leading role in the creation of a National Workers' & Shop Stewards' Movement. All this was done in his spare time: he also had a full-time job as an engineer at G. & J. Weir's Cathcart works, where he was the most well-known militant. Besides these commitments, which would have been more than enough for half a dozen men with only a normal amount of energy, MacManus found time to help in the struggle in Ireland. In 1915, James Connolly visited Glasgow and told his old SLP comrades that the authorities had suppressed their journal, the *Irish Worker*. So the SLP undertook to print it clandestinely on the Party's press at Renfrew Street. In his autobiography Tom Bell stated, 'Comrade Arthur MacManus was especially keen on doing this; working night and day to get it out, and arranged for the shipment of the paper, which he took over personally to Dublin.'[11] He regularly carried the issues over to Ireland, wrapped in a parcel marked 'Glass', until the authorities discovered the ruse.[12] So determined was MacManus that he even made the journey one stormy night after he had fallen off his bike and broken his collar bone.

But MacManus's dedication was far from unique. Willie Paul, John S. Clarke, Tom Bell and a number of others subordinated all personal considerations to the task of keeping the SLP going and spreading socialist ideas. Without the bravery and self-sacrifice of its members, the Party would have collapsed. Selling *The Socialist* and holding public meetings were hazardous undertakings, which could result in being beaten up by young patriots or arrested by the police. 'The police court is becoming quite a familiar place with members of the Glasgow branch,' *The Socialist* stoically reported.[13] Despite this persecution, propaganda work continued and, partly as a consequence, the mood of the public began to change.

But the Asquith government's own actions were much more important in changing public attitudes. People's war euphoria began to evaporate when they experienced long hours of work for low wages, with rapidly rising prices. Inevitably, war places an added burden on a country's economy, but this was magnified in Britain by Governmental mistakes. Asquith miscalculated both the duration of the conflict and the extent to which it would devour economic resources. He compounded these errors by relying on market forces rather than direct state control to attain a sufficient level of war production. The laws of supply and demand, as most economists will admit, are appropriate for making marginal adjustments, not for massive re-allocation of a country's economic forces. A large increase in demand, such as took place in the initial period of the First World War, is likely to send prices shooting up. Higher profits encourage industrialists to increase output. While this procedure may appear admirable to capitalists, others may have a rather different idea, wondering why a few people should wax rich at the public's expense. As soldiers fell, the profits of the Merchants of Death rose. What made matters worse, in the opinion of the sizeable section of the general public, was another aspect of the operation of market forces: for demand to exceed supply under normal circumstances may be none too calamitious, but when the supply is ammunition – and enemy troops are advancing – then one is liable to be slightly less sanguine. The 'great shell scandal' of 1915, when some British troops ran perilously short of explosives, aroused considerable indignation.

Gradually, the truth began to percolate through. From their own experiences and occasional stories appearing in the Press, a lot of people began to realise that many employers were benefiting from the mass slaughter. War might be terrible – but it was terribly profitable! Referring to shipping, the *Daily Mail* said:

> The net earnings of the trade are estimated to have risen from £20 million in 1913 to £250 million in 1916. The profits are so great that a steamer is reported to pay for her entire cost in two voyages.[14]

In the House of Commons on 23 December 1915, Frank Goldstone MP capped this story by instancing a ship that had paid for itself in a single voyage. In 1915, two Tyneside shipping companies, Cairn Line and Moor Line, actually made profits that exceeded their capital value. Profits were equally astronomical in the manufacture of military

supplies. Soon after the declaration of War, the *Daily News* reported
that revolvers that had hitherto cost the government two guineas each
were now being bought for four guineas while those that had cost five
guineas had now been raised to ten.[15] W.W. Ashley MP told Parliament
that the War Office had purchased a million wooden ammunition
boxes at 13s 6d when the production cost was only 1s 2d.[16] Arms
manufacturers like Projectile Co. Limited, which only made a profit
of £18,880 in 1914, made £194,136 after tax in 1916.

Any intelligent person was liable to contrast the treatment of the
never-had-it-so-good industrialists with the less favourable treatment
accorded to the men who actually did the fighting. The *Daily Express*
reported that a soldier who had lost the use of limbs due to frostbite
would receive no pension since it could not be directly attributed to
enemy action.[17] Similarly, the *Daily Chronicle* said 300 widows would
receive no pension since, according to the War Office, their husbands'
illnesses had 'only developed in the course of service.'[18] The
Manchester Guardian carried the story of a soldier's wife, the mother
of six, on the meagre allowance she received, was unable to pay the
increased rent. She was 'dragged partially dressed from her bedroom
landing on to the street, and there beaten with an umbrella.' The court
fined the landlord — her assailant — a mere £10.[19]

Women were particularly vulnerable to exploitation as a result of the
pressures of the war. Unskilled and unorganised, millions of them were
drafted into factories to take the place of men who had gone to fight.
Female labour was cheap labour. Employers could make women work
long hours for much lower pay than men. At G. and J. Weir's Glasgow
foundry women were paid 15s a week making big shells. At Lusty's soup
factory wages were even worse — twopence an hour plus an extra twopence an hour for overtime:

> The basement in which the women work is wet and steaming. In one
> morning 24 women plucked and cleaned 500 fowls, some of which are
> said to be crawling with maggots.

According to Sylvia Pankhurst's paper, the *Workers' Dreadnought*, there
were many places where women worked 70 hours a week for only 22
shillings.[20] The long hours plus the inexperience resulted in frequent
accidents, some fatal. What was more, working in an explosives factory
turned women's hands, face and hair yellow. Obviously, the long hours
of work and the conditions under which it took place were liable to lead
to physical deterioration. It was probably no coincidence that in

Sheffield, where large numbers of women were employed in the engineering factories, infant mortality figures almost doubled: from 11,912 deaths in 1913 to 22,281 deaths in 1915.

But it was not merely women: no section of the working class could remain immune to the harmful effects of the war. The cost of living rose sharply without an equivalent rise in wages. The price rises were particularly marked in the case of food. Official figures show that retail food prices rose in the first twelve months of the war by an average of 32 per cent in large towns and 29 per cent in small towns and villages.[21] Most disturbing to the poor and those with large families was the increase in the price of bread – it rose from 5½d to 8d or more. Yet, when the Prime Minister was questioned in Parliament about these increases, he displayed remarkable complacency. Attempting to justify the Government's failure to take counter-measures, he said that these price rises had been no worse than those brought on by the Franco-Prussian war.[22]

Not surprisingly in the circumstances, industrial unrest began to grow. Faced with an erosion of their real wages and a worsening of their working conditions, workers bestirred themselves and began to resist.

The first major industrial revolt came from the Clyde. There tensions were felt more acutely then elsewhere. It was the area that had many large factories where workers, crowded together, gained a sense of unity. The introduction of modern production techniques had made men conscious of the methods used by management to economise at their expense. A tradition of militancy had developed. The war tended to reinforce the sense of grievance. From many parts of Britain, people flocked into Glasgow to work in the munitions factories. This simply worsened the appalling housing shortage in the city, where half the population lived in two-room houses and an eighth in single rooms. The newcomers, according to the official historian of the Ministry of Munitions, were compelled to endure 'the inclemency of the weather, the overcrowding, and the indifferent cooking in such lodgings as were available'.[23]

The engineers' pay claim provided the spark. In January 1912, the Clyde ASE district committee signed a three-year agreement that gave men a rate of 8½d an hour. Since then, both profits and prices had risen considerably. The district committee felt it was justified in making a formal claim for an extra twopence an hour, payable after the existing agreement expired. But the engineering employers sought to delay negotiations. Only the ASEs threat of a stoppage led them to make an offer. Then it was merely for a farthing, with a further half-

penny three months later. Irate engineers at Weir's banned overtime.
Meanwhile, socialists — mainly SLP members and the group around
John Maclean — held factory-gate meetings, relating the immediate
struggle to the general question of capitalism. While ASE officials,
anxious to avert a stoppage, desperately tried to seek a compromise,
to cool the situation and restore normal working, the tendency was
in the opposite direction. At factory after factory throughout Clydeside, engineers went on strike: the attitude of their union officials had
simply served to exasperate them all the more. 'The one fact that struck
home,' Arthur MacManus later remarked, when referring to the dispute,
'was the necessity of the workers doing for themselves what the officials
were too cowardly to attempt.'[24] Opposed by the employers, Government and their own union machinery, the Clydesdale workers resolved
to set up their own rank-and-file organisation, which eventually became
known as the Clyde Workers' Committee. Two special features characterised this newly-formed body① first, it embraced people from a variety
of trades, and therefore could not be controlled by the officials of any
one union; and, second② it was democratic. 'By pledging themselves to
accept no decision other than that arrived through the Unofficial
Central Committee and endorsed by *all* the workers in the District
Meetings, a possible split in the ranks was averted.'[25]

Union officials did everything possible to divide the men. J.T. Brownlie,
the ASEs general secretary, delivered a patriotic address to a rowdy
meeting at the Palace Theatre, Glasgow, but the engineers told him
they were determined to stay out — regardless of what their union
said — until the full twopence had been conceded. On 24 February
1915, the employers' offer was rejected in a ballot of the men by a ten
to one majority. Finally, the Government's intervention, offering
arbitration, and threatening serious counter-measures if it were refused,
brought the first faltering within the strikers' ranks. Seizing the
opportunity, the union officials called for a return to work on 3 March;
to assert its own authority, the Clyde Workers' Committee called for a
united return the following day, and that was what happened.

This first strike ended in failure. The strikers did not achieve their
objective, gaining only a temporary bonus of a penny. Since this was
exactly the amount gained by Glasgow dockers, without resorting to
a stoppage, it seems probable that the strike did not increase the final
size of the award. Moreover, after the dispute had ended, the Clyde
Workers' Committee — at that time known as the Central Labour
Withholding Committee — went out of existence. A few of the leading
figures did, however, continue to meet informally.

The significance of this first industrial battle was that it frayed the tempers of both employers and workers, producing a climate encouraging conflict. One can only make surmises about the reasons for the various attitudes adopted. Perhaps employers, having won the strike and seemingly smashed the Central Labour Withholding Committee, thought they were in a good bargaining position. They may well have wanted to teach the militants a lesson. Or maybe the exigencies of war, the need to boost production, compelled them to give the screw another twist, further increasing output without equivalent pay increases. Whatever it was that propelled employers into this activity, they did not see that the workers, too, had changed. Far from being demoralised by defeat, it had acted as a spur to strengthening organisation on the shop-floor. In the key Clydeside factories, militancy reached fresh heights after the return to work. Instead of regarding the strike as a catastrophic defeat, it was seen as a temporary setback, soon to be avenged.

In these circumstances, employers and trade unionists were clearly on a collision course. Managements decided to probe the enemy's positions. In July 1915, a shop steward named Marshall at Parkhead Forge, a stronghold of militancy, was dismissed and arraigned before the courts, accused of 'Slacking and causing others to slack'. A three-month sentence was imposed upon him. Immediately, workers made collections for Marshall's dependents and threatened to strike unless the sentence was withdrawn. Rather tardily, the authorities released Marshall and he returned to Parkhead.[26] Soon after this incident, the courts fined seventeen workers from Fairfield shipyard for going on strike. Three of the men chose prison rather than pay the fine. John Maclean launched a campaign to secure their release, but his efforts gained little response. They had to do their time. Then came the case of Robert Bridges' a shop steward at Weir's, who was charged with 'molesting' a worker by asking him for his union card. Two hundred of Bridge's workmates accompanied him to the proceedings and made their position abundantly clear: no fine would be paid and imprisonment would cause an immediate stoppage.[27]

Grievances about rent increases accompanied this industrial unrest. ILP members around Councillor John Wheatley strove unsuccessfully to obtain a legal prohibition of rent rises. Agitation on the issue was conducted by Maclean, MacDougall, MacBride and other socialists.[28] They used the same technique of factory-gate meetings as had been employed a few months earlier as the prelude to the Clyde engineers' strike. A Women's Housing Association, led by an energetic housewife,

Mrs Barbour, formed tenant committees. In May 1915, it felt
sufficiently strong to call for a rent strike. Soon 15,000 tenants had
refused to pay. Would-be rent collectors received rough treatment,
being smeared with flour and refuse before being kicked out.

An amazing aspect of the rent strike was the attitude of many
employers to it. The managing director of Harland & Wolff's Govan
Shipyards said: 'We are very pleased to hear that the tenants of Govan
are refusing to pay these rent increases, and we sympathize entirely
with them.'[29] Likewise, 'the manager of Fairfield told a deputation
that they would allow no workmen of theirs to occupy any house of
any person victimised for refusing to pay a rent increase.'[30]
Employers may have adopted this stand as it was popular, an attempt
to curry favour with the men. Another reason could have been the cold
calculation that a rent increase would inevitably steel workers in their
demand for higher wages: keeping rents down helped to keep down
labour costs.

In October 1915, a massive demonstrations in St. Enoch's Square,
Glasgow, demanded the Government curb rent-racketeers. The
following month an official Commission of Enquiry was appointed.
Meanwhile, the rent strike continued in many parts of the city, while
elsewhere landlords, anticipating controls, hurried through further
rent rises, a fact that only served to exacerbate tenants' feelings. On 17
November 1915, eighteen munition workers were summoned for the
non-payment of rent. As a result, several local shipyards, including
Harland and Wolff and Fairfield, immediately downed tools and,
marched to the court. En route, they stopped at the school where
John Maclean was a teacher, and he joined in the procession. Maclean
addressed a 10,000 strong demonstration outside the court, and this
was really the occasion on which he first came into prominence: it
was he who spoke for the strikers, making it plain that no return to
work would take place until the charges were dropped. They were.[31]
It was also Maclean who wrote to Asquith, the Prime Minister, saying
what would happen if rents were permitted to rise:

> That this meeting of Clyde Munition Workers requests the Govern-
> ment to definitely state not later than Saturday first, that it forbids
> any increase of rent during the period of the war and that, this
> failing, a general strike will be declared on first Monday, November
> 22nd.[32]

Hurriedly, the Government, fearful of the consequences of strikes

spreading throughout the munitions industry, introduced the Rent
Restriction Act. This tied rents all over Britain to the pre-war level.
Both locally and nationally, the agitation had been spectacularly
successful.

As the rent struggle had approached its climax, another sign of
mounting discontent appeared – the revival of the Clyde Workers'
Committee. Its newly-appointed leaders issued a leaflet, explaining
that the Committee had been formed 'for the purpose of concentrating
the whole forces of the Clyde Area against the Munitions Act.' The
aim was 'simply and purely defensive': the defence of precious and
hard-won rights – essential for the preservation of trade union
strength – from erosion by wartime legislation. Union officials,
anxious to maintain full productive effort, had signed agreements that
gravely weakened labour's bargaining power. It was 'an act of
Treachery to the Working Class,' declared the leaflet. 'Those of us who
have refused to be Sold have organised . . . determined to retain what
liberties we have, and to take the first opportunity of forcing the
repeal of all the pernicious legislation that has recently been imposed
upon us.'[33] The ultimate object was to achieve a much greater unity
and strength of the working class, sufficiently powerful to put 'the
workers in complete control of industry.'

The CWC held regular meetings in a hall at Ingram Street, Glasgow,
customarily attended by up to 300 workers, some representing strong
shop-floor organisations in their factories, others only a small nucleus
of colleagues. Despite weak links with some factories, the Committee
could claim to voice the opinions of a large section of Clydeside
workers. It was a body with a revolutionary potential. Except for its
secretary, James Messer, and later David Kirkwood, both of whom were
ILPers, all the other leaders could claim to be revolutionaries – Muir,
MacManus, T. Clark and many others from the SLP; Gallacher, its
chairman, belonging to the group around John Maclean, was in the
BSP.

The first challenge to the CWC was dilution, the substitution of
unskilled – sometimes female – labour for skilled. Policy on this
issue, drawn up in a document written by Muir, was agreed by the
Committee in December 1915, just before Lloyd George, the Minister
of Munitions, visited Glasgow to discuss the topic. In his policy statement, Muir accepted dilution as a necessary and progressive step, an
inevitable move in capitalist development. Yet, at the same time,
dilution represented a menace to organised labour. Government could
renege on its promise to restore pre-war trade union conditions; women,

paid much less than men, would by that time have become proficient, and it would be in the employers' interests not to replace them. The Clyde Workers' Committee's policy was nationalisation of all industry, with workers having a direct and equal share in the running along with management. When it became obvious to the CWC that such sweeping changes would not be introduced by the Government, nor could they be forced upon the Government, it laid down guidelines for plant bargaining. The two most important principles enunciated in the document compiled by Muir were, first, that income should not be determined by sex, previous training or experience, but upon the amount of work performed; and, second, that a workers' committee should be empowered to see this stipulation was carried out.

Armed with its policy, the Clyde Workers' Committee prepared its tactics for Lloyd George's visit. It was agreed that negotiation with him would not be on a piecemeal basis, factory by factory, but conducted by the Committee as a whole. So, on 23 December Lloyd George visited Weir's and Albion Motors — only to find no workers prepared to talk with him; only at Parkhead Forge did he gain a hearing. On the following day, he met the Clyde Workers' Committee. No agreement was reached. Lloyd George hoped that Glasgow workers generally would adopt a more favourable attitude to his proposals. He planned to address a big meeting of trade unionists on Christmas day, then not a Scottish public holiday, in St Andrew's Hall.

Arthur Henderson, the Labour leader and member of the Coalition Government, took the chair. From the outset, it was plain there would be difficulties from an overwhelmingly hostile audience. The Glasgow *Forward* reported Henderson's introductory remarks:

I am delighted to have the opportunity of appearing in this hall with the Minister of Munitions — (What about the hall for the workers) — to lay before you the great issue of the present moment so far as the war is concerned. (Ay! and profits) You are all aware of the fact that we are probably engaged in the greatest war — (At home) — that ever the old country has been concerned with. The issue that was raised in August 1914, when the neutrality — (Oh, heavens, how long have we to suffer this?) — of a brave and independent people was trodden on in a most shameful way. (That's enough).

When we began the war — (We don't want to hear that. Get to the Munitions Act) — I am endeavouring to show you the country was not prepared, and the fact that we were not prepared (Loud interruption: 'Cut it short!' 'Come away wi' Davy!') — Mr. Lloyd

George (loud hissing and booing) will presently address you — (more booing and hissing and some cheering) — on the dilution of labour.

The scheme of dilution that Mr. Lloyd George will recommend to you did not come from any employer. It came from a Committee — (interruption) — upon which there were seven trade unionists. (Traitors. Give us their names. Was John Hodge one o' them?)

I am quite prepared to give you their names. I do not want to hold any thing back. The first name I will give you is the chairman of the ASE (booing and hissing). My friends may jeer at his name, but he has been elected chairman since the scheme of dilution came up. (Dirty.) Another member of the committee was Mr. Kaylor — re-elected to the Executive (Away with him).[34]

The rest of Henderson's introduction was punctuated in the same style. When he sat down, the Minister for Munition rose to speak amid cat-calls and the singing of the 'Red Flag'. Lloyd George attempted to ingratiate himself with his audience. He referred to Labour leaders like Ramsay MacDonald as 'my greatest personal friends' and described the state-run munition works as 'great socialist factories'. But it was to no avail. The situation grew more and more out of hand, and eventually, the meeting broke up in disorder when Johnny Muir rose from the middle of the hall and started to state the workers' case in reply to Lloyd George. 'Seldom has a prominent politician, a leading representative of the Governing class, been treated with so little respect': this verdict, which appeared in John Maclean's journal, *Vanguard*, is almost certainly correct.[35]

The exigencies of war compelled the Government to acquire increasing control over the economy and, of the vast battery of regulations and restrictions had a built-in anti-working-class bias. This became clear not merely on the Clyde, but to people elsewhere. Even a paper like the *Sunday Chronicle* admitted: 'The Munitions Act, ostensibly and probably genuinely meant for the sole purpose of getting rapid production of shells, is in effect an Act to limit wages. Every Engineer in the land knows that.'[36]

The *Sunday Chronicle* hoped that engineers, imbued with a spirit of self-sacrifice, would willingly forego higher wages in the national interest. But patriotic appeals were becoming threadbare. Workers saw that burdens were increasingly being placed on their shoulders, not those of other classes in society. When the journal the *Motor Trader* cited instances of landlords preventing war work being done on their premises because it was outside the terms of their leases, no Government action was taken.[37] Nor did the authorities do anything to stop well-to-do young men evading the army by posing as key figures in family businesses, who should therefore have exemption.[38] In fact, many of them did nothing but loaf about — the Munitions Act was not used against them — whereas trade unionists were liable to be fined or imprisoned: traditional workers' rights could easily be construed as impediments to production. The Munitions Courts, supposedly impartial, had, by 27 November 1915, convicted 2,012 workers and only 86 employers.[39] That the Munitions Act had a built-in bias in favour of capital and against labour was being increasingly realised. Farmers petitioned for agricultural labourers to be included under the provisions of the Act: unless farmworkers were legally compelled to remain on the land, their employers would have to pay them higher wages to counteract the attraction of higher rates in industry.[40]

In an attempt to sell State controls and regulations to workers, some Government apologists argued that they were progressive. Traditionally, Labour Party politicians had seen the extension of State activity, curbing private enterprise's ambit of operation, as a step forward, and it was on this notion that the appeal was based. But, more and more, workers were beginning to understand the fallacy inherent in this position:

> In economic home policy the old State Socialism of the Fabian Society is somewhat discredited. There were socialists who rejoiced, in the early days of the war, that now Socialism had come. The Government controlled banks, railways, prices, everything. Now they have carried Socialism to the point of punishing all who will not take part in the war. If this is Socialism, the less we have of it the better. What is desirable is not increased power of the State, as an end in itself, but greater justice in distribution and, still more, better opportunities for initiative and self-direction on the part of those who do not happen to be capitalist. We need economic democracy as well as political democracy; we need the complete abolition of the system of working for wages. Something of the youthful revolutionary ardour of syndicalism is needed if labour is to have a free life. The men who do the work ought to control the policy of their industry.[41]

These remarks, written by Bertrand Russell, touched a responsive cord in the minds of many workers.

In the early stages of the war, the authorities could regard socialists as harmless eccentrics, people whose weird message had no impact on the public. But the situation changed as industrial unrest grew and socialists became the spokesmen for the expanding army of discontented people. In these circumstances, the state abandoned its attitude of grudging tolerance, and resolved to use its full arsenal of weapons against the enemies from within. Repression was the answer to the growing socialist menace.

Leading individuals were singled out for persecution. The first important instance was that of William Holliday. Described as 'a very reserved man, modest and unassuming', he nevertheless was a bold and uncompromising platform speaker. During the Boer War, he had defied jingoistic crowds in Birmingham Bull Ring, and had become well-known in the Midlands as an out-door speaker. He chaired the first conference of the Advocates of Industrial Unionism in 1906, and subsequently played an important part in the Birmingham SLP. From the beginning of the First World War, he spoke against it in the Bull Ring with increasing success. One Sunday night, speaking from his usual platform, Holliday declared: 'Freedom's battle has not to be fought on the blood-drenched soil of France, but nearer home. Our enemy is within the gates.' As he went on to say, he was not concerned with the outcome of the battle at Hill 60 but what happened to the striking miners of the Black Country — 'They are men. They have my sympathies' — he was pulled off the rostrum and taken to jail. On 28 May 1915, he was sentenced to three months' hard labour under the Defence of the Realm Act. Largely as a result of the initiative of William Paul, a William Holliday Defence Fund was set up. It received support from trades councils, NUT branches, Socialist Sunday Schools, Daily Herald League, ILP and SLP branches, Scottish BSP branches and many other sources. Money was raised for an appeal, and at Birmingham Quarter Sessions on 5 July 1915, Holliday was acquitted.[42]

Success was short-lived. Labour leaders spoke at an army recruiting rally in Birmingham Town Hall on 17 October 1915 and the SLP replied by holding a protest meeting in the Bull Ring. Holliday was speaking when he was again stopped and taken to the police station. This time the authorities made no mistake. William Holliday was jailed. He died in prison, aged 46. Rowdies unsuccessfully attempted to break up a Holliday memorial meeting, addressed by William Paul and Jimmy Stewart, in the Bull Ring on 28 May 1916. Although a large number of policemen were there at the time — *The Socialist* says 'many of them were disguised as men' — the forces of law and order did not stop the violent disruption. 'What better tribute could they pay to the dead warrior of Labour than break up the demonstration held to honour his work.'[43] Money had to be borrowed to pay for Holliday's funeral. He left a wife and eight children.

Like William Holliday, John Maclean first fell foul of the authorities for making statements prejudicial to recruitment. He, too, was prosecuted under the Defence of the Realm Act on 27 October 1915. The charge against him arose from remarks made during his speeches. Replying to a persistent heckler, who kept shouting, 'Why don't you enlist?', Maclean replied: 'I have been enlisted for fifteen years in the socialist army, which is the only army worth fighting for. God damn all other armies.'[44] In the course of his trial, evidence from prosecution witnesses unwittingly revealed the extent to which anti-war feeling had developed on the Clyde. The Sheriff asked a policeman, 'What was the size of the audience at the time?' 'About three hundred,' came the reply. 'You mean to say,' demanded the astonished Sheriff, 'that three hundred citizens of Glasgow heard a man say, "God damn the King's army", and did not resent it?' 'No one spoke,' replied the policeman. Referring to another occasion, a detective was asked why he did not take action while the meeting was taking place. He answered: 'Our interference would have resulted in a riot.'[45] What worsened matters was that John Maclean used the court to explain and justify his revolutionary principles. At the end of the trial there were shouts of 'Three cheers for the Revolution' from the public gallery and a large crowd outside sung *The Red Flag*.[46]

The case was heard in the aftermath of the victorious rent strike. With this still clear in people's minds, the authorities had to act with discretion. If they had made Maclean, the hero of that struggle, into a martyr there might well have been grave repercussions on Clydeside. So the Sheriff contented himself with passing a mild sentence. Faced with a £5 fine or five days' imprisonment, John Maclean chose the latter. The punishment did not gag him long nor act as a deterrent.

Unable to silence its critics, the Government sought to deprive them of a platform. Meeting halls were cancelled, sometimes at the last minute, when alternative arrangements could not be made. Also, magistrates could ban meetings. One of the first times this happened was in November 1915. Two thousand handbills had been issued advertising a lecture at Glasgow Lyric Theatre on 'Glorious Episodes in British History'. Suddenly, it was prohibited. That the authorities should take this severe step over a lecture with such an innocuous-sounding title may appear surprising. But the speaker was to have been John S. Clarke. He normally began his 'glorious episodes from British history'

with the beheading of Charles the First, graphically illustrated with
lantern slides, and went on to inspiring events like trade unionists
defying the Combination Acts and other laws to win the right to
organise. Once when John S. Clarke was addressing a meeting, the
police stood outside, waiting to arrest him. He foiled them with a
simple 'disguise', as David Kirkwood explains:

> He left the hall, passing on his way a bunch of detectives. He walked
> through them all easily by carrying his own hat. I know nobody who
> is so different without a hat. When John S. Clarke wears a hat, he is
> like a douce Glasgow business man; but he is so bald that, when he
> removes his hat, he looks like Grock the clown![47]

This kind of victory, while good for morale, was short-lived. Soon John
S. Clarke was forced to go into hiding. By March 1916, the journal
Plebs said suppression had become a common occurrence: 'Meetings
have been cancelled by the score, and even where meetings have been
held, summonses against speakers have been issued and fines imposed.'

When even these measures proved insufficient, the Government
turned its attention to the working-class press. It banned *Forward*, a
mildly Left journal, for publishing a report of the Lloyd George
meeting in Glasgow. John Maclean's *Vanguard* was also seized for
having the audacity to reprint *Forward*'s report. On 2 February 1916,
the police raided the SLP headquarters. They smashed the printing
machinery and confiscated the forthcoming issue of the Clyde
Workers' Committee paper, *The Worker*. Next day two CWC officials,
Gallacher and Muir, were arrested along with Walter Bell, the SLPs
business manager. They were charged under DORA with attempting
'to cause mutiny, sedition or disaffection among the civilian population and to impede, delay or restrict the production of war material
by producing, printing and circulating amongst workers in and around
Glasgow *The Worker*.' Depicted as dangerous enemy agents, the three
men initially were refused bail. But this aroused a massive response:
10,000 'workers decided to have a holiday in honour of the occasion.'
After a day's stoppage, the court relented and the three were released
on bail.

Resistance from workers did not deter the State from continuing its
offensive. On 11 April 1916, John Maclean faced indictment on six
charges, which ranged from inciting soldiers to lay down their arms to
willing workers 'to sell or pawn their alarm clocks, sleep in in the
morning and not go to work.' Maclean received a three-year sentence.

Then came the turn of those associated with *The Worker*'s production:
Muir and Gallacher each got twelve months, Walter Bell was imprisoned for three. Meanwhile, the authorities continued their activities
outside the courts. The leading militants at Weir's, MacManus, Bridges,
Kennedy and Glass, were dragged from their beds in the middle of the
night and deported from Glasgow. The same treatment was accorded
to Kirkwood, Haggerty, Shields and Clarke, the leaders of the men at
Parkhead Forge. Jack Smith, the convenor at Weir's, received an 18
month sentence. On 11 May 1916, Jimmy Maxton and James
MacDougall, Maclean's right-hand man, were both sentenced to a
year's imprisonment.[48]

This repression robbed the Clyde Workers' Committee of its leadership, and of the political services of accomplished men like John
Maclean. Undoubtedly, by doing this, the Government succeeded in
making the introduction of dilution much smoother than it might
otherwise have been. At the same time, the Government achieved
it at a cost to itself. On Clydeside, socialist organisations grew in
numbers and, at least at shop floor level, workers continued the
struggle. Moreover, by its action, the Government gave a gratuitous
lesson in political understanding: workers could clearly see that the
State was not a neutral body; it squarely backed the employers in
every battle. Indeed, William Weir, who had gained the reputation
of being one of the worst types of employers in Scotland, devised the
assault plan used by the Government against the Clyde Workers'
Committee.[49]

In the opinion of Cabinet Ministers, the position had become so
grave that all weapons, no matter how dirty and sinister, were deployed to crush the opposition. Some people, accustomed to the
British State acting in a reasonably liberal and tolerant manner, were
shocked when the mask was stripped off and all the ugly features of a
totalitarian regime revealed – the mass use of *agents provocateurs*
and police spies, the concoction of false evidence, and the holding of
individuals without trial. At most, very mild protests against repressive measures came from Labour MPs; much more outspoken were a
handful of radical Liberals who opposed Lloyd George. For example,
J. King, the MP for North Somerset, spoke in the Commons on 8
March 1917, criticising the expenditure of £620,000 in the year 1916
on these activities. He talked about the 'employment of immoral, disreputable and ungentlemanly means' by police agents. He cited Carl
Graves, a convicted criminal. When he had come before the courts,
R. Munro, the prosecutor, described him as a dangerous man and

asked for an exemplary sentence. Within two months of completing his prison-term, Graves was approached by Munro, by then Secretary of State for Scotland, and employed to spy on militants in Glasgow.

Another Liberal MP, W.M.R. Pringle, complained that the Ministry of Munitions used another way of gleaning information:

> I have personal knowledge of cases where important leaders in the trade union movement in this country have been approached for the purpose of spying upon their fellows and making secret reports in regard to their actions to the Government.[50]

The introduction of conscription in 1916 provided the State with a further club with which to beat its opponents. Some socialists, like pacifists and religious objectors, refused to fight. There was initially no provision for conscientious objection, and therefore such people could find themselves forceably taken into army barracks, ordered to don military uniform, and charged with mutiny for disobeying a command. Scenes of terrible brutality would often ensue. Henry Sara, later to become one of the founders of British Trotskyism, was dragged into the barracks at Harrow Road, London, had his clothes ripped off him, and was then beaten by soldiers. Afterwards he was taken to Hurdcott camp, where he was told to form fours. Again he refused, and was sent to Parkhurst prison.[51] J.P. Kay received even worse treatment: at Winchester camp, when he refused to obey orders, an officer bayoneted him three times.[52] In his book on war resisters, David Boulton gives the names of 73 men who died as a direct result of the treatment they suffered at the hands of the military or in prison.[53]

Probably the cruelty exercised was indicative of the growth of anti-war feelings among the young, and of the authorities finding themselves under pressures. There had been an indication that some British soldiers did not regard their German counterparts as filthy Huns on Christmas Day 1915. Troops from the opposing armies met in no-man's-land, chatted, played cards, and even had a game of football. Among those who took part in this memorable meeting was Herbie Bell, a lifelong socialist from Wallsend. He describes how both British and German soldiers said they were heartily sick of the war and realised it was not being fought in their interests but on behalf of the rich.[54] Occasionally draconian action was taken against soldiers who did not display sufficient enthusiasm for fighting. Three Durham miners were executed at Boullecourt, France, in 1916, and subsequent attempts to get the army to divulge the full details proved to be unsuccessful.[55]

Once the Government resolved to permit conscientious objection,
some socialists applied for exemption. A tribunal, after rigorous
questioning, decided whether to uphold their claim, send them into
an industry vital to the war effort, or reject their claim, in which case,
assuming they still refused to go in the army, they were liable to be
imprisoned. Usually tribunal proceedings were sombre affairs − so
much depended upon their outcome − but there were sometimes
moments of wry humour, such as when a military representative
asked an SLPer: 'Are you engaged on work of national importance?'
To which the SLPer replied: 'No, I'm engaged on work of international
importance.'[56]

When Karl Liebknecht appeared before a German army court martial
on 3 May 1916, a verbatim account of his courageous speech against the
war appeared in *The Socialist*. As a gesture of international solidarity,
as well as to promote anti-war sentiment here in Britain, many SLPers
made similar speeches. George Hutchinson, of Bolton, after serving a
four-month sentence, was brought before the court a second time. He
declared:

> I would be failing in my duty to the international working class if I
> do not oppose, with all my strength, the institutions of militarism
> and capitalism. To me, they are inseparable. I believe that the action
> I am now taking is in the best interests of the wage earners of this
> and every other country, and believing so, I am fully prepared to
> accept punishment. As Karl Liebknecht, Rosa Luxemburg and
> other anti-militarists of Germany are being severely punished for
> their part in the struggle for international solidarity, so I and my
> comrades have been, and are being, cruelly punished for what we
> consider absolutely necessary for the principles of industrial liberty
> and political freedom.

When Hutchinson was sentenced to a further two years' imprisonment,
he shouted 'Long live The International.'[57]

Many SLPers, wishing to avoid prison if possible, did not register as
conscientious objectors but instead joined the 'flying corps' − so
named because this intrepid band of men spent most of their time
flying away from the police and the military. They would visit a town,
sell socialist literature, perhaps hold a public meeting, and rush off to
evade capture. A network of places throughout Britain grew up which
would harbour socialists on the run. Even in remote spots like the
Lake District staging-posts existed: at Hill Top Farm, near Lake

Windermere, a number of wanted men, grateful for hospitality provided,
carved their names on a big boulder.[58] In Leicester, a small room near
the Clock Tower provided a haven. When this became common
knowledge, the *Leicester Mail* fulminated about this 'veritable hotbed
of sedition . . . a disgrace to the town.' In these premises, the newspaper continued, absentees were 'given a good time, being well
supplied with food, playing cards, literature and music.' One man who
the police had been seeking for months regularly went cycling round
the district at dusk. He was said to possess two revolvers. Another two
men had tramped 80 miles to reach the city: 'They slept out at nights
in barns and fields, and unwashed, ragged and nearly bootless arrived
in Leicester.' The newspaper story ended by warning:

> That the SLP is a direct menace to society is proved by the fact that
> its leaders are at present in prison for sedition, and that its activities
> were mainly responsible for the serious labour troubles in the Clyde
> district some little time back.[59]

The *Leicester Mail* was not entirely correct. Admittedly, some SLP
leaders were in prison, but others were still on the run. The regular
appearance of *The Socialist* owed much to members of the 'flying
corps'. Among those primarily responsible were John S. Clarke and
William Paul. John S. Clarke spent most of his time at Turner's farm,
Arleston, near Derby, where he earned his keep working as a labourer
and spent his spare-time writing articles.[60] Willie Paul was far more
ingenious. Being a theoretician of some eminence, he seems to have
asked himself: 'What would Karl Marx have done in such circumstances?'
and to have taken himself off to the Reading Room of the British
Museum. There, he not only wrote for *The Socialist* but completed a
book, *The State: Its Origins and Functions*, which is today a neglected
Marxist classic. Paul remained undisturbed in the BM, presumably
because the British Museum was not a haunt of the Special Branch.[61]
    The secret police strove hard to infiltrate militant organisations and
to smash the network of people who befriended the 'flying corps'.
Sometimes it gained success, as in the SLP stronghold of Derby.[62] Mrs
Wheeldon was a kind-hearted middle-aged woman, active in the
Suffragettes before the First World War. One of her daughters, Hetty,
was engaged to Arthur MacManus. He, of course, often visited her home
at 907 London Road, and so did many others since Mrs Wheeldon
arranged accommodation in Derby for members of the 'flying corps.'
A police spy, calling himself Alex Gordon, called on her, posing as a man

on the run. She fixed him up with lodgings. Previously, he had attempted to ensnare militants from a number of parts of the country in his plot. Nobody was prepared to fall into the trap, but eventually Mrs Wheeldon showed interest.

Her trial opened at the Central Criminal Court, London, on 11 March 1917. She claimed that she possessed four phials of poison because Alex Gordon had persuaded her to join in his scheme, which was to secure a mass break-out of war resisters by poisoning the guard-dogs at a detention centre near Liverpool. The prosecution, on the other hand, claimed Mrs Wheeldon possessed the poison because she wanted to assassinate the Prime Minister and Arthur Henderson. According to the Attorney-General, she intended 'to get a position in a hotel where the Prime Minister stayed and drive through his boot a nail that had been dipped in poison.'[63]

In his *Last Memoirs*, Willie Gallacher described the prosecution's case as 'melodramatic nonsense', while Tom Bell expressed the verdict of left-wingers about the case:

> The trial was a most disgraceful frame-up. The prosecution point-blank refused to put 'Gordon', their chief witness, into the witness box for cross-examination. The mother got ten years and the other members of the family five years imprisonment each.[64]

In prison, Mrs Wheeldon suffered terribly. She was released after she had served only two years of her sentence and died a few weeks later. She was buried, her coffin draped with a red flag, in Nottingham Road cemetery, Derby. The *Derby Daily Express* reported the proceedings under the headline 'Sensational Incidents at Graveside: Rhetorical Sneers at Prime Minister'.[65] The reason for this was that, although still on the run himself, John S. Clarke turned up at the funeral and gave a graveside oration. He accused Lloyd George and Henderson of being responsible for Mrs Wheeldon's death through their employment of agents provocateurs. Clarke went on to say:

> There are several ways of murdering our valiant women fighters. There is a straightforward, brutal way of sheer murder, which killed Rosa Luxemburg. And there is the secret, sinister, cowardly and slower method, which killed Mrs Wheeldon.[66]

John S. Clarke, who was already well known as a poet, resolved to express his feelings in another way. He had an unfortunate knack of

writing the epitaphs of people he detested before they were actually dead,
perhaps as an encouragement to them to shuffle off this mortal coil, and
he penned:

> Epitaph on Alex Gordon
>
> Agent Provocateur of the British Government
> during the great war to safeguard democracy.
>
> Stop! stranger, thou art near the spot
> Marked by this cross metallic,
> Where buried deep doth lie and rot,
> The corpse of filthy Alex.
>
> And maggot-worms in swarms below
> Compete with one another,
> In shedding tears of bitter woe,
> To mourn — not eat — a brother.[67]

This poem became well-known among class-conscious workers. It was a
popular recitation at social gatherings. The feeling of repulsion was so
strong that, according to Tom Bell, 'Gordon was shipped to South
Africa for a time to save his skin.'

When things calmed down, Gordon returned to Britain. The bad
publicity had apparently created severe mental strain. He entered a
Derby newspaper office, brandishing a gun, and had to be removed by
the police.[68] Then he tried to clear his name by giving an interview to
the *Daily Herald* on 28 December 1919. He told the paper his real name
was F. Vivian. He had worked for the Government as a labour spy for
quite a time. He received £2 10s a week plus an occasional £2 bonus.
The headquarters of the International Workers of the World in White-
chapel Road and the Communist Club in Charlotte Street had been
raided after he had visited them. Gordon attempted to justify himself:

> I was not consciously a secret service man. By the time I was told
> that the Government had got me . . . the Government agents had a
> hold over me which made it absolutely impossible for me to break
> away from them.

This did not satisfy his critics. John S. Clarke, by this time editor of
The Worker, launched a further attack on 'dirty Alex', and Gordon
replied by threatening a libel action. But this failed to materialise. A

court case, with the glare of publicity about its methods, was probably
the last thing the Secret Service wanted to happen. Nothing further was
heard of Alex Gordon. It seems reasonable to conclude that, in some
way or another, the Secret Service silenced him.

Speaking in Parliament, J. King stated he knew three other instances
of the use of agents provocateurs similar to Alex Gordon. Ramsay
MacDonald, the Labour leader, also pointed to dangers inherent in
the employment of 'agents provocateurs, who make their money by the
manufacture of crime.'[69] The same opinion was expressed, in retrospect,
by the *Manchester Guardian*:

> During the war a system of industrial espionage was established in
> the Ministry of Munitions. That Department learnt in course of time
> what a dangerous instrument it was. The system, introduced under
> cover of war, has now been established as part of our domestic
> machinery as a branch of the Home Office . . . Spying of this kind
> at the worst produces plots and conspiracies manufactured or
> stimulated by the spies themselves: at the best it drives discontent
> underground and makes it more dangerous. The men who employ
> these spies are credulous, and the spies themselves have every motive
> for finding trouble. They are men who do dirty work which no man
> of character would touch.[70]

After likening the position to that prevailing during the Napoleonic
Wars, when the Government employed large numbers of spies and
agents provocateurs, the *Manchester Guardian* said that 'such methods
are peculiarly repulsive to Englishmen'. It then went on to ask for the
full facts about these activities to be revealed: 'Some day the whole
truth of the proceedings of this kind that did so much to embitter the
munition workshops during the war, will be made public, and the
sooner the better.'

Of course, what the *Manchester Guardian* wanted has never
happened. Successive governments, zealous to guard as secrets the techniques employed against working-class organisations, have refused to
reveal the facts. But one thing is clear: when the British State feels
threatened by a class foe, and it did feel threatened during the First
World War, it will use any method, no matter how despicable and dirty,
in the struggle.

Trade unionists as well as opponents of the war had to endure a
repression more vicious than at any period since Chartist times. But
despite all the State's actions, they continued to function and achieved

considerable successes.

Notes

1. Statement by R. Page Arnot in the *Bulletin of the Society for the Study of Labour History*, Autumn 1966, p.11.
2. G.D.H. Cole, *Labour in War Time*, p. 62.
3. Ibid, p. 138.
4. *Daily Express*, 22 November 1915.
5. *Daily Chronicle*, 14 August 1914.
6. *Merthyr Pioneer*, 14 August 1914.
7. R.M. Fox, *Smoky Crusade*, p. 193.
8. *The Socialist*, September 1914.
9. Ibid, January 1915.
10. Ibid, November 1914.
11. Thomas Bell, *Pioneering Days*, p. 49.
12. Ibid. Also, *The Socialist*, September 1915.
13. *The Socialist*, September 1914.
14. *Daily Mail*, 5 February 1916.
15. *Daily News*, 20 November 1914.
16. House of Commons, 30 May 1916.
17. Pamphlets exposing war profiteering included *Profits and Prices* (BSP, 1916); *Profits and Patriotism* (ILP, 1916); and *The Conscription of Wealth* (National Labour Press, 1917)
18. *Daily Chronicle*, 7 February 1916.
19. *Manchester Guardian*, 30 September 1915.
20. *Workers' Dreadnought*, 21 August 1915, 9 September 1915, and 4 December 1915.
21. Board of Trade *Labour Gazette*, quoted G.D.H. Cole, op. cit., p. 119.
22. H. Asquith, House of Commons, 11 February 1915.
23. History of the Ministry of Munitions, vol. 4, pp. 29-44. I.S. Maclean's 'The Labour Movement in Clydeside Politics 1914-1922' emphasises the environmental reasons for discontent.
24. *The Socialist*, January 1915.
25. 'On the Clyde: A Study in Solidarity', by A. MacManus, *Plebs*, March 1916.
26. *Glasgow Herald*, 19 February 1915.
27. *Vanguard*, November 1915; W. Gallacher, *Revolt on the Clyde* (1949) p. 62.
28. Nan Milton, *John Maclean* (1973) p. 93.
29. *Forward*, 5 June 1915.
30. Ibid, 12 June 1915.
31. Nan Milton, op.cit., p. 90.
32. W. Gallacher, op.cit., pp. 54-5.
33. Beveridge Collection on Munitions, vol. 3, p. 95.
34. *Forward*, 1 January 1916.
35. Dr James Hinton's essay, 'The Clyde Workers' Committee and the Dilution Struggle' in A. Briggs and J. Saville's book *Essays in Labour History, 1886-1923* (1971) reaches the same conclusion.
36. *Sunday Chronicle*, 28 November 1915.
37. *Motor Trader*, 6 October 1915.
38. *Manchester Evening News*, 17 April 1916.
39. *Daily Express*, 29 December 1916.
40. *Daily News*, 18 December 1916.

41. *Ploughshare*, August 1916. Bertrand Russell was imprisoned in Brixton jail for writing an article saying troops would be used to intimidate strikers.
42. *The Socialist*, August 1915.
43. Ibid, May 1915.
44. Nan Milton, op. cit., p. 100.
45. Tom Bell, *John Maclean* (Glasgow, 1944) p. 45.
46. Nan Milton, op. cit., pp. 100-1.
47. D. Kirkwood, *My Life of Struggle* (1935) p. 134.
48. J. McNair and James Maxton, *The Beloved Rebel* (London, 1955), p. 65.
49. PRO Mun. 5/70. David Kirkwood described Weir as 'one of the worst types of employers' in the *Glasgow Sunday Mail*, 7 October 1934.
50. House of Commons, 5 August 1917.
51. *The Socialist*, May 1916.
52. *Workers' Dreadnought*, 7 April 1917.
53. David Boulton, *Objection Overruled* (1967) p. 266.
54. BBC Radio Newcastle has an interview with Herbie Bell in its archives.
55. The attempts were made by C.H. Norman and reported in *Railway Review*, 3 February 1922, and *Forward*, 15 April 1922.
56. *The Socialist*, October 1916.
57. Ibid, July 1917.
58. Interview with Lester Hutchinson, former MP for Rusholme, on 18 March 1972. Lester's father, Richard Hutchinson, provided one of the havens for the 'flying corps' near to Blackpool.
59. *Leicester Mail*, 9 June 1916.
60. Interview with Joe Crispin, an ex-NCLC lecturer, 16 June 1972. Frank Burton and Tom Crispin, Joe's brother, also took refuge at Turner's farm.
61. Interviews with Archie Henry, 7 August 1972, and Lester Hutchinson, 18 March 1972. Fortunately William Paul's classic has been reprinted by Proletarian Publishers of Edinburgh.
62. For full account see my article in the *Socialist Worker*, 10 June 1972.
63. F.W. Chandler, *Police Spies and Provocative Agents* (Sheffield, 1936) pp. 109-10. For Police version of the Wheeldon case see Sir Basil Thomson's article in *Sheffield Weekly Telegraph*, 7 March 1923.
64. Thomas Bell, *Pioneering Days*, p. 126. Also, W. Gallacher, *Last Memoirs*, p. 139.
65. *Derby Daily Express*, 21 February 1919.
66. *The Socialist*, 27 February 1919.
67. The poem is reprinted in John S. Clarke's book, *Poems, Satires and Lyrics* (Glasgow, 1919).
68. *Workers' Dreadnought*, 3 January 1920.
69. House of Commons, 8 March 1917.
70. *Manchester Guardian*, 6 August 1919.

7 SOCIALISTS IN TRANSITION

The First World War had an immense impact on British society. Socialist organisations were transformed by the heat of conflict, and greater unity and disunity came simultaneously into being. The unity stemmed from an unparalleled persecution which tended to make real left-wingers forget doctrinal differences and become brothers in misfortune. Comradeship grew and mutual help was given, regardless of political affiliation. Old animosities and distrust were swept aside by socialists who realised that the fundamentals they agreed upon, opposition to the war and the need for industrial militancy, were of more importance than those that divided them. Reinforcing this attitude was an appreciation of the fact that the tensions created by world war would probably produce glittering opportunities. No longer need socialists remain spectators, commenting on events from the sidelines; they now had a chance to mould events and have a say in the writing of history. Yet, if this was to be done, they had to learn to co-operate with each other in the struggle for the common goal.

The greater disunity arose because, by action and utterance, Labour politicians revealed that they did not share this common goal. The meaning of Social Democracy was spelt out in practice: support for the war, speeches at recruiting rallies, endorsement of the government's harsh industrial code, persecution of left-wingers. When Labour leaders actually joined the government, becoming personally responsible for anti-working-class measures, it merely served to emphasise their role. Arthur Henderson's hostile reception at the Glasgow meeting, described in the last chapter, was indicative of this growing distrust. Besides being responsible for keeping wages down and strike-breaking, as a member of the inner cabinet Henderson had direct complicity in the brutal way the British government crushed the Easter Uprising in 1916. When news reached Parliament that the army had summarily executed James Connolly, Arthur Henderson led Labour MPs in spontaneous applause.[1]

Two trade union officials, George Barnes, of the Engineers, and William Brace, of the Miners, also belonged to the Coalition government. At the Home Office, Brace helped in the enforcement of repressive industrial regulations as well as the employment of agents provocateurs and spies. But it was in rather another fashion that Brace drew attention to himself, as the *Sunday Chronicle* pointed out:

> Who is the greatest 'swell' in the House of Commons? Who wears the most carefully cut overcoat, the most shiny silk hat (and at the most jaunty angle), and who walks with the most subdued consciousness of the fact that he is shiny and well-dressed and that no speck is ever upon his clothes? His name is William Brace, a miner. He worked down on the coal-face when a boy. Now, although not in the cabinet, he is a Minister, a member of the Government, and he adorns the Treasury Bench.[2]

Doubtless workers, more worried about the effect of rising prices upon the pay packets, were unimpressed by Brace's sartorial splendour.

From the outset of the war, the Socialist Labour Party had much graver matters to concern itself with than the cut of a minister's overcoat. Its most pressing problem was a miniscule membership, an inadequacy making it impossible to function effectively. Although actual numbers were not given, it seems probably that they were around 200: in 1915 the SLPs annual conference shows the Party possessed only eight branches, exactly the number it had in 1904. What had changed in those intervening eleven years was the size of the periphery. Thousands of workers had bought SLP pamphlets, often Marxist classics published at the exceedingly low price of a penny, in addition to reading the SLPs journal. Therefore, the Party's influence depended upon being able to influence its sympathisers, drawing them into joint activity.

While there was almost complete unity within the SLP in 1914, the Party's contacts, more susceptible to outside pressures, were initially hesitant. So the case for and against the war was openly debated in the columns of *The Socialist*. The journal sought patiently to explain, winning people over to an opposition stance. Unlike other socialist groups who sought to breathe life again into the Second International, the SLP saw, in the orgy of patriotism indulged in by the Labour leaders of the various belligerents, a vindication of its analysis.

For this reason, the SLP immediately endorsed the call for the formation of a new international. In November 1914, it reprinted an article from the *Berner Tagwacht*, organ of the Swiss SDP, by the Dutch Marxist, Anton Pannekoek. The article stated that the growth of giant trusts had led to the development of imperialism; that parliamentarianism and bureaucracy had enfeebled the Second International; that just as capital's power had become more concentrated, so, with the burdens of militarism and taxation, 'the power of the proletariat grows too'; and, fourth, that the current crisis demanded the creation of a new international.[3]

Throughout discussions on re-groupment, the SLP reiterated that all organisation had to be built on sound socialist principles. Without this, however spectacular early successes might be, the project would be doomed to failure. By 1916, as workers became more and more war-weary, the SLPs membership had doubled and the circulation of its journal trebled. But Tom Bell, who chaired the SLPs annual conference that year, declared that this expansion was fraught with danger: 'In his judgment, it was not desirable to promote the formation of branches of mushroom growth . . . (new recruits) should understand the principles of the Party thoroughly first.'[4] Theoretical clarity remained the pre-condition for sound progress.

Tom Bell went on to review the growing rank-and-file resistance within the trade unions, and cited the mounting militancy among railwaymen, building workers and miners. 'This new spirit,' he said,

> this change of front, this revolt against leaders, was mainly due to the SLP. For example, the powerful minority amongst the Welsh Miners, who defied their leaders and brought on a strike during the war, was composed of men who had been in touch with the SLP literature and Marxism.

Although the SLP appears to have had very few members in South Wales, its publications were widely read and studied there. A few months after Bell's chairman's address, *The Socialist* listed 35 Marxist Social Science classes, many in South Wales, and advised members to attend. Among the class secretaries were Noah Ablett at Mardy and Arthur Horner (later secretary of the National Union of Mineworkers) at Yashir.

From early in the war, the SLP learnt to collaborate with socialists who had similar, but not identical, views. When Landsbury's *Daily Herald* refused to publish accounts of its anti-war activities, the Daily Herald League sent them to the SLP. Ralph Fox, one of its leading members, became a regular contributor to *The Socialist*. In 1915, the Glasgow branch cooperated with members of the SLP and the BSP to hold a highly successful week of socialist propaganda. John Maclean and former SLP members, like Neil Maclean, spoke from the same platform as Bell, MacManus and others. This growing unity continued when the authorities began to resort to repression. A Free Speech Defence Campaign was launched on the Clyde, supported by a wide spectrum of left opinion. In a slightly different guise it continued when

militants were arrested. The Committee led the protests, calling for
their release. Likewise, with the increasing number and influence of
shop stewards throughout British industry, it was SLPers who saw the
need to form a national organisation to co-ordinate their activities. The
Party learnt to emphasise points of agreement, to call for united action,
and to state differences only when absolutely necessary.

One of the first targets of the Government were the socialist newspapers that spread ideas contrary to official policy. To counter this
threat, the SLP realised it was vital to support journals under attack,
even where policy disagreements existed:

> How insane, therefore, is the jubilation of the Aberdeen BSPers,
> who have actually written to the local papers congratulating the
> Government for suppressing the *Labour Leader*. No doubt these
> fellows disagree with the *Labour Leader*. So do we; but it is not a
> matter of the publication of the *Labour Leader* that is at stake — it
> is the right of all of us to state our views under any circumstances.
> If the *Labour Leader* goes under, then it will be child's play to
> suppress the organ of the BSP, *Justice*.

When an issue of a journal was seized, the SLP usually registered a
protest and, to underline it, reprinted the article that had led to the
suppression in the columns of its own paper. As a result, *The Socialist*
over the years contained many reprints. In 1912, the 'Don't Shoot'
leaflet, for which Tom Mann and others were imprisoned, appeared
in its columns. Similarly, the account of Lloyd George's visit to
Glasgow that appeared in the *Forward* was published in *The Socialist*,
as did articles from *The Worker* when it was banned. The SLP carried
this policy of defiance to considerable lengths: extracts from banned
issues of satirical journals and Tolstoyan pacifist papers were reprinted
— simply to hit back at the Government.

Where it was not merely one issue that was being suppressed but the
journal itself, then the SLP was prepared to place its printing facilities
at the disposal of those who were under attack:

> When the Government threatened to prosecute those who dared to
> print *The Suffragette*, the Socialist Labour Press at once offered to
> print the paper, despite the fact that as an organisation we had little
> in common with principles propagated by that journal. The same
> thing happened when the police of Ireland attempted to victimise
> the paper published by the Irish Transport Union. The paper was

printed by the SLP and, in order to guarantee its safe arrival in
Dublin, a member was sent with the printed copies to dupe the
police, who had intimated their intention of seizing the issue when
it reached Dublin. In this manner we have upheld the freedom of
the Press as a principle to be jealously guarded.[5]

Many have criticised the SLP as sectarian. True, in the period before
the First World War, a time of isolation, tendencies of this character
did exist within the Party. All organisations of revolutionaries, operating in times not conducive to their ideas, develop the same tendency.
It was as true of the nineteen-fifties and sixties as it was of the pre-
1914 period. But it is often worthwhile to investigate further precisely
who are those people who fling the accusation of sectarianism. Usually
they are people who are unsympathetic to left wing politics. When
they attach the label of 'sectarian' to an organisation, they are really
criticising its revolutionary essence, its preparedness, indeed determination, to adopt a principled stand.

The main objection that can be levelled at the SLP during the First
World War was not sectarianism but the failure on occasions to put
forward sound theoretical principles because it might endanger unity
in the immediate struggle. Far from being too narrow, too rigid, the
Party failed to make distinctions that should have been made, regardless of the unpleasant scenes that might have ensued. Probably the
reason for this is that, conscious of breaking down the barriers that had
divided socialists in the past, the SLP swung too far in the opposite
direction, tacitly making concessions to achieve united action with
other groups that were in the long run damaging.

Take the important issue of membership of the SLP. In the past,
every potential member had to sign a declaration stating that he
accepted a number of basic propositions of Marxism. By 1916, however, a person could quite easily be made a member. T.A. Jackson
describes in his autobiography how he was told he was presenting the
case for the SLP in a debate at Leeds. When he protested that he did
not belong to the SLP, he was told that he had been made a member
the previous evening.[6] While there may have been little harm in this,
since Jackson had moved on so many issues so close to the Party's
policies, there is nevertheless a case for obtaining a firm commitment,
both as to conduct and finance, before admitting somebody to the
ranks.

But the slackness did not end at this point. There are definite signs
that the SLPs attitude to belonging to its ranks, the conduct and

commitment expected from a member, strayed well below the standards of democratic centralism. This can be shown by comparing three accounts, those of Bell, Gallacher and Kirkwood, of the discussions that occurred in 1914 about the attitude socialists should adopt to the war. Tom Bell writes:

> A special Party meeting was called to discuss the war situation. A keen debate ensued, in which three lines were taken. The first line, led by MacManus and myself, was definite, open hostility to the war; the second, led by the late John W. Muir, was that in the event of invasion we should be prepared for National Defence; the third line was to look upon the war with an academic interest, as an event of world importance that would hasten the inevitable collapse of capitalism.[7]

Bell goes on to say practice resolved this theoretical problem. When members experienced what war really meant, and when angry mobs of jingoists strived to smash SLP public meetings, even Johnny Muir changed his mind and became as hostile to the war as the rest of the membership.

The Kirkwood memoirs confirm much of what Tom Bell wrote:

> In September 1914 I was still a member of the Socialist Labour Party. At a meeting of the Glasgow Branch a discussion took place as to our attitude towards the war. I moved that as a branch we should declare our opposition to the war and start agitation for the purpose of stopping it. An amendment was moved that we support the war. The mover was John W. Muir, then editor of our paper, *The Socialist*, a quiet, thoughtful man of fine character and much respected. My motion was carried. Muir resigned his position as editor.[8]

William Gallacher's version of the meeting is rather different:

> Another outstanding figure was David Kirkwood, who finished with the SLP early in the war. Johnny Muir, who was editor of *The Socialist*, the SLP organ, was trying to argue a case for a socialist defending 'his own' country, at a special meeting in their hall in Renfrew Street. In the midst of the discussion, and while Johnny was arguing a certain point, Davy jumped up and shouted, 'Naw, naw, Joanie, that'll do nae, the workers have nae country. Ah'm

feenished wi' ye.' He shook the dirt of Renfrew Street from his
feet and found a new haven and ultimately an empire in the ILP.[9]

A small, intriguing point: Gallacher writes his account as if he
attended the meeting he describes. If this happens to be the case, then
it makes it difficult to reconcile the fact that Gallacher, a member of a
rival political party, the BSP, could be privy to internal debates of the
SLP with the frequently-given picture of the SLP as a highly exclusive,
rigidly sectarian organisation. Far from wanting to keep workers who
disagreed with it at arms length, the SLP sought to establish a dialogue
and convince them.

Two important issues help to explain how the Party functioned and
the extent to which it controlled the activities of its members. The first
is the relationship between David Kirkwood and the SLP and raises the
question of actually when he left the Party. The second is the conduct
of Johnny Muir, the only leading SLPer to succumb to social patriotism.

So far as David Kirkwood is concerned, it would appear that he was
still a member of the SLP in May 1916. *The Socialist* of that month
carried an account of the imprisonment and deportation of militants,
many of whom were party members. The paper published the following
entry:

> SLP Roll of Honour
> William Holliday, John W. Muir, Walter Bell, David Kirkwood,
> Arthur MacManus, Thomas Clark.
>   The above comrades fought valiantly for the working class and
> conducted themselves in a manner revealing heroism and determina-
> tion. The SLP is proud that comrades of such sterling merit were
> drilled and disciplined beneath its banner.
>   The SLP contains many such fighters who will not flinch in the
> struggle before them.

From that, it would appear as if Kirkwood must have been a member
of the SLP in May 1916 and therefore must also have been an SLPer in
December 1915, when Lloyd George visited Glasgow. At that time, the
decision of the Clyde Workers' Committee was that they would only
see the Minister of Munitions as a collective body, not individually. All
factories except Parkhead Forge, where Kirkwood was convener,
obeyed this decision. In a similar manner, Parkhead disregarded the
Clyde Workers' Committee policy on dilution of labour. Quite uni-
laterally, Parkhead broke ranks. Kirkwood states he got John Wheatley

to draft the proposals, which were broadly accepted by the Management.[10] An historian, Dr James Hinton, gave his opinion of the harmful effect this had on the whole struggle:

> From the standpoint of the SLP leadership of the Clyde Workers' Committee the Parkhead agreement represented a resounding defeat for 'the principle of workers' control'. It involved the abandonment of their dilution policy, the collapse of the Committee's attempt to force the Commissioners to recognise and negotiate with the Committee as a whole, and it engendered a bitterness against Parkhead in the other strongholds of militancy that was to be instrumental in the defeat of the movement two months later.[11]

Whatever the bitterness against Kirkwood on the floors of Clydeside factories, there is no indication that it extended to the SLP leadership. No criticism of him appeared in the columns of *The Socialist*. When, along with other militants, Kirkwood was deported from Glasgow and compelled to live elsewhere, the SLP staunchly backed him. Even after he had left the Party, *The Socialist* continued to take a favourable line. At the 1917 Labour Party conference, David Kirkwood, still a deportee, launched a full-blooded attack on the government's industrial policy and Arthur Henderson's membership of the cabinet. In detail, *The Socialist* reported the scene at the Labour Party conference, adding 'ILPers deserve every credit' for it.[12] It also sprung to his defence in June 1917, when Lloyd George sought to buy off Kirkwood with the offer of a well-paid government job. 'It is simply amazing,' said *The Socialist*, 'how many people judge others from their own standards.'

Such magnanimity is rarely exhibited among left-wing organisations towards a member who leaves and decides to join a rival. That the SLP did praise Kirkwood, though he had quit its ranks, is a sign of fair-mindedness and of the unsectarian approach that characterised the Party in this period. But the episodes also reveal a weakness in the SLPs approach. It appears that the Party merely expected agreement on questions of fundamental political principle — the objectives to be attained — but never imposed a discipline on its members so far as tactical issues were concerned. As a consequence, Kirkwood was free to take his own line on dilution, disregarding the Clyde Workers' Committee policy, despite it having been drawn up by a fellow SLPer, Johnny Muir. Such conduct would not, or at least should not, be permitted in a revolutionary organisation today.

The same applies to the second issue, the conduct of Johnny Muir. It is clear that Tom Bell's version, quoted above, is too generous. An article which appeared in December 1914, quite definitely shows Muir took a pro-war line at the time. He may afterwards have changed, although there is no evidence for this as he confined his writings mainly to industrial affairs. Undoubtedly, he played a major role in Clydeside struggles. As we have already seen, it was Muir who stood up at Lloyd George's meeting to put the workers' case; it was Muir who drafted the Clyde Workers' Committee policy on dilution; it was Muir who edited the CWCs journal, *The Worker*, which reached the impressive circulation of 15,000.[13] Yet when Muir, along with Gallacher, was arrested, he made a pitiful spectacle. Instead of hurling defiance at his persecutors, as SLPers usually did in court, he attempted to dissemble. He told the judge he had done nothing to impede the progress of the war effort; at work he had striven to smooth out differences that arose between management and men; and he had been opposed to every strike. A director of Barr & Stroud testified on his behalf. But this did not save him: Muir and Gallacher, who behaved in precisely the same way, received prison sentences of a year.[14] Referring to their poor performance in court, Gallacher retrospectively wrote: 'If Maclean held high the banner of revolutionary struggle, we dragged it, or allowed it to be dragged, in the mire. Even now it is hard to think of it without a feeling of shame.'[15]

Such behaviour not only reflects upon the individual but also the organisation to which he belongs. It shows a deficiency in the SLP, the weakness of its discipline, that it failed to repudiate Muir publicly. The only extenuating circumstance appears to have been that he was being prosecuted for an article that appeared in *The Worker* which he did not write. Had he divulged the authorship, then a man with a large family might have gone to jail in his place.

Although no direct evidence has appeared to support this conjecture, what happened in court may have been influenced by the title of the article and the date of the proceedings. The offending piece was headed 'Should the Workers Arm?' and the trial took place in April 1916, the same month as the Easter Uprising in Dublin. Clearly, it has been firmly established that the SLP knew about the military preparations secretly taking place in Ireland and maintained close contact with Connolly. Walter Kendall, the historian, goes so far as to declare that the SLP was 'involved in the preliminaries to the Easter Rising of 1916.'[16] Were that so, then the accused may well have been afraid that much more weighty evidence and a much more severe charge could come if they tried to make things difficult for the prosecution.

However, a more plausible explanation for the behaviour of Muir and Gallacher at the trial can be found elsewhere. Perhaps they were overwhelmed, knocked off balance, by the ferocity with which the authorities clamped down on Clydeside militants. They appear to have sought advice from John Wheatley who, though he was in the ILP, was frequently consulted by socialists of every political grouping. It was he who acquired for them the services of Rosslyn Mitchell, the solicitor, and of a barrister. Feeling the intense pressure of State repression, Muir and Gallacher seem to have agreed with their counsel to make an orthodox defence.

The fact is that this kind of backsliding is more likely to occur in organisations that do not keep effective control of their membership, and this, in turn, depends upon the formulation of policies on tactical issues, a thing which the SLP did not do. The reasons for this failure seems to have been threefold: first, there was the acute problem of resources, the inability to create and maintain a strong centre, capable of directing day-to-day activities; second, there was the fragmentation of industry, the existence of widely divergent levels of development, that made the formulation of common tactics exceedingly difficult; and, third, there seems to have been an attitude of fatalistic determination, a belief in the therapeutic properties of struggle as such, that merely bringing workers into action gave them a fresh insight into the way capitalism operates — and into their own power as a class. Whatever the outcome of a particular battle, workers would be brought closer to the SLP.

Having this attitude necessarily lessened the importance of tactics. The SLPs emphasis was placed on building rank-and-file organisations, the vehicle for struggle, without being too finicky about theoretical disagreements. Naturally, the Party viewpoint was put forward. Yet it was never pushed to the extent that it led to splits because, it was believed, life itself would eventually vindicate the SLPs position. This approach had numerous practical consequences. When the first conference of Workers' Committees was held in Manchester on 5-6 November 1916, the SLP would have liked to have seen a strong and powerful executive, leading the Shop Stewards' Movement.[17] However, the majority of delegates, their ideas moulded by pre-war Syndicalism, favoured a federal-type structure, leaving autonomy in the hands of the local groups. The conference was poorly attended, with London, Manchester and Barrow the only English committees represented. If further growth was to occur in England, then militants, many of whom had syndicalist ideas, had first to be attracted to the movement and then, gradually, weaned away from their erroneous ideas. Therefore, the SLP did not press its views. The same approach was made to the Clyde Workers' Committee, in which SLP members played the leading role. While openly revolutionary themselves, SLPers recognised that most of the CWCs membership was not: 'It must not be thought that the rank-and-file are socialists. The Committee was formed to stem the onslaught on the privilege won by organised labour in the past.'[18] Most of the militancy on Clydeside existed among skilled engineers in the munitions factories. To John Maclean, this was entirely wrong. He criticised SLPers for not struggling within the CWC to get it to adopt a clear, all-out anti-war line. He went on to point out that if the Committee achieved its declared aim, nationalisation with workers' participation in management, then it would involve the CWC in direct complicity with the war. The workers in management would be trying to produce more shells for France.[19]

Almost certainly, if Maclean's proposal had been accepted and fought for vigorously with the Committee, it would have led to a split and probably the end of the CWC. To the SLPers, this appeared as an appalling prospect. They wanted the Clyde Workers' Committee to continue and flourish. Not only was it an organisation with revolutionary potential, but it also provided SLPers with a base from which they could attempt to form a national organisation of shop stewards. John Maclean, on the other hand, appears in practice to have been preoccupied with local problems at this time. Significantly, in view of his subsequent leanings towards a brand of Scottish nationalist socialism, he does not seem to have thought of the consequences for Britain as a whole. To enlighten a few workers, to create a greater socialist consciousness among them, was more important than keeping the Clyde Workers' Committee intact so that it could play a leading role in the formation of a national rank-and-file movement.

In the same way that John Maclean related himself to industrial struggles in Scotland, he eschewed playing a leading part in the internal fight inside the BSP to rid the Party of Hyndman and his clique. His line was not to battle to win the BSP from Hyndman, but to create his own embryonic organisation in Glasgow around the journal *Vanguard*. This may have made sense in a Scottish context. The BSP was very weak in Scotland. Where it did exist, it almost entirely accepted the Maclean line, and since the BSP leadership, ensconced in London and primarily concerned with political intrigues in the metropolis, left the Scottish branches alone, there may have appeared little reason why

Scots should attempt to interfere with the BSP leadership. John
Maclean contented himself with a letter to *Justice* early in the war,
dissociating himself from the jingoistic pronouncements of Belford
Bax. He did not make any further intervention.[20]

From the outset of the war, the BSPs position could be characterised as 'chauvinistic Marxism'. Unlike the German Social Democrats,
and many in Britain who succumbed to patriotic fervour in the early
days of the war, the BSP had already decided its duty was to King and
Country. The Party's conference in 1911 passed a resolution that called
for the strengthening of the Royal Navy. This stimulated *Vorwarts*,
organ of the German Social Democratic Party, to exclaim that the BSP
'had taken up a position on armaments diametrically opposed to that
of the Socialist Parties of the World.'[21] The BSPs line in 1914 followed
logically on from what it had said in 1911. Its executive committee
declared: 'Recognising that national freedom and independence of this
country are threatened by Prussian militarism, the party naturally
desires to see the prosecution of the war to a successful issue.' To that
end, the EC instructed branches to speak from public platforms with
representatives of other political parties whenever the national interests
of Britain were being furthered.[22] As 'good' Marxists, the BSP sought
to unite theory with practice: besides supporting the war, it urged its
own members to flock to the colours. A special 'Comradeship Company'
of socialists, recruited under the guidance of Hunter Watts, served in
the trenches.[23]

Opposition within the BSP began in a half-hearted manner. Speakers
were at pains to make it clear that what they wanted to see was an
Allied victory before they went on to criticise the party's line on
subordinate issues, such as its support for army recruitment campaigns.
But this lack of fire did not save the opposition from the wrath of the
Hyndman leadership. Because they appeared not to be completely
behind the BSPs policy on the war, they were accused of being German
agents. This was Hyndman's political style: a preparedness to smear anybody who did not share his frenetic patriotism. While proud of the
BSPs stand on the war, he was ashamed of the pacifism of the ILP.
Writing in the French journal, *Le Canard Enchainé*, Hyndman railed
against 'the Scotch clique of peace-at-any-price, which for many years
had dominated and held the leading strings of the Independent Labour
Party.' His venom spilled forth enveloping some politicians who
supported the war, albeit with less enthusiasm than displayed by himself: 'I would very much like Messrs. Ramsay MacDonald, Keir Hardie
and W.C. Anderson to go and talk to all these men (British troops on

active service) and try and whiten, even slightly, the executioners of civilians and women and children in Belgium and France.'[24]

As the war continued, the BSPs attitude became even more vehement. The ILP was accused of being in the pay of Prussian militarism. Any socialists who favoured ending the war were described as being guilty of 'villainy'. Germany was denounced as 'the enemy not only of the democracy and Socialism but of the entire human race.'[25] The BSP leaders resolved to create a broad organisation within the working class, the Socialist National Defence Committee, to 'resist the anti-British, pro-German pacifist elements in this country' and 'to insist that the war must be pursued to a complete triumph.'[26]

The SNDC held its first public meeting in London on 21 July 1915. The speakers, who included Hyndman and Thorne, mostly made highly emotional orations. Ben Tillett had just returned from visiting British troops in France, where he had remarked: 'I felt ashamed of being a civilian. I felt ashamed at the knowledge that every one at home was not working as well as he could work. There shan't be a slacker left when I get back.'[27] Naturally, his speech consisted of an attack on strikes and a call for increased productivity. John Hodge, chairman of the Parliamentary Labour Party, welcomed the formation of the Coalition Government, little more than a month old. But the speech that did the most to stir patriotic hearts came from a Frenchman, Marcel Cachin, who subsequently was prominent in the French Communist Party and editor of its journal, *L'Humanité*. He told his audience: 'So long as a single German soldier remained in France or Belgium, there could be no compromise; it was the sacred duty of every socialist to help in driving out the invader.'[28]

A few of the BSP opposition had decided to attend the SNDC meeting. One of them, E.C. Fairchild, rose to his feet and suggested that British socialists should write to their German opposite numbers. He favoured a negotiated peace, a peace without annexations. His contribution, however, angered the patriots. Soldiers in uniform were brought in to the meeting. Fights broke out, and many of the BSP opposition were badly mauled. Among them was Albert Inkpin, the party secretary, who was 'thrown out with blood streaming down his face and neck.'[29]

The harassment of the BSP opposition did not end there. One evening, H.W. Alexander returned home to find two detectives waiting in his sitting-room. He believed that leading members of the BSP were responsible: they had informed the police about his activities and those of others who disagreed with the official party line. Probably the accusation was true. On 23 December 1915, *Justice* published an article headed: 'Who and what is Peter Petroff?', which incited the authorities to arrest him. This was a particularly cruel move since Petroff, a veteran of the 1905 Russian Revolution who had been active in the BSP since 1908, could have been in grave trouble. Government officials were aware that Petroff would be quickly disposed of by the Tsarist regime, and for this reason one of them recommended to the Ministry that he be returned to Russia:

> Peter Petroff, a Russian Socialist of a very dangerous type. The easiest thing to do with Petroff is to have him repatriated, when, from all that I am told, he will be shot within 24 hours of landing in Russia.[30]

This was the proposal that was being considered by the authorities in January 1916. Peter Petroff had been arrested the month before, only a few hours after the publication of the article in *Justice*. Also arrested was his German-born wife, who was put in Aylesbury jail. There she was forced to take a bath and use utensils just after they had been used by a prostitute with advanced venereal disease. The Liberal Peer Lord Sheffield, raising the question of Mrs Petroff's treatment in Parliament, said: 'This matter is felt to be an outrage and is causing immense bitterness.'

The viciousness with which the Hyndman leadership dealt with them tended to arouse support for critics inside the party. Yet, if they were unwittingly helped by Hyndman, they were hindered by themselves. Their own indecisiveness and lack of clarity were obstacles to success. They failed to see the international implications of the collapse of European social democracy in 1914, as the Bolsheviks and SLP had done. Having faith in traditional forms of organisation, the BSP confined its mental horizon to what could be achieved under the aegis of the Second International. It regarded the International Socialist Bureau as the potential saviour of the situation, the force that would pull the working-class of Europe back from Armageddon. At the BSP 1915 annual conference a resolution was passed 'that every effort should be made to maintain the status of the International Socialist Bureau in order that its influence may be used in the direction of peace at the earliest opportunity.'[31] However noble and idealist such sentiments were, they were without a spark of realism. They overlooked the fact that Vandervelde, chairman of the ISB, belonged to the Belgian cabinet and had made it clear that he had no intention of convening a meeting of the ISB so long as a single German soldier remained on Belgian soil.

This impractical policy had practical results. As a consequence of its veneration for the ISB, the British Socialist Party shut its ears to the growing volume of working-class opposition to the war. When, in September 1915, delegates from twelve countries, representing workers living on both sides of the battlefields, met at Zimmerwald, the line of the BSP was downright equivocal. *Justice* reported the proceedings at Zimmerwald; underneath it carried a report that 'eighty German spies had been arrested and are now in prison in Berne' — a definite attempt by H.W. Lee, *Justice's* editor, to smear Zimmerwald as an enemy plot. The EC of the British Socialist Party, however, was more generous. Although not adopting any stand on the Zimmerwald manifesto, the EC expressed the hope that the conference would prompt the International Socialist Bureau into taking speedy action. Later, the ECs attitude to Zimmerwald hardened: in December 1915, it said it was 'not in favour of any move to form a new international organisation apart from or in opposition to the International Socialist Bureau.'[32] Since the ISB did not function, this meant doing nothing.

Yet, even had there been the remotest chance of action, it is unclear what the British Socialist Party would have wanted the ISB to do. The Hyndmanite right-wing, of course, were wholeheartedly behind the war effort. On the other hand, the left-wing critics were diffident about adopting an unequivocal anti-war stance. One of the most prominent spokesmen, E.C. Fairchild, moved a motion in October 1915, declaring that the 'continuation of the war . . . imperils the future of socialism'. This statement, however, was prefaced with: 'Whilst all action should be rigorously avoided, calculated to endanger national defence . . .'[33] Likewise, another outspoken left-winger, Joe Fineberg, attacked 'This capitalist war', yet added the rider, 'It would be a disaster for Europe if Germany were victorious.' In the same vein, a further critic of Hyndman, H.W. Alexander, claimed to be an internationalist but went on to say 'But that did not prevent him being a nationalist, prepared to defend his own country.'[34]

The opposition within the BSP suffered from another limitation. It saw the path to peace as coming through an agreement of socialist parties to work in unity for this objective, and made its own adoption of an anti-war campaign contingent upon such an agreement. Before being prepared to take a stand, the BSP thought all troops should withdraw from occupied territories — a demand that placed the onus upon German Social democrats to force the German government to

make the first move. Then the BSP critics saw peace being reached
through international negotiation; this did not have the remotest
similarity with the revolutionary position of the Bolsheviks and SLP,
who saw that the roots of the war were to be found in capitalism and
only through an overthrowal of capitalism could a lasting peace be
secured.

The assessment of Walter Kendall, of the BSP in this period, is undoubtedly correct:

> Lenin classified socialists into the following three groups, according
> to their attitude to the war. There were open chauvinists; those
> 'capable of leading revolutionary work in the direction of civil war';
> and 'the confused and vacillating elements' in between. By the
> terms of Lenin's division, Hyndman and his allies represented the
> open chauvinists, John Maclean and his followers the revolution-
> aries, leaving the 'confused and vacillating elements' as the majority
> of the BSP.[35]

Whatever the ideological quibblings of the majority of the BSP, merely
to express doubts was sufficient to arouse the anger of Hyndman and
his group. When it was decided in February 1916 to publish a journal,
The Call, in which these reservations would be stated, it was too much
for the chauvinists within the party to countenance. They accused
those who made pleas for peace as 'acting under instructions from
Berlin'. As the executive failed to endorse the Hyndman line completely, it, too, was said to be gaining its inspiration from Germany.
Leading members of the BSP, opponents of Hyndman, found themselves being shadowed by police agents, and suspected that it was
fellow party members who had acted as informers.[36]

The position inside the British Socialist Party was untenable. The
split occurred at the Salford conference on 23-4 April 1916. Held in
an atmosphere of intimidation, a move was made early on in the proceedings to hold the conference in private, allowing delegates a greater
opportunity to express their views. Hyndman and his followers objected to this proposal. Amid attempts to reach a compromise, tempers
became frayed. A speech from the national treasurer, H.W. Alexander,
brought uproar. Pointing at Hyndman, Dan Irvine and Jack Jones, he
declared: 'Colleagues of these men are responsible for Scotland Yard
dogging the footsteps of men like myself.' Pandemonium followed.
Hyndman strove to gain a hearing, but 'snarling cheers drowned everything he had to say.' 'Stewards began to move menacingly forward',

attempting to restore order so Hyndman could be heard. They were
met with boos. Apparently shocked by the scene, Fairchild tried to
persuade delegates to give Hyndman a hearing. But it was futile. When
the resolution was eventually put, conference carried it by 76 votes to
28. Whereupon Hyndman and his supporters withdrew from the conference.[37] In June 1916, he formed his own party, known as the
National Socialist Party.

The opposition, led by Alexander and Fairchild, acquired control
of the BSP. It did not possess the journal, *Justice*, which belonged to
the Twentieth Century Press, most of whose shareholders were
supporters of Hyndman. So *The Call* became the official weekly organ
of the BSP. In its columns, the plea was repeatedly made for peace
through negotiations. Emphasis was placed on the spurious nature of
the Allied war aims and on the huge profits being made by arms and
manufacturers. Yet *The Call* was careful not to oppose the war openly.
Nor did it raise the demand for socialist revolution as a necessity if
capitalist wars were to be ended forever.

The BSPs failure to adopt a position similar to the Bolsheviks
limited the amount of co-operation that revolutionary socialists could
have with it. A further restricting factor arose from the nature of the
party and the outlook of its members. Although no definite figures
exist on the social composition of the BSP, the observations of J.T.
Walton Newbold probably are not without significance:

> The BSP contains a fairly numerous lower middle class element, a
> small shopkeeper and craftsman element, with little industrial
> resistant force and no economic indispensability. These do not
> altogether harmonise with the workers in big industry, and there
> has become apparent inside the BSP as inside the ILP a wistful
> disappointment, a sorrowful discontent, with the industrial prole-
> tariat.[38]

J.T. Walton Newbold, himself an ILPer, appreciated the importance
of industrial work and therefore collaborated with the SLP. He became
a frequent contributor to *The Socialist*, writing articles which embodied
painstaking research. His long piece 'Capitalism on the Tyne', with a
detailed account of the ownership and profits of North-Eastern companies, caused a sensation because it revealed many of them had links
with enemy firms and had even supplied the torpedoes with which
British vessels had been sunk. Mass-produced by the SLP, J.T. Walton
Newbold's article appeared in a leaflet, sold at six shillings for a

thousand copies.

An invaluable contributor to *The Socialist* from the BSPs ranks was
Alexander Sirnis. Little is know of him yet he played a vital part as a
link man, spreading the news about the anti-war struggle in other countries. It was he who made *The Socialist*'s coverage of the international
working-class movement better than that of any other journal, giving,
for instance, the verbatim speech of Karl Liebknecht before his court
martial in 1916, and translating Lenin's articles for the first time into
English. Sirnis did this despite being in the throes of a terminal illness.
Indeed, in some sense, his personal tragedy may have helped. Suffering
from tuberculosis, he went to a Davos sanatorium for treatment. There
is no evidence that he met Lenin while staying in Switzerland, but his
Press reports clearly show that he had close links with both the German
Spartacists and the Russian Bolsheviks. When he died in November
1918, he was engaged in translating Lenin's pamphlet, *The Collapse of
the Second International* into English.[39]

In September 1917, Sirnis decided to leave the BSP, giving as his
reason that it was 'floundering in the bog of political opportunism'. He
cited the way the BSPs executive called for the Allies to be saved from the
treachery of the Tsar and the way in which *The Call* had contrasted
Lloyd George, the despotic dictator, with Asquith, the previous Prime
Minister, who was 'benevolent and meek', instead of realising it was the
difference between Tweedledum and Tweedledee. Sirnis's final criticism
was of the BSPs failure to take the struggle for industrial unionism
seriously.

This latter point was a big barrier to co-operation between the SLP
and BSP, at least on a party-to-party basis. Yet, individually, co-operation could, and did, occur. The BSP did have some talented trade union
militants within its ranks, even if they failed to play a big part in the
BSPs decision-making process. Many of them came into contact with
SLPers through the shop stewards' movement and the links forged in
industrial conflicts transcended party differences. For instance, F.H.
Peet, chairman of the shop stewards' movement nationally, acted as
Arthur MacManus's election agent at Halifax in the 1918 general
election.

The fact was that the SLP realised its strength lay in the soundness
of its organisation and the correctness of its policies. Nothing could be
allowed to stand in the way of making corrections to those policies
whenever mistakes became discernible:

By other sections of the Labour Movement, we have been blamed for the ferocity of our criticism. But the average SLP member is also an unsparing critic of his own party and its policy. We have always retained the right to criticise other organisations because our members have always retained the right to criticise their own organisations.[40]

While attaching such great importance to ideas, the SLP seized every opportunity in the course of the First World War, for joint activity. In a sense, it was merely an extension of the united action in the shop stewards' movement. Regarding industry as so important, it was natural that the kind of working arrangements between socialists established on the shop floor should be extended elsewhere.

The organisation with which the SLP had the greatest kinship was Sylvia Pankhurst's Workers' Socialist Federation, a predominantly women's organisation based on working-class support, primarily in the East End of London. Starting as campaigners for female suffrage, Sylvia Pankhurst and her supporters came to see that women's liberation required more than the vote; it needed the overthrow of capitalist society. They fought an unrelenting struggle, often coming into conflict with the forces of law and order. With the WSF, there were none of the inhibitions prevalent in the BSP. When the authorities clamped down on the SLP Press in November 1918 for publishing reports about British intervention in Russia, the WSF, although its own press had twice been raided by the police and the *Workers' Dreadnought* confiscated, did not flinch in offering assistance. The SLP was grateful: 'This offer was the only assistance offered us by an organised section of the Socialist Movement.'[41]

In the supreme test — that of its attitude to revolution — the Workers' Socialist Federation acquitted itself well. Of all the currents in the British left-wing movement, the WSF came out by far the most strongly in support of the Irish Easter Uprising.[42] Not content with simply stating its line in the *Workers' Dreadnought*, a daring attempt was successfully made to gain — and then publicise — eye-witness accounts of the savagery of British repression in Ireland. An 18-year-old girl, Patricia Lynch, set off for Dublin. Somehow, she had evaded the watchful eyes of the authorities, who were determined to maintain a news black-out and arrest all who sympathised with the Irish rebels. Fortunately, on the train Patricia Lynch had the good luck to meet a sympathetic army officer, who allowed her to pose as his sister. In this way, she reached Dublin and saw what was happening for herself. When she returned to London, her reports appeared in the *Workers'*

Dreadnought under the title 'Scenes from the Irish Rebellion'. They excited such interest, both in Britain and abroad, that the paper sold out. Several more editions had to be produced. Subsequently, her account was printed as a pamphlet, *Rebel Ireland*, with a preface by Sylvia Pankhurst.

The significance of Patricia Lynch's reports is perhaps best conveyed by Ralph Fox: 'We hailed the Irish Uprising as the first crack in the as yet undisputed rule of the imperialists.'[43] Of much greater importance was the second crack, the one that plunged Tsarism to its doom. The Russian Revolution and its very considerable influence in Britain will be considered in the next chapter. It is important to realise that it was under the pressures generated by these two events — the Easter Uprising and the Russian Revolution — that new outlooks and fresh opportunities began to emerge for the socialist movement in Britain.

Notes

1. For a time, Arthur Henderson tried to deny he cheered Connolly's execution in Parliament. However, after the Glasgow *Forward*, of 25 September 1920, contained a description of the scene, he made no further denials.
2. *Sunday Chronicle*, 29 October 1916.
3. *The Socialist*, November 1914.
4. Ibid, May 1916.
5. Ibid, March 1916.
6. T.A. Jackson, *Solo Trumpet*, p. 128.
7. Thomas Bell, *Pioneering Days*, p. 102.
8. David Kirkwood, *My Life of Revolt*, p. 86.
9. William Gallacher, *Last Memoirs*, p. 27.
10. D. Kirkwood, op. cit., p. 118.
11. James Hinton, *The First Shop Stewards' Movement* p. 151.
12. *The Socialist*, February 1917.
13. *Glasgow Evening News*, 30 March 1915.
14. *Daily Record and Mail*, 14 April 1916.
15. W. Gallacher, *Revolt on the Clyde*, p. 119.
16. Walter Kendall, *The Revolutionary Movement in Britain* (1969) p. 373.
17. D.M. Chewster's thesis, op. cit., p. 167. Also B. Pribicecic, *The Shop Stewards' Movement and Workers' Control, 1910-1922*, p. 99.
18. *The Socialist*, April 1916.
19. *Vanguard*, 30 December 1915.
20. *Justice*, 17 September 1914.
21. Ibid.
22. Ibid, 1 October 1914 and 22 October 1914.
23. Ibid, 22 April 1915.
24. *Le Canard Enchainé*, 7 March 1915. Also F.J. Gould, *Hyndman, Prophet of Socialism* (1928) p. 202.
25. *Justice*, 27 May 1915.

26. Ibid, 24 June 1915.
27. *Reynolds News*, 20 June 1915.
28. *Justice*, 5 August 1915.
29. Ibid, 27 September 1915.
30. Letter of Patterson to Lewellyn Smith, 17 January 1916, in Beveridge Collection, vol. 3, p. 111.
31. BSP Conference Report, 1915, pp. 38-41.
32. BSP Conference Report, 1916, pp. 44-5.
33. *Justice,* 28 October 1915.
34. BSP Conference Report, 1916, p. 7.
35. W. Kendall, op. cit., p. 97.
36. Ibid, p. 99.
37. BSP Conference Report, 1916, p. 3.
38. *The Socialist*, August 1918.
39. Ibid, December 1918.
40. Ibid, January 1919.
41. Ibid, October 1918.
42. *Workers' Dreadnought*, 6 May 1916.
43. Ralph Fox, *Smoky Crusade*, p. 216.

8 BRITAIN AND THE RUSSIAN REVOLUTION

The February Revolution, which deposed Tsar Nicholas II, won almost universal approval among British politicians. On 22 March 1917, Parliament sent fraternal greetings to the new Provisional Government. The motion was moved by Bonar Law, a prominent Conservative and Leader of the House. Members from all sides echoed his sentiments. And the Prime Minister, speaking a few days earlier, welcomed what was described as 'one of the landmarks in the history of the world.' Lloyd George regarded the Revolution as 'the first great triumph of the principle for which we entered the war . . . the cause of human freedom.'[1]

British politicians did not express such praise without good reason. They expected great things from the Russian Provisional government. The old Tsarist regime – corrupt, inefficient and unpopular – failed to fight the German army effectively. Inept Russian generals squandered millions of lives in pointless battles. It was thought that the new government, having much greater mass support, would be able to mobilise effective resources for the war effort. The new regime would be an asset politically, too. The Tsarist government had been an embarrassment to Allies striving to depict themselves as struggling for 'freedom' and 'democracy', while having the most grotesque despot in Europe on their side. Now Russia appeared to be moving in the direction of a Western-style democracy. Allied propaganda would be more credible.

There were economic grounds, too, for welcoming the political changes in Petrograd. British businessmen and financiers had invested large sums of money in Russia and vast mineral wealth and productive resources still remained to be tapped. The big obstacle to further profitable investment had been the old regime, which did little to promote economic growth. Now Tsarism had been swept aside, the door seemed open to foreign capitalists bent on lucrative opportunities. As Brigadier-General G.C. Poole, writing from Russia, told the Foreign Office:

> The great advantage of works in Russia is that there is a home market which would take up all the output. I am of the opinion that many large manufacturers in Great Britain would be only too glad to expand their businesses into Russia, if only they could have the

171

active support of the government.[2]

Optimism in London's official circles waned as it became clear that the Provisional government was losing command of the situation. The February Revolution, a re-shuffle of the top echelons of society, had done nothing to alter harsh reality. Backward Russia continued the unequal battle with the sophisticated German war machine. Tensions within Russia mounted, and the people, denied the basic necessities of life, clamoured for peace, land and bread. With this agitation, the Bolsheviks grew in influence — and the Provisional government became increasingly unpopular.

Whitehall did what it could to arrest this process. The material aid that could be spared for Russia was strictly limited. The main form of help was ideological. Speakers and publications went to Russia, and forged copies of *Pravda* were printed in London for use against the Bolsheviks.[3] In July 1917, it was proposed that the British government should step up this kind of intervention. Two million pounds were to be spent in the first three months, with an extra half million every month after that, in the attempt to shore up the Provisional government.[4] But these efforts proved to be of no avail: they did not halt the Provisional government's fall from popularity, the erosion of the centre and the polarisation of political forces. Confronted with the alternative of military dictatorship or Soviet power, British officials favoured the army. A desperate communication sent from Lord Milner, visiting Russia, to the Prime Minister on 8 September 1917, told Lloyd George:

> General Knox is here, greatly perturbed about Russia. He thinks the situation almost desperate, the last chance being Kornilov . . . Time is short if anything is to be done to help him.[5]

The Times editorial took the same line, favouring the destruction, by Kornilov's 'savage divisions', of the Soviets:

> A self-constituted organisation of idealists, theorists, anarchists, syndicalists, who are largely of the international Jew-type, who have hardly any working men or soldiers among them, and some of whom are known to be in the German pay.[6]

If the Soviets were such a collection of oddities, it is difficult to explain how they had enough cohesion and unity of purpose to seize power. Conservative-minded readers, however, did not worry themselves

unduly with this problem: newspapers assured them that the Bolshevik
Revolution was like a freak summer storm, unexpected and unpleasant
but not likely to last. On the day after the Revolution, the *Morning
Post* reported: 'The followers of Lenin have usurped power in Petrograd,
but they have given no evidence that they represent Russia as a whole,
and it is questionable if they will survive.'[7]

As it became clear that Bolshevik control was more firm than had
been thought, the Press changed its tone to one of alarm. The
Manchester Guardian feared that Bolshevik propaganda for peace could
spread the virus of revolutionary ideas among the combatants of both
sides.[8] *The Times* expressed disquiet about the expropriation of wealth:

> The new government, or, as it is styled, the Council of Commissioners
> of the People, gave the world a sample of the legislation with which
> it proposes to regenerate Russia. The main features of the series of
> enactments are the spoilation of one class and the transference of its
> property to another.[9]

Between February and October 1917, the British government's attitude
to events in Russia was transformed from euphoria to dismay. A similar
change occurred in the Parliamentary Labour Party, which had long
acquired the habit of agreeing with the government on questions of
fundamental principle. The feeling that the representatives of British
workers could best speak to the representatives of Russian workers led
the Labour Party to resolve, in March 1917, on a delegation to Russia.
Lloyd George and his colleagues welcomed the news.[10] It would help
to inspire the Russian Provisional Government's war effort and perhaps
banish thoughts of a separate peace. As a gesture of goodwill, F.E.
Smith, the Attorney-General, gave one of the delegation, Will Thorne,
his magnificent fur coat so he might better withstand the rigours of the
Russian climate. This caused a storm of disapproval in left-wing circles.
For some time, F.E. Smith had spearheaded the government's repressive policy against militants and had recently put the prosecution case
at the notorious trial of Mrs Wheeldon (see page 144). On many factory
floors, it was suggested that Smith and Thorne had much more in
common than the sharing of an expensive coat.[11]

In Russia, some folk held the same view. Thorne and his two companions were once accused of being British government spies. But they
were able to tour Russia extensively, and probably, on balance, helped
the Allied cause. When they returned to Britain, both the Prime
Minister and the King were anxious for reports.[12] Lloyd George must

have considered the expedition worthwhile for he decided to seek Labour Party assistance on another mission to Russia. Over the years, the British ambassador, Sir George Buchanan, had become well-known for his close and friendly relations with the Tsarist regime. In the changed circumstances, this made him 'no longer the ideal British representative.' The cabinet, therefore, asked Arthur Henderson 'to make a personal sacrifice and go to Petrograd.'[13]

Henderson's main task was to counteract Bolshevik propaganda. He addressed meetings in Russia, telling his audiences that British workers thoroughly backed their government's resolve to fight the war until final victory was achieved. He did score some successes. At Petrograd, he told a crowd of 5,000 that he had lost his son at the front. The meeting was so moved that the entire audience rose to its feet to sing the Russian Requiem. Proceedings ended, according to *The Times*' report, with 'a scene of indescribable enthusiasm. Men and women, moved to tears, demanded a general mobilisation, and cries of: "We all are ready to march against the foe." '[14] Elsewhere, Henderson's call to arms did not strike such a responsive chord. One reason was that Russians were becoming increasingly suspicious of the role both he and his French counterpart, Albert Thomas, were playing in the Russian Revolution. In a speech reported in *Pravda*, Lenin sought to expose their activities. He described them as

> partisans of the 'union sacrée', a principle forged by the enemies of the working class who have ensnared to their side the labour aristocracy. Whoever extends his hand to Henderson or Thomas extends it as well to Lloyd George and Ribot, to the English and French bankers.[15]

Lenin called them 'bourgeois-trained socialists.'

A hostile reception greeted Henderson when he addressed the Moscow Workers' and Soldiers' Council. Critics pointed out that his political opinions bore a close resemblance to those of the Russian workers' class enemies. In reply, Henderson said 'that if the Russian bourgeoisie held the same point of view as the English workers the latter were not to blame.'[16] It appears that the Workers' and Soldiers' Council remained unconvinced.

One reason why Henderson had visited Russia was to persuade Russian socialists not to send representatives to a conference to be held in Stockholm. It was being organised by the Dutch Social Democrats. Delegations from belligerent countries on both sides would, it was

hoped, attend. But this was anathema to the Labour Party: to frater-
nise with the enemy was wrong, even if the enemy were fellow social
democrats. The Labour Party suggested that a conference should be
held in London, which only social democrats from Allied countries
would be permitted to attend. At first, Henderson put forward this
line. But when he saw the quickening process of military and political
disintegration, he changed his mind. To attend the Stockholm conference might, he thought, help to bolster the dwindling fortunes of
the Provisional Government. Kerensky and his fellow ministers had to
appear to be desirous of peace if they were to retain sufficient popular
support for continuing the war.

In the deteriorating political situation, Henderson experienced an
increasing estrangement. Admittedly, in the upper section of Russian
society his message still was well-received. He was able to report to the
Prime Minister: 'I have noticed a distinctly more reasonable tone
appearing in conversation with business men since I have been here.'[17]
Yet, this was poor compensation for the widening gulf between himself and the Russian masses. Henderson found himself in a state of
complete non-comprehension. As Bruce Lockhart, the acting British
Consul-General in Moscow, wrote: 'The comrades in the Soviets
bewildered him. He did not understand their language. He did not like
their manners.'[18] So unreasonable were the Bolsheviks that they broke
into his hotel and stole his papers to investigate his links with the
British government. His humiliation was complete when they 'liberated'
his clothes! Without doubt, Bruce Lockhart was right when he said that
the Russian assignment 'had the advantage of curing Mr Henderson of
any revolutionary tendencies for the rest of his life.'[19]

Of course, it is doubtful whether Henderson — or the Labour Party
— were ever even warmed by the spark of revolution. To the majority
of the official leaders of British working-class organisations, the
October Revolution in Russia was a complete disaster. Ramsay
MacDonald told his Leicester constituents that Lenin led a party of
'thoughtless anarchists . . . whose minds were filled with violence and
hatred.'[20] Philip Snowden described the October Revolution as 'tragic
indeed', and the ILP was at pains to explain it did not accept
Bolshevik methods.[21] Henry M. Hyndman, still considering himself a
Marxist, wrote an article on 'Why we must repudiate the Bolsheviks'
for the *Sunday Pictorial*:

I am proud to state that I can reckon most of the leading revolutionaries of Europe and Asia among my friends. But they, in all their

uprisings against abominable tyranny were never guilty of such crimes
as those which Lenin and Trotsky and the Bolsheviks generally
are committing . . . Democracy and Socialism are now endangered
by their conduct.[22]

Probably the most outspoken condemnation came from Jimmy
Thomas, the railwaymen's leader. He thought that the Bolsheviks'
tyranny was more terrible than the Tsar's; the Kaiser was morally
superior to Lenin.[23]
   Support for the Bolsheviks in Britain was sparse. Only the Workers'
Socialist Federation and the Socialist Labour Party gave the October
Revolution a complete and unreserved blessing, and tried to assist the
Bolsheviks by their own revolutionary activities in this country.
Although news from Russia was fragmentary and sometimes false,
their journals sought to sift through the information and arrive at a
Marxist analysis. While this was wrong on some points, limited in
others, it nevertheless remains a remarkable testimony to the acuity
with which British revolutionaries were able to judge developments
in another land.
   In April 1917, *The Socialist* included a special supplement on the
Russian Revolution. The main article attempted to assess the significance of what had happened:

> Insofar as the Russian Revolution has cleared away the parapher-
> nalia of medieval Feudalism, it is a glorious step in social evolution
> and as such all socialists welcome it: but across the triumph of
> Russian capitalism there looms the spectre of International
> Socialism.

It went on to cite what it considered the main needs to be learnt from
the Russian Revolution: (i) for industrial organisation to secure the
control of industry, (ii) for political action to wrench the State from
the capitalists' grasp, (iii) for the press to be controlled by the workers
and (iv) for educational classes to equip comrades for agitational work.
   The same issue of *The Socialist* contained a report from George
Chicherin, a Russian refugee living in London, who was later to join
the Soviet government and become its Foreign Minister. He described
what happened at a mass meeting in the Great Assembly Hall, Mile
End Road, which, attended by Russian refugees and others, celebrated
the downfall of Tsarism:

It was an unforgettable demonstration of enthusiasm, unbounded joy and revolutionary feeling. Over 7,000 persons were present, and many thousands were unable to get in and had to go away . . . again and again delirious outbursts of boundless enthusiasm filled the immense hall.

Chicherin also published a resolution which had been passed by the Russian Socialist Group on 17 March 1917. This warned of misrepresentation in the British Press, which depicted the Russian revolutionaries as wanting the war to continue. It castigated the British Labour Leaders for trying 'to utilise the revolutionary movement in Russia for the interests of the Entente.' It also said that 'the establishment of the bourgeois parliamentary regime in Russia demands from the class conscious proletariat of Russia the more urgent straining of all its forces . . . against capitalism, against war and for Socialism.'

The June 1917 edition of *The Socialist* contained an article, 'Socialism or Jingoism', by Lenin, 'the famous Russian socialist leader of the revolutionary section in the Council of Workmen and Soldiers' delegates.' Translated by Alexander Sirnis, it attacked the social patriots, citing as examples MacDonald in Britain, Millerand in France, and the majority of the SDP in Germany. In the same issue, the editor commented on the famous 'sealed train' journey made by Lenin and other Bolshevik exiles from Switzerland through Germany and on to Russia. He pointed out that the Allies had done everything within their power to see that Plekhanov and the social patriots living abroad could quickly return to Russia while, at the same time, they impeded revolutionaries wanting to return. Lenin, Zinoviev, and the rest were correct in seizing their opportunity, said *The Socialist*.

The August editorial warned that the Russian people's newly-won freedom was being threatened by 'Russian and Allied Capital (is) playing a sinister game.' It went on to say:

If the Soldiers' and Workmen's Councils are to be a success, they must be revolutionary, not reformist. They must breathe freedom, not stale politics and futile palliatives. They must be live revolutionary organisations of the rank-and-file, not wire-pulling things of officials and would-be leaders.

The September issue of *The Socialist* contained another article by Lenin, this time on 'The Progress of the Russian Revolution.' The following month the SLP made its assessment on the position, trying as

well to relate events in Russia to politics in Britain. The salient points
made were as follows:

1. The forces that were united in the struggle against Tsarism were
not united on other issues.

2. 'The bourgeoisie in Russia are weak. Most of the capital in
Russia is of Franco-British origin. This is why the imperialist aims of
Milyukoff — the incarnation of the bourgeoisie — are identical with the
aims of the Allies.'

3. 'The peasants, who form the right wing of the Russian labour
movement, desire the break-up of the feudal land and its collective
redistribution.'

4. It was no accident that the Provisional government linked its
military offensive against the German army with hurling slanders at
Lenin and the industrial workers. 'The greatest obstacle in the way of
the capitalist class was the uncompromising attitude taken up by the
Maximalists led by Lenin. This movement, the real socialist group,
realised the true international working class position. It does not aim at
the immediate establishment of Socialism, which at present is impossible in such an economically backward country as Russia; but it sought
to use its power to strike a blow for international peace and to win the
maximum concessions possible for the Russian workers.

6. Capitalists both in Russia and abroad thought the Maximalists
could easily be strangled. But not so. 'The Maximalists struck terror into the hearts of imperialists: Lenin and the Maximalists had to be
crushed.'

7. 'True to its universal character of subtle hypocrisy, the capitalist
class charged Lenin with being a recipient of German gold and in league
with the Kaiser. In the conspiracy every renegade of the Labour Movement, from the editor of *Clarion* upwards, had a hand.'

8. Kornilov attempted to capture the State 'in order to restore order
and subdue the workers. Here we observe the historic function of the
State — a point we recommend to Mr Ramsay MacDonald and his
middle class friends.' (This is a reference to a recent ILP policy statement which declared the State was not an instrument of class rule; it
represented 'the well-being of the community.')

9. 'The reason why the capitalist press of the Allies has so fiercely
attacked the regimental and army committees of the soldiers is because
those committees pledge the soldiers not to give up either their arms or
ammunition to any other bodies than the workers' own committees!'
(Order No. 1, Section 5 of Workmen's & Soldiers' Committee). This

order anticipated and prevented the possibility of the troops being
disarmed in the Petrograd area and being left helpless before the much
vaunted 'savage divisions' of Kornilov and his propertied supporters.

10. General Lukovsky, threatened with insurrection by his soldiers,
says he will let in the enemy. 'Let there be no mistake about it, the
Russian and Allied propertied interests would much rather see the
minions of the Kaiser safely entrenched in Petrograd than the properti-
less workers of Russia. Yet, on the face of these facts, there are independent Labour pacifists in this country, spoon-fed with middle class
sap, who deny the existence of the class struggle.' It was President
Thiers, of France, who sought the aid of Bismarck to crush the Parisian
workers in 1871.

11. 'The press of this country praised Kornilov in his attempt to
establish a dictatorship of property owners upon the massacre of the
workers. Did not *The Times* – the echo of the government and high
finance in this country – say that "ruthlessness would be better than
weakness"? Let the British workers ponder over these words. They
reveal to what depths British capitalism will descend in the struggle
against Labour. They prove that those sentimental and independent
labourists who declaim against the class war are dangerously stupid
regarding the intentions of Capital.'

In the opinion of *The Socialist*, the events in Russia 'vindicated the
policy and tactics of the SLP.' Often it referred to Lenin and the
Bolsheviks as 'our Russian comrades', and there was no attempt to conceal the fact that the SLP agreed with what they were doing. When the
Provisional government was overthrown, *The Socialist* expressed its
jubilation under the heading 'Hail Revolutionary Socialist Russia',
and went on to analyse this momentous event:

The affairs in Russia have proved mysterious to many people. This
is due to the fact that, while Russia has carried through a revolution,
it has been accomplished in a country at a low stage of capitalist
development. The great driving force in the revolution was the
clear-sighted working class. But the Russian workers were educated
by the International Socialist Movement. That is to say that the
social theories of the Maximalists have been furnished by close
examination of history and of the higher developed capitalist countries. Clear-sighted students of history like Lenin are aware what the
Cromwellian revolution did for English workers. They know that the
moment the middle class revolutionaries destroyed the monarchy

they sought to stamp out the only movement in that revolution which had any bona fide democratic pretensions — the Levellers. Likewise in France, when the French middle class triumphed over the Feudal regime, it next directed its attention to crushing the modest demands of the working class. History clearly shows that when any propertied class accomplishes a revolution, it becomes conservative from the moment it gains the reins of government.

When, therefore, the socialist workmen of Russia threw in their lot and assisted in destroying Tsarism, it was not with the intention of placing the capitalist and landlord class — the Milyukovs and Kornilovs — in power unconditionally. Our Russian comrades know their history, and they know what capitalism means. They therefore formulated a series of demands which they insisted upon being put into operation. First and foremost among these demands was the stopping of the war. To that end, they repudiated the undoubted imperialist aims of the Allies.[24]

The October Revolution clarified British politics, just as the February Revolution had blurred political differences. It took courage to back the Bolsheviks with words and deeds, whereas almost everyone could, with comfortable conscience, applaud the downfall of Tsarism. The wide diversity of people who supported the February Revolution was shown in Britain on a number of occasions, but never more vividly than at the Leeds Convention of June 1917. This Convention has become part of the mythology of the Labour Left and of the Communist Party. Veteran CP historian R. Page Arnot wrote a few years ago: 'The convention was a great success.'[25] Many other historians have endorsed this verdict.

A closer examination leads to a different conclusion. Called to express the support of the British working class for the Russian Revolution, the convention had a key resolution moved by Ramsay MacDonald. The second resolution, declaring the convention's support for 'the foreign policy and the war aims of the Russian Provisional government,' was proposed by Philip Snowden and seconded by E.C. Fairchild, of the BSP. A further motion, calling for the creation of Workers' and Soldiers' Councils in Britain, was moved by W.C. Anderson, an ILP Member of Parliament.

In essence, most of the leading spokesmen of the Leeds Convention were right-wing politicians on holiday, indulging in the rare luxury of revolutionary speechifying. From their standpoint, this fitted the needs of the times. By adopting a left posture, they hoped to increase their own credibility among British workers, who were becoming more and more disgruntled. With an extremist stance they aimed to steal the thunder of the real militants, retain control of working class organisations, and steer the movement into harmless channels. In fact, W.C. Anderson had already given the game away. More significant than his speech to the Leeds Convention was the warning he had given to Parliament three weeks earlier:

> I have been very much astonished indeed, in visiting various places recently, at seeing a feeling springing up in this country which I did not believe possible — that is, a deep revolutionary feeling springing up among many of the workmen of this country . . . I do assure you that you will be astonished and, *unless you are very careful*, you will bring the country to the very verge of revolution. Only a week ago, I saw 70,000 people — the estimate was made not by any Labour people, but by one of the local newspapers — march through the streets of Glasgow with bands and banners, every one of the members of that procession wearing the revolutionary colours.[26] [My emphasis — R.C.]

In moving the motion calling Workers' and Soldiers' Councils, W.C. Anderson MP was not hoping to create the basis for Soviet power — far from it: Anderson's aim was to nip in the bud any movement in that direction.

In foreign as well as home affairs, right-wing politicians believed that it could be possible to make tangible gains from a few leftish phrases. By sending congratulations to the Russians and by appearing to be genuine revolutionaries themselves, MacDonald and his friends thought it might give them greater influence with the Russians. They hoped it would make the task of Henderson, Thorne and the other Labour politicians who journeyed to Russia, just that bit more easy. But this did not occur: the Russians, aware that it was merely left posturing, became even more suspicious.

The SLP and WSF also understood the role of these parliamentary gentlemen: that they wanted the Leeds Convention to be a first-rate theatrical performance, full of socialist sound and fury but signifying nothing. Nevertheless, this did not mean revolutionaries ought to dismiss the convention out of hand. Sylvia Pankhurst realised that the 1,150 delegates included many who were seeking the left alternative; to adopt an abstentionist attitude would leave them at the mercy of MacDonald and his colleagues.[27] So the revolutionaries not only participated in the proceedings at Leeds, but followed up by using what pressure they had to call for the setting up of Workers' and Soldiers' Councils. Perhaps, they reasoned, revolutionary life might yet be breathed into what would otherwise be a still-born project.

Significantly, the fear that something capable of threatening the existence of the capitalist social order might arise as a result of the Leeds Convention troubled even His Majesty King George V. And, ironically, it was Will Thorne, an ex-militant gas worker, taught to read and write by the daughter of Karl Marx, who performed the role of King's Comforter:

> The King seemed greatly disturbed about the famous Leeds conference and asked me if I knew anything about it. I said, 'Yes, I know all about it. I've read all the proceedings.' I also told him about the telegram that had been sent from the conference that made the Russians think we were spies, and he was amused at my story of some of the incidents that had happened over the message.
>
> 'Do you think any ill will come from this conference at Leeds and the decisions that were made there?' the King asked me. 'No,' I said; 'I've seen these things happen many times before in days gone by, and in my humble judgment there will never be a physical violent revolution in this country. But there will have to be many political and industrial changes within the course of the next few years.'
>
> This seemed to relieve his mind, and he spoke to me in a most homely and pleasant way. I was very pleased.[28]

Not only the King, but others in the top echelons of society, had misgivings about the Leeds Convention: even shadow-boxing sometimes develops into the real thing. By accident, a peaceful demonstration in Petrograd led by the police agent Father Gapon sparked off the 1905 Russian Revolution. How could one be sure that similar untoward events might not arise from even playing around with the notion of Workers' and Soldiers' Councils? Was there not a danger that the leadership, at present in the hands of innocuous 'moderates' like MacDonald and Snowden, might slip into other, revolutionary, claws? The authorities resolved to act.

The committee appointed by the Leeds Convention made plans for further meetings. Six regional conferences were to be held, as well as a national conference in London's Memorial Hall, Farringdon Road. The police had other ideas. They persuaded the owners of the public halls to cancel the bookings at short notice. Where this could not be done —

in Glasgow, for example – they invoked the Defence of the Realm Act and simply forbade the conference. The meetings of the Lancashire, Cheshire and North Wales committee were to have been held in the Milton Hall, Manchester. When the ban was imposed, it took place in the Stockport Labour Church. Similarly, when the London committee was denied the Memorial Hall, it switched to the Brotherhood Hall in the East End. But Sir Basil Thomson, head of the Special Branch, arranged for a reception party to meet the delegates. Leaflets announcing that a pro-German meeting was taking place were issued, and they urged East Enders to: 'Remember the last air raid and roll up.'[29]

The police seem to have gained the co-operation of the Army, which sent along loyally patriotic soldiers. Gleefully, Sir Basil wrote in his diary on 27 July: 'They will have a rude awakening tomorrow, as I have arranged with the *Daily Express* to publish the place of their meeting and a strong opposition may be expected.'[30]

The Whitehall-sponsored violence and vandalism was a total success. A mob of 8,000 surrounded the building, and, according to *The Observer*, one of the rioters had a real tomahawk. The *Daily News* had a picture of the hall being wrecked while the police looked on. When John Maclean arrived, half-an-hour after the conference was supposed to have started, he was confronted by 'a howling mob of male and female Dervishes.' The conference completely broke up.[31]

Most of the organisers of the regional conferences were respectable, middle-class citizens who did not expect violence. With the exception of Tom Quelch, none of them seem to have been associated with left-wing organisations. Faced with such determined opposition, they capitulated and nothing further was heard of Workers' and Soldiers' Councils.

The affair did, however, have a footnote in the form of a Parliamentary Question. Arthur Ponsonby, a dissident Liberal MP, asked if the King's Regulations regarding the Army were being 'strictly and impartially enforced.' I. Macpherson, for the War Office, replied that soldiers were not permitted to join Soldiers' and Workers' Councils. This provoked another query from Ponsonby: if they were denied the right to attend, would they also be denied the right to break up Soldiers' and Workers' Councils? There was no answer forthcoming.

That the plans formulated at the Leeds Convention were abortive did not mean the Government's troubles were over, that it had no need to worry further about the Russian Revolution. The triumph of the Bolsheviks acted as a great stimulus to revolutionary groups in Britain, whose influence was expanded in any case as a result of the growing

industrial unrest. Another threat faced the Government: the large number of Russian emigrés, many of them supporters of Lenin, who lived
in Britain and who would do everything in their power to transmit
Bolshevik ideas.

Britain's 19th-century policy of an 'open door' to victims of overseas persecution had, naturally, greatly increased the foreign population.
A Royal Commission on alien immigration reported that the figure in
1881 of 135,000 had become 286,000 by 1901. Many of the new
entrants had been refugees from Tsarist tyranny – Russians, Poles and,
of course, Jews. It was officially estimated in 1917 that in London
alone there were 30,000 Russian political refugees[32]. Like a seismo-
graph, they reacted to every convulsion in their homeland . . . and that
created problems for the British Government.

The first brush between the authorities and the Russian emigrés had
occurred early in the war, when HM Government had decided to assist
its ally the Tsar by dealing with some of the undesirables. The
(Russian) Seamen and Firemen's Union, outlawed in Russia itself, had
its headquarters first in Istanbul and then in Egypt. In both places, the
Russian Government exerted its influence and succeeded in getting the
union offices closed down. They were then moved to Antwerp and,
following the German invasion of Belgium, were transferred to London.
In December 1915, British police raided the offices of the union,
seizing all the papers and documents there. The house of the union's
leader, Anitchkine, was searched and he was taken to Scotland Yard.
Told that the police had nothing against him and he could go home, he
refused to leave until all the papers and documents were returned.

Meanwhile, other Russian emigrés were being harassed. Trotsky's
journal *Nashe Slovo*, published in Paris, circulated widely. Indeed,
according to Trotsky's friend, Alfred Rosmer, its circulation in Britain
was as big as it was in France.[33] After its suppression on 15 September
1916, the work was continued by other bodies. By 1916, the Lettish
Social Democratic Party claimed to have issued 40 appeals against the
war, with a total circulation of half-a-million copies. Some of these had
found their way to emigrés in Britain, as did other items of subversive
literature. As a consequence, a large number of refugees held and
expressed anti-war views. This fact began to have an impact outside
emigré circles. For example, *The Socialist*, with severely limited space,
still carried a lot of material from these sources. To illustrate this
point, examination of four months' issues (October 1915 to January
1916) shows that the paper carried: A Revolutionary Manifesto from
Russian Poland (October 1915); An Open Letter to German Social

Democracy by Lettish Social Democracy (October 1915); Russian
Political Prisoners & Exiles Relief Committee – report (December
1915); and Resolution on Zimmerwald conference from Russian Social
Democratic Party, London Group (January 1916).

The British authorities decided to curtail these activities, and this
could only be done by repression. Harassment, arrest and the smashing
of organisations was used. A particularly sinister weapon augmented
these measures: refugees were threatened with being sent back to
Russia where, like Petroff, they would be murdered.

Almost immediately, the emigrés took counter-measures. They
formed the Political Prisoners and Exiles Relief Committee. This body
contained representatives of the Russian Social Democratic Party,
the Jewish Alliance of Lithuania, Poland and Russia, the Polish
Socialist Party and the Lithuanian Socialist Federation. Mrs Bridges
Adams acted as secretary of the Committee, with George Chicherin as
her assistant. Their choice of secretary was wise: Mrs Bridges Adams, a
tireless and courageous woman, for a long while had taught English
to foreigners and her activities had given her extensive contacts among
the emigré population. Many refugees in difficulties had acquired the
habit of turning to her for advice and assistance. At the same time, Mrs
Bridges Adams was a Marxist. Almost from its inception, she had
belonged to the Plebs League and had striven to spread socialist ideas
among working women.[34] Simultaneously, she had fought for equality
of opportunity in the State-run educational system. As a result of her
prodigious efforts, extending over several decades, she had acquired a
wide range of contacts among Suffragettes, trade unionists and
socialists as well as emigrés.

Under her guidance, the Political Prisoners and Exiles Relief Committee concentrated on influencing the labour movement. It produced an
'Open Letter to Organised Workers of Britain'. The police immediately
raided Mrs Bridges Adams' house, confiscating 600 copies of the letter.
She was again raided when the Committee prepared a leaflet on the
right of political asylum for distribution at the 1916 TUC Congress in
Birmingham. Mrs Bridges Adams was detained for 30 hours. She
returned home to find her home ransacked. Such visits by the police
and Special Branch soon became a frequent happening. Her house, 96
Lexham Gardens, off Earls Court Road, – known as Bebel House after
the German socialist leader – was the headquarters of the Relief Committee and the centre for a lot of socialist activity.

Attempting to justify the attentions paid to her by the authorities,
Lord Derby told Parliament that Mrs Bridges Adams was secretary of a

society of 'a dangerous character'. He went on to say that 'she was closely connected with two men named Petroff and Maclean.' Another of her companions was Anitchkine, the Russian seamen's leader, who was suspected of passing information to the enemy. 'If people like to keep the company that this Mrs Bridges Adams does,' Lord Derby continued, 'they must expect to come under suspicion.'[35]

The Political Prisoners and Exiles Relief Committee did not succeed in forcing the authorities to stop their repressive measures. After three raids, the Russian Seamen & Firemen's Union ceased to function. Peter Petroff and his wife were arrested, and other refugees were imprisoned. On 1 December 1916, that customary haunt of the left, the Communist Club in Fitzroy Square, was raided without a search warrant. Twenty arrests were made, and considerable brutality used. The Club's secretary reported: 'The soldiers broke into the wine cellars and liberally helped themselves to the content. They also appeared to be badly in need of playing cards, fountain pens, walking sticks, watches, etc.'[36] Over-enthusiastic and wanting to set an example, the intruders destroyed a lot of property belonging to the Garment Workers' Union, which happened to use the same premises. This kind of conduct could not fail to arouse disquiet in trade union circles and tended to arouse sympathy for the refugees. Almost definitely, Lord Sheffield was right when he said in the House of Lords: 'Scotland Yard became a little uneasy when they found their action was not merely against isolated groups of Russians but attracting the attention of active labour societies in Britain.'[37] Union journals often printed articles sympathetic to the refugees. The authorities realised that this was very difficult to stop: it was one thing to suppress an emigré fringe organisation; it was quite another to have a direct confrontation with British trade unions. So, reluctantly, they overlooked the matter. Yet, as Mrs Bridges Adams wrote in 1922:

During the past year I have spent much time in rearranging, for future use, newspaper cuttings from the chaos they were left in after various police raids on my house, and I have been amazed at the daring and outspoken character of Anti-Tsarist propaganda I was able to carry on in trade union journals.[38]

Additional trouble faced the British authorities as the Russian Revolution unfolded in 1917. Refugees in this country were becoming politically more active. Whereas the authorities had been able to rely hitherto upon the Tsarist censor to stop seditious communications, Britain now had to introduce its own censorship. Some news still percolated through and refugees, more outspoken than previously, sought to spread the information. At the May Day rally in his Leicester constituency, when Ramsay MacDonald attacked Lenin as a 'thoughtless anarchist', a Russian in the audience led the opposition.[39] Similarly, when Thorne, on his return from Russia, made anti-Semitic references to Lenin and Trotsky, Russian refugees in London issued a reply.[40] While Labour leaders like Henderson and Thorne had been treated with a suspicion verging on hostility when visiting Russia, a much different attitude was adopted to individuals whom the British government regarded as dangerous extremists: in June 1917, the All-Russian Congress of Workmen's and Soldiers' Councils passed a resolution sending fraternal greetings 'to comrade John Maclean, now sitting in gaol for preaching internationalism.' In the same month, 200 Russian seamen left their warship anchored in the Clyde to join a demonstration on Glasgow Green protesting against the imprisonment of John Maclean and of Peter Petroff, who was a hero of the 1905 Revolution, in which he was twice wounded.[41]

Much more serious from the British government's standpoint were the internal consequences which threatened a large portion of its surveillance of subversives in this country. What is well known is that the Soviet Foreign Ministry published secret treaties concluded by the Tsarist government, revealing imperialist deals with France, Britain and others. What is less well known is that the Soviet Foreign Ministry also revealed the archives of the Tsarist secret police. The names of agents working undercover among Russian refugees in Britain were divulged. Similarly, much to the embarrassment of Her Majesty's government, these archives showed that Scotland Yard and the Special Branch had collaborated closely with the Russian secret service in its persecution of refugees. The entire network of agents, both British and Russian, as well as the painstaking work of surveillance of revolutionaries, were in jeopardy.[42] To minimise the threat, the Home Office ordered that George Chicherin, probably the individual most closely in communication with the Soviet government, should be interned in January 1918.

Persons could be imprisoned; ideas could not. Yet every attempt was made to do so. The Home Office issued new regulations that stated that all material had to be submitted to the censor before being circulated. This led to the BSP journal, *Call*, of 17 January 1918, being confiscated. It carried a manifesto on Russia. The SLP criticised the BSP for submitting to the government's new procedures — 'We disagree with it for placing its manifesto on Russia before the censor; a thing neither

Lenin nor Trotsky would do' — but this did not stop the SLP from offering its own printing press for the BSP to use.[43]

Threat of suppression did not deter *The Socialist*. In February 1918, the issue that commented on the confiscation of *The Call* carried an article by Litvinov on the life of Lenin as well as an article by Lenin himself on 'The Aims of the Bolsheviks'. The following issue carried a translation by Sirnis of the Control of Factories decrees passed by the Soviets. At the same time, it had a letter from 'our Russian Comrade Chicherin' in which he briefly explained how Bolshevik ideas originated. Lenin, he said, developed his ideas well before the revolution: 'He expressed his ideas in numerous newspapers and reviews, freely sold in London bookshops.' Trotsky's *Nashe Slovo* had also been easily obtainable, he said.

The SLP saw itself as possessing the same outlook and policies as the Bolsheviks. It explained: 'The theories of Lenin as put into operation by the Russian Maximalists are similar to those advocated by the SLP.' Later, in a piece headlined 'Triumph of the SLP Tactics in Russia', it tried to indicate, in terms of practical politics, what was necessary:

> The SLP is the only party in this country which has compelled the ILP and BSP to realise that socialist tactics do not mean how to juggle men into Parliament. Socialist tactics mean the education of the proletariat and the organisation of the political weapon to destroy capitalism, backed by the industrial unions taking over the means of production.
>
> For years the SLP has been sneered at and jeered at, but now Russia, in the transition towards the Socialist Republic, shows the SLP is right.[44]

The authorities seem to have paid the SLP the compliment of regarding them as the British Bolsheviks, the most dangerous group of revolutionaries in Britain: suddenly, a wave of repression was unleashed. On 13 June 1918, the police raided the SLP headquarters and confiscated 10,000 copies of Trotsky's pamphlet, *War or Revolution*. On 6 July 1918, the SLP press was raided. All paper and every drop of ink was seized. Two new linotype machines were dismantled. This did not dishearten the Party:

> The attempt to wreck our press shall in no way deter us from carrying on our work. Those who understand what the class struggle means also realise that the workers in their march to Socialism must

encounter many obstacles and many defeats. These reverses, however, are good things in one sense — they rid our ranks of faint
hearts, compromisers and weaklings.[45]

The SLP had anticipated these actions. The Party had a number of
printers lined up who, in the event of difficulties, had agreed to
produce *The Socialist*. The first was E.H. Williams, of 232 Devons
Road, Bow, who printed the August issue after the ILP press had
refused. Then the authorities placed a ban on him, causing considerable
financial loss. The next was also a London printer, J.F. Edwards, who
had the task of printing the memorable September 1918 edition,
which carried a first-hand account of the British attempt to overthrow
the Soviet government.

It seems that Maxim Litvinov received coded wireless messages from
Moscow and that the British government had succeeded in breaking the
code. Therefore, immediately Litvinov heard of the Bruce Lockhart
plot, the police moved in to arrest him. He was only just able to despatch the news to *The Socialist* before they arrived. It reached the
editor when the paper was already half printed and the whole edition
had to be re-set.

The lead story said that 'our comrade Litvinov is arrested', and went
on to explain why the paper was appearing late. Then it gave the report
Litinov dictated before his arrest:

On 2 September, a plot organised under the supervision of the Chief
of the British Mission Lockhart, the French Consul General Grenard,
and the French general Laterne was liquidated.

The plot had for its aim to seize the power of the Soviet of the
People's Commissaries by bribing the chiefs of the Army Corps of
the Soviet Army and to proclaim a military dictatorship in Moscow.

In possession of the plotters were found forged secret communications of the Russian Government with Germany and a forged
treaty with Germany. All with the object of creating a suitable atmosphere after the *coup d'etat*, which would allow the dictatorship to
declare war on Germany.

The whole of this organisation, which was a well thought out and
thoroughly organised scheme, and which acted by means of bribery,
was stopped.

The plotters were protecting themselves with diplomatic
immunity.

One of Lockhart's agents, Lieutenant Reilly, passed 1,200,000 roubles in 10 days.

The September issue of *The Socialist*, of which an extra 7,700 copies were printed, also contained an article by Lenin entitled 'No Compromise with Opportunists'. Again, the paper found itself in trouble with the authorities and in need of a new printer, and yet again the *Workers' Dreadnought* offered to share its columns with the SLP until fresh arrangements could be made. But it was not necessary. The Party, aware of the tightening grip of officialdom on the freedom of the Press, had made contingency plans to print *The Socialist* clandestinely. By the end of 1918, the editor worked from a tent in a field at Heald Green, near Manchester.[46]

Every effort was made to get the maximum protest against the government's repressive measures. Hundreds of trade union branches passed resolutions deploring interference with socialist journals and with the jailing of political prisoners. In December 1918, a joint manifesto on the curtailment of civil liberty, entitled 'A Call to Labour', was jointly issued by the ILP, BSP and SLP.

But the government was in no mood for compromising. Besides promoting the Bruce Lockhart plot for overthrowing Soviet rule by internal subversion, the United Kingdom had now become involved in more overt efforts. Military intervention began when British troops were landed at Vladivostock, then at Archangel. Large supplies of arms and ammunition were supplied to the White armies fighting against the Bolsheviks. Playing such a leading role in the crusade against communism abroad, the British government saw no reason to relax its vigilance at home.

Equally, revolutionaries saw the fight in a global context. The SLP considered that the government's campaign of suppression had been directed against it for exactly this reason:

> The government realised that its onslaught against socialism in Russia could only be successful by attempting to smash the one press in Britain that dared to stand up for Bolshevism.[47]

In the war of intervention, the SLP thought it had an exceedingly important role to play in helping its Russian comrades:

> How can we help Russia? We can best assist the Soviet Republic by extending and intensifying our activities in this country. By attending to our own problems and organising to solve them we can

force the government to attend to *us* instead of seeking to strangle the Soviet Republic.

Many means, sometimes quite ingenious ones, were employed to thwart the authorities. For example, one of the main reasons why the SLP fought three seats at the 1918 general election was to circumvent official restrictions. The Party considered that the government would be reluctant to confiscate literature, produced under the pretext of being for election purposes, for fear of creating a backlash among the electorate. As a result, a lot of material was printed that otherwise would have been forbidden under the Defence of the Realm Act. The SLP's election manifesto, 'A Soviet Republic for Britain — a plea for the formation of Workers' & Soldiers' Councils' — spelt out in detail what would have to happen to bring about a social revolution in this country.

The historian Walter Kendall suggests that the SLPs three candidates fought their elections with the aid of Russian finance, coming into Britain in the form of diamonds, not gold. Small, compact, highly valuable, diamonds were an ideal commodity for smuggling purposes.[48] One SLPer definitely made the hazardous journey through strife-torn Europe, crossing and re-crossing the lines of opposing armies, to go to Russia and back. Naturally, everything was done to keep secret both his identity and mission. Discreet inquiries suggest, however, that William Stoker, jun., of Wigan, undertook this difficult, dangerous task.[49]

The most interesting things Stoker returned to England with were five short pieces, none of which contained new ideas or theoretical profundity. Appearing without explanation in a Russian supplement, their origin and purpose still remains quite clear: they were leaflets distributed by the Red Army to British soldiers in the armies of intervention. To quote from a typical leaflet, one of them ends:

> Fellow working men, refuse to be suppressors of your own class. Form Soldiers' Councils in your regiments. Send your representatives to your officers and demand to be sent home. And when you get home, destroy the sham capitalist democracy reigning there and establish a true Republic of Labour, as we have done in Russia.

A few months later, *The Socialist* admitted what was happening:

> Literature *does* reach the shore of England from Russia, and most of the leaflets and manifestoes printed in England are delivered, by

various means, to the British troops on the Russian front. Our government will find out when the troops return to this country.[50]

The British Press referred alarmingly to the spread of Bolshevism. In November 1918, the *Daily News*, talking about the revolution that had just broken out in Germany, attributed it to 'the flood of Bolshevik agitators' coming in from Russia. The paper went on to describe these revolutionaries who 'made of steel and indiarubber, are absolutely untireable, and have four times the energy of ordinary human politicians.'[51] Commenting on these observations, *The Socialist* remarked that 'happily "the boys of the Bolshevik breed" are not entirely unknown in Britain.' The SLP did nothing to disguise its programme. At the 1918 general election it made its position quite clear to the public:

> We are denounced as 'British Bolsheviks'. We do not seek to conceal our views. We are proud of the title. The SLP is the only political organisation that stands wholeheartedly and uncompromisingly for the Soviet idea. Let it be known: We are the British Bolsheviks![52]

Clearly, by the end of 1918, a struggle of international dimensions existed. It stretched from Moscow to Glasgow, from Leningrad to London. The forces of counter-revolution and the forces of revolution were locked in bitter conflict in every country. With the reciprocal validity of Leibknecht, the British rulers could say: 'The enemy is at home.' They had to contend with British Bolshevism as well as the Russian variety.

Notes

1. House of Commons, 14 and 17 March 1917.
2. Letter of Brig. Gen. F.C. Poole to Lord Milner, 31 July 1917. H.O. 197 (1917) C.18/21(4).
3. *Forward*, 12 March 1921.
4. Letter of Brig. Col. Poole to Captain Ormsby-Gore, 31 July 1917. H.O. 197 (1917).
5. Lord Milner to the Prime Minister, 8 September 1917. A.F. Kerensky, *The Catastrophe* (New York, 1927) p. 315, alleges that General Knox subsidized a Kornilov pamphlet. Lord Milner also told Kerensky to back Kornilov.
6. *The Times*, 13 September 1917.
7. *Morning Post*, 9 November 1917.
8. *Manchester Guardian*, 27 November 1917.
9. *The Times*, 20 November 1917.
10. CAB. 28/2 107(9), 28 March 1917.

11. *The Socialist*, August 1917, refers to the coat and John S. Clarke even wrote a poem about it. Also E.A. and G.H. Radice, *Will Thorne, Constructive Militant* (1974) p. 79.

12. Will Thorne, *My Life's Battles* (1925) pp. 194-5. The Russian Provisional government also wanted MacDonald to visit Russia, but British seamen blacked the ship. (Lord Elton, *The Life of J.R. MacDonald* (1939) vol. 1, p. 317.)

13. CAB. 23/2 144(1), 23 May 1917. In his article, 'Arthur Henderson, the Russian Revolution and the Reconstruction of the Labour Party', J.M. Winter deals with the Henderson mission to Russia in detail. (The Historical Journal, 1972, pp. 753-73.)

14. *The Times*, 18 June 1917.

15. V.I. Lenin, *British Labour and British Imperialism* (1941) pp. 172-3.

16. Letter of Bruce Lockhart to Sir George Buchanan, 23 July 1917, F.O. 438/10.

17. Letter of A. Henderson to Lloyd George, 1 July 1917, F.O. 371/2997.

18. R.H. Bruce Lockhart, *Memoirs of a British Agent* (1934 ed.) pp. 187-8.

19. *The Times*, 14 June 1917: Bruce Lockhart, ibid.

20. *Leicester Post*, 7 May 1917.

21. *Labour Leader*, 15 November 1917 and 7 March 1918.

22. *Sunday Pictorial*, 21 January 1918. Also C. Tsuzuki, *H.M. Hyndman and British Socialism* (Oxford, 1961) p. 240.

23. Hansard, cxii (1918) 58-9. It is interesting to note that, on the fiftieth anniversary of the October Revolution, the London *Evening Standard* approached a number of prominent Labour leaders and asked them which side they would have backed if they had lived in Russia in 1917. Barbara Castle, R.H.S. Crossman and Roy Jenkins all replied they would have been on the side of the Bolsheviks. What needs to be said is that their historical predecessors certainly were not.

24. *The Socialist*, December 1917.

25. R. Page Arnot, *The Impact of the Russian Revolution in Britain*, p. 64. An assessment of the Leeds Convention similar to my own is to be found in the *Fourth International*, vol. 4, No. 3, November 1967, by Alan Clinton and George Myers.

26. House of Commons, 14 May 1917.

27. *Workers' Dreadnought*, 9 June 1917.

28. W. Thorne, op. cit., p. 195.

29. *Workers' Dreadnought*, 4 August 1917.

30. Sir Basil Thomson, *The Scene Changes* (1939) p. 383.

31. *Daily News* and *The Observer*, 30 June 1917; Nan Milton, *John Maclean*, p. 142.

32. Figures given in House of Commons, 7 February 1917.

33. Letter from A. Rosmer to W. Kendall, cited in W. Kendall, *The Revolutionary Movement in Britain, 1900-21*, pp. 376-7.

34. Information about Mrs Bridges Adams given by Lord Sheffield in the House of Lords, 7 March 1917, and J. King MP, in the House of Commons, 8 March 1917. Mrs Bridges Adams was very annoyed by the indifference shown by Labour and ILP Members of Parliament to the plight of Russian refugees. She had to rely on two dissident Liberal politicians to champion her cause. For her Marxist background, see W.W. Craik, *Central Labour College* (1964) p. 82, pp. 102-3.

35. House of Lords, 7 March 1917.

36. *The Socialist*, February 1917.

37. House of Lords, 7 March 1917.

38. *The Socialist*, 12 January 1922.

39. *Leicester Post*, 7 May 1917.
40. *Workers' Dreadnought*, 16 June 1917.
41. *The Call*, 28 June 1917. Nan Milton, op. cit., p. 108.
42. House of Lords, 30 January 1918.
43. *The Socialist*, February 1918.
44. Ibid, March 1918.
45. Ibid, August 1918.
46. Tom Bell, *Pioneering Days*, p. 176.
47. *The Socialist*, September 1917.
48. W. Kendall, op. cit., p. 252, quoting from the Pankhurst Papers.
49. *The Socialist*, 18 September 1919. Tom Bell, op. cit., p. 176, briefly
     mentions reprinting 'Bolshevik leaflets issued to troops.'
50. *The Socialist*, 12 June 1919.
51. *Daily News*, 15 November 1918.
52. *The Socialist*, December 1918.

9 1918-1920: A MISSED REVOLUTIONARY CHANCE?

The prospects appeared gloomy for the British ruling class as the First World War neared its end. It faced a swelling tide of industrial discontent. Workers became increasingly exasperated by rising prices, food shortages and repeated appeals for further sacrifices. New and dangerous leaders emerged from the ranks to express their feelings of disenchantment and to channel discontent along lines which seemed to threaten capitalism's very existence. Faced with this challenge, the British Government had little ground for manoeuvre. It sought to bolster the public's flagging morale by making promises. It held up the vision of a better society, with homes fit for heroes, where everyone could enjoy the fruits of victory. The problem was that, at the same time as the government encouraged these expectations, its ability to fulfil these promises continued to dwindle.

The First World War left the British economy considerably weakened. In human terms, the losses had been great. Three-quarters of a million men, most of whom were young, with the major portion of their working lives in front of them, had been killed in the fighting. A further 1,700,000 had been wounded. The provision of scanty pensions for the most seriously crippled caused an annual drain on the exchequer of £100 million. On top of these physical losses, there was the rundown in productive capacity. Some industries had been compelled to make do with antiquated equipment so that more resources could be devoted to producing machines of war. Even where after 1918 it was possible to produce on a competitive basis, many foreign markets that had been the preserve of British firms had gone forever. Unable to buy British during the war, many countries had either found other sources of supply or developed their own industries. In some cases, customers had now become competitors. As a consequence, the recapturing of lost overseas markets was an exceedingly hard task. The whole situation was aggravated by the state of the world economy: the considerable uncertainties and dislocations made the re-establishment of international trade difficult and was particularly badly felt by a country like Britain, so dependent upon foreign trade.

All this was taking place against a background of the emergence of a new world power. By 1918, the United States was definitely the strongest capitalist country. In the course of the war, America had suffered negligible losses. For most of the time, she had not been a belligerent but had acted as a quarter-master, making money by supplying the combatants. As the United States productive capacity and output increased, so did the indebtedness of other countries to her. By contrast, the United Kingdom had been compelled to sell some of its foreign assets and its investments in Russia had been confiscated. What was more, a question-mark had not merely been placed over Britain's foreign assets but also its colonies. There were the rumblings of nationalism in Ireland, Africa and Asia. The clamour for Indian independence had resulted in a number of serious incidents. At Amritsar, troops fired on an unarmed demonstration, killing 379 and wounding a further 1,200 people. This act of imperialist savagery aroused widespread condemnation. It also had a special significance: the world was witnessing the beginning of the decline of the British Empire as well as of Britain itself.

Clearly, Lloyd George and his fellow ministers faced a situation fraught with dangers. Probably at no time since the 1840s has a government been faced with such a serious challenge. No wonder they had to give considerable thought to the possibility that there would be an attempt to overthrow the existing social order. The head of the Special Branch was quite explicit. 'We cannot hope to escape some sort of revolution,' declared Lord Burnham, 'and there will be no passionate resistance from anybody.'[1] Likewise Field Marshall Sir Henry Wilson told the cabinet that, in his opinion, 'a Bolshevik rising was likely.'[2]

The government resolved to combat the menace, and if this was to be done effectively, information had first to be acquired about the nature and disposition of the enemy. So a cabinet sub-committee was set up, which met regularly, to monitor the activities of subversive organisations and make suggestions about whatever counter-measures the government could adopt. Plainly, the surveillance was most rigorous and thoroughgoing. Even items of little consequence were carefully documented. For example, it is recorded that Jimmy Stewart, of Wallsend SLP, had acquired shop premises which he used for teaching Social, Economic and Industrial History. 'He calls his shop a Labour College. The classes are attended by a few youths from 18 to 21.'[3] Equally trivial, but indicative of a concern for minutiae, is this reference to I.P. Hughes, of Liverpool:

A young man named Hughes described himself as a shop steward and Bolshevik, and said he had been trying to educate his work mates, but that they were not sufficiently advanced to understand his teaching. His creed seemed to be purely Syndicalist.[4]

What must have been highly disturbing to the authorities, as they carefully documented subversive activities, was the rising curve of working-class discontent. In previous chapters, the battles on Clydeside of 1915-16 have been discussed. Subsequently, the struggle was mainly centred south of the border. In the autumn of 1916, trouble flared up in Sheffield. The cause was the insistence of the War Office that a young engineer named Leonard Hargreaves, previously exempt, should nevertheless join the army. Failing to get this decision countermanded through official channels, Sheffield shop stewards got 10,000 munition workers to down tools. They also sent a fleet of motor-cyclists to other industrial centres calling for sympathetic action. It was a direct challenge to the government's right to conscript men – and the Sheffield Shop Stewards won. Leonard Hargreaves returned to his bench at Vickers, and the Ministry was forced to negotiate a 'Trade Card Scheme', exempting engineers from military service.[5]

To some extent, the government retrieved the situation later. In March 1917, 10,000 workers at Barrow went on strike because of alleged cuts in piece-work rates. They appealed, like the Sheffield men, for support from elsewhere. But none was forthcoming. The cabinet, having discussed the dispute, decided to issue a proclamation, threatening arrest and imprisonment for anybody who came out in solidarity. As a consequence, the Barrow men remained isolated, and after a fortnight returned to work.[6]

The authorities' success proved to be short-lived. In April 1917, the Rochdale firm of Tweedale & Smalley tried to extend dilution, which up till then had been confined to munitions work, to private contracts. This was a violation of national agreements and trade unionists were soon out. The strike spread to many parts of the country until it encompassed all the major industrial centres, with the exception of Clydeside and Tyneside. More than 200,000 workers were involved and 1½ million working days lost, making it the largest unofficial strike in British history.[7] In a desperate situation, the government endeavoured to stir up patriotic feelings by sending the King and Queen on visits to the main strike areas. When this failed, it arrested ten of the men's leaders. Effectively, this beheaded the strike. With them in prison, awaiting trial, the government opened negotiations with the union bureaucrats of the ASE. Pliant and cautious, J.T. Brownlie and his colleagues, who had opposed the unofficial stoppage from the outset, were quick to arrive at an agreement. After the men were back at work and the situation de-fused, F.E. Smith went as the government's emissary to the imprisoned shop stewards. He offered to drop the charges on condition that they accepted the agreement reached by the officials of their own union. This they agreed to do.[8]

Irrespective of how skillful the government's tactics happened to be, the successes it scored merely gained a temporary respite. Within a short time, the industrial scene had again become stormy. In November-December 1917 a dispute over bonus payments at White & Poppes led to 50,000 workers in the Coventry area going on strike. And worse was to follow in 1918. Led by militants, the South Wales miners came out in May and, later in the year, the usually docile textile workers of Lancashire struck. The result was that 1918 had the highest number of working days lost through industrial disputes of the whole First World War, a total of 5,875,000 days. Clearly, the government had failed to curb the industrial militancy.

The administration and its supporters anticipated the worst. In the Air Ministry's weekly orders, it stated that firing on rioters must be effective. Commenting on this, the journal *Aeroplane* declared that the RAF 'would have but little mercy on a Bolshevik mob . . . the RAF pilots and observers have had much practice during the German retreat in operating against mobs on roads and in streets.'[9] The *Glasgow Evening Times* also gloated over 'the irresistible logic inherent in the bayonet and bullet.'[10] Nor was this point lost on Winston Churchill, then Minister of Munition, who referred to the role of the tank corps: 'They will be valuable in savage frontiers, and they obviously have police value in India, Ireland and at home.'[11]

It was very much in this frame of mind that the government responded to the 40 Hours' Strike early in 1919. Faced with the prospect of large scale unemployment, the Clyde Workers' Committee sought a solution through a campaign to lessen the working week. It tried, with limited success, to spread the stoppage to the whole of Scotland. Trouble broke out on 31 January 1919. A delegation of men's leaders had gone to Glasgow City Chambers to meet the Lord Provost. While they were in the building, an argument occurred on the south side of St George's Square. A big crowd had assembled there, awaiting news from the talks, when a tramcar was heedlessly driven at them. This caused tempers to rise. The police drew their batons, and mounted police charged the crowd. About 40 people were injured, some of whom were merely innocent bystanders. Officialdom greatly exaggerated the incident. The Secretary of State for Scotland,

R. Munro, informed the cabinet that 'in his opinion, it was more clear than ever that it was a misnomer to call the situation in Glasgow a strike — it was a Bolshevik uprising.'[12] As a consequence, the government quickly despatched six tanks and 100 lorries to Glasgow by train. Strike-bound Central Scotland was placed under army occupation, with machine-gun posts at strategic places.

Military intervention in industrial disputes in this way was highly exceptional. While force might be used, sometimes in abundant quanti- ties, against hapless colonials, successive British governments have tended to behave with greater restraint when dealing with workers at home. As Marx observed in the *Manifesto*, the State in the final analysis is a body of armed men. Nevertheless governments had discovered through experience that it was usually prudent to keep the military in reserve; to let it be the last argument of kings, not the first. Force used unwisely could be counter-productive.

But in the post-First World War situation, there were other reasons why the authorities would be chary of committing the troops in civil strife: they were not sure of the soldiers' reliability. Throughout the services, disaffection was rampant. In January 1919, 10,000 soldiers mutinied at Folkstone and refused to return to France. A further 4,000 in Dover demonstrated in sympathy. In the same week, 1,500 men from Osterley Park seized army lorries and went to Whitehall to protest. Within a short while, similar acts of insubordination had occurred in units throughout the Home Counties. Aboard *HMS Kilbride* matters became even more out of hand: on 13 January 1919, its seamen hauled the Red Flag up its masthead, declaring 'Half the Navy are on strike and the other half soon will be.'[13]

The government must even have had qualms when it returned to that customarily stolid and reliable protector of capitalist property, the British Bobby. A trade union had been formed in the police force. In May 1919, 1,000 London policemen went on strike while on Merseyside half the force came out. For months afterwards, the authorities had misgivings about the reliability of the police if an awkward situation should arise.[14] Clearly, had the government wished to use the police or the armed forces in a violent confrontation with the workers, then it could easily have found things getting out of hand. So other means of quietening the angry multitude and bringing Britain back to a state of capitalist normality had to be found.

Lloyd George and his Ministers aimed to achieve these objectives by devious and subtle methods: first, to smash unofficial rank-and-file movements or, where this proved to be impossible, render them harmless through incorporation into the established structure; second, to lessen the strength of the official trade union movement, thereby making it more pliant and obedient to the needs of industry and the capitalist state; and third, to harass and persecute left-wing organisations so that their activities were disrupted and they failed to have an impact on the course of events.

The government was fortunate because it faced rank-and-file movements which were fragmentary and lacked co-ordination. In many industries, they remained feeble or non-existent. Where they did exist, their limited membership and different stages of development made united action next to impossible. They had, moreover, come into being as a consequence of the special conditions prevailing during the war. Once union leaders were no longer hamstrung by wartime laws and regulations, they could move nearer towards expressing some of the aspirations of their union's membership, thus lessening reliance at factory floor level on shop stewards. Likewise an issue like dilution and Trade Card scheme ceased to be matters of great import, and the main areas around which rank-and-file bodies centred their struggles appeared to vanish overnight. Even as early as 17 January 1919, the *Workers' Dreadnought* was reporting that most workers' committees had gone out of existence.

The government aimed to hasten this process. This could be accomplished by refusal to negotiate with unofficial bodies, arresting their leaders and letting industrial disputes continue until the rank-and-file organisations had been smashed. This is precisely what happened to the Clyde Workers' Committee in 1919. On 27 January, 40,000 shipbuilding and engineering workers struck. The following day the figure had swollen to 70,000. But after the Battle of St George's Square, all the Committee's leading members — Gallacher, MacManus, Shinwell, etc., — were charged with riotous assembly. By 3 February 1919, when it had become obvious that the strike would not spread, the drift back to work began. This defeat of the Clyde Workers' Committee marked the end of it as an effective organisation. Left £5,000 in debt after fighting the legal cases, the CWC never again called workers out on strike.[15]

The pattern was repeated elsewhere. An attempt, roughly at the same time, by Belfast workers to secure a 44-hour week ended in defeat. Similarly, in his autobiography, Harry Pollitt described how the River Thames Shop Stewards' Committee, a well-organised body which ran its own paper, choir and orchestra, was smashed as a result of industrial defeat early in 1919. On Tyneside's shipyards, the collapse of a strike in February 1919 virtually eliminated rank-and-file organisation, which in any case was only rudimentary. Likewise Barrow shop stewards' committee took a battering and, in May 1919, was compelled to suspend publication of its journal, *Northern Light*.[16]

Associated with this employers' offensive was an attack on the jobs of individual militants. Even in its period of ascendancy, when the shop stewards' movement was at its point of greatest strength and with full employment created by wartime conditions, the committee found it difficult, if not impossible, to stop victimisation. For example, 56 men were dismissed from Hotchkiss et Cie's factory in Coventry in 1918, including shop stewards and the leader of the Coventry workers, David Dingley, without effective resistance taking place.[17] But in the conditions prevailing after the war it became much easier for management to weed out the militants; as J.T. Murphy clearly admitted in July 1919:

> At Vickers, Sheffield, it is questionable whether there is a single, active shop steward or literature seller left in the place. They have practically all been cleared out under the cloak of unemployment. The same applies to many prominent people on the Clyde.[18]

The government also appreciated the effect of joblessness. A report on revolutionary organisations in the cabinet papers mentioned that 'the fear of unemployment is exercising a steadying influence'. Elsewhere there is reference to the conflict and disunity engendered within the working class by lack of employment. On Clydeside, demobilised soldiers discovered that Irishmen, brought over during the war, had taken their jobs in the shipyards. This, naturally, aroused extensive anti-Irish feeling.[19]

Lack of unity within the working class and the smashing of rank-and-file organisations helped to make the industrial scene more tranquil. The government sought to further this process by assisting surreptitiously the trade union bureaucracy's fight with its left-wing critics. As was pointed out, in the cabinet's survey of British revolutionary movements in 1920, much agitation resulted from small groups of politically-motivated people, securing influence within the lower echelons of trade unions. Referring to the disputes in the railways, textiles and transport, the survey stated, 'In spite of the fact that the basis of the claims advanced was economic, as distinct from political, unrest was largely the work of the revolutionary minority which had captured the branch and lodge machinery.'[20] Frequently, the inefficiency of union officials provided the basis upon which the left-wing critics extended their influence. Wherever possible, the government aimed to disrupt this activity, to create confusion in the ranks, by the timely arrest or harassment of militants.

Gradually, the combined effect of the government and employers' strategy was to strengthen the power and authority of union leaders over their membership. The wild boys, the unofficial leaders thrown up from the factory floor, with no respect for constitutional proprieties or inhibitions in fully pursuing workers' demands, became less and less important. Replacing them was the stolid, well-paid and highly respectable union official, who would not dream of breaking a law or endangering the capitalist system which he cherished.

Even where shop stewards continued to function, they operated in a different context and in a different way. Now they had become part of the unions' official machinery, with clearly defined duties and responsibilities. In this manner, their teeth were drawn. They no longer possessed the power or freedom they previously had. Vanished was the kind of independence that James Messer, secretary of the Clyde Workers' Committee, described in a letter he wrote in 1917: 'The relations between the Committee and the official side of the trade unions may be taken as nil.'[21]

As the union leaders gained ascendancy, it made the task of Lloyd George and his ministers much easier. The cabinet now had to deal with gentlemen very much more reasonable. They felt a natural bond of sympathy for a union man like J.H. Thomas, who came rushing back from America in an attempt to avert a dispute. As he informed his members in the union's journal: 'I must candidly admit that the mere threat of a stoppage, or the danger of rupture, is at all times sufficient to absorb my whole being and to prompt my instant return to London.'[22] Clearly, Lloyd George was correct when he declared about J.H. Thomas in a cabinet meeting, 'He wants no revolution. He wants to be Prime Minister.' At another cabinet meeting, he added, 'I have complete confidence in Mr. Thomas's selfishness.'[23]

But it did not have to be sordid self-interest that led union leaders to betray their members and capitulate to the government. Lacking a proletarian worldview, determination and a will to win, they would always surrender rather than endanger the fabric of the existing social order. Indeed, the weakness of their position was most clearly displayed at the time they appeared strongest: when they were able to defeat the Lloyd George government's reactionary policies, they instinctively drew back, afraid that the ensuing chaos could lead along the perilous path to revolution.

This is plainly shown in the dealings of Lloyd George with the Triple Alliance, an alliance of miners, railwaymen and transport workers, designed to increase their collective power. In 1919, the Triple Alliance leaders went to Downing Street to see the Prime Minister. The proceedings there are described by Aneurin Bevan in his book, *In Place of Fear*:

I remember vividly Robert Smillie describing to me an interview the leaders of the Triple Alliance had with David Lloyd George in 1919. The strategy of the leaders was clear. The miners under Robert Smillie, the transport workers under Robert Williams, and the National Union of Railwaymen under James Henry Thomas, formed the most formidable combination of industrial workers in the history of Great Britain. They had agreed on the demands that were to be made on the employers, knowing well that the government would be bound to be involved at an early stage. And so it happened. A great deal of industry was still under government wartime control and so the state power was immediately implicated.

Lloyd George sent for the Labour leaders, and they went, so Robert told me, 'truculently determined they would not be talked over by the seductive and eloquent Welshman.' At this Bob's eyes twinkled in his grave, strong face. 'He was quite frank with us from the outset,' Bob went on. 'He said to us: "Gentlemen, you have fashioned, in the Triple Alliance of the unions represented by you, a most powerful instrument. I feel bound to tell you that in our opinion we are at your mercy. The Army is disaffected and cannot be relied upon. Trouble has occurred already in a number of camps. We have just emerged from a great war and the people are eager for the reward of their sacrifices, and we are in no position to satisfy them. In these circumstances, if you carry out your threat and strike, then you will defeat us.

' "But if you do so," went on Mr. Lloyd George, "have you weighed the consequences? The strike will be in defiance of the government of the country and by its very success will precipitate a constitutional crisis of the first importance. For, if a force arises in the state which is stronger than the state itself, then it must be ready to take on the functions of the state, or withdraw and accept the authority of the state. Gentlemen," asked the Prime Minister quietly, "have you considered, and if you have, are you ready?" From that moment on,' said Robert Smillie, 'we were beaten and we knew we were.'

After this the General Strike of 1926 was really an anti-climax. The essential argument had been deployed in 1919. But the leaders in 1926 were in no better theoretical position to face it. They had never worked out the revolutionary implications of direct action on such a scale.[24]

More perceptive than many socialists, Lloyd George's cabinet recognised the essential conservative role played by the Labour leaders. In periods of acute class tension, they could be guaranteed to place their full weight behind the preservation of the status quo. As the Tory leader Bonar Law said, referring to the Triple Alliance:

Trade union organisation was the only thing between us and anarchy, and if trade union organisation was against us the position would be hopeless.[25]

Likewise some union leaders were prepared to recognise the part they were performing. T.E. Naylor, of the London Compositors, told the government to remember that, had it not been for their moderating influence, 'the revolution would undoubtedly have broken out.'[26]

As it was, the union leaders went along with the government's policy. Essentially, this was a question of playing for time: ministers wanted the talking between both sides of industry to continue until the revolutionary tide had subsided and the state considered itself thoroughly in command of the situation. So, on 27 February 1919, a National Industrial Conference met. It discussed far-reaching plans for the regulation of industry, the improvement of conditions and the introduction of a universal 48-hour week. The employers' representatives appeared amiable, almost ingratiating in their desire to understand the workers' point of view. Admittedly, they seemed to be more eager to pass resolutions asking the government to initiate improvements than to accept the onus — and expense — on their own shoulders. Yet, nevertheless, they gave the impression that concessions would be made. But as the danger to the social order receded, it became clear that neither the employers nor the government intended to implement the decisions reached. The National Industrial Conference had merely been a talking-shop, a public relations exercise designed to gull the workers.

The same was true of the Sankey Commission on the coal industry. When it issued its interim report, in March 1919, it proposed higher pay, a seven-hour day, later to be reduced to six, and condemned 'the

present system of ownership'. In its final report, published three
months later, the majority of the Sankey Commission called for the
nationalisation of the coal industry. Initially, some of the miners'
union, suspicious of the government's intentions, had been reluctant
to participate in the Commission. Their misgivings, however, had been
allayed when Bonar Law spoke of the earnest sincerity of the government and made the matter a question of his personal integrity. He
wrote to the secretary of the miners' union, Frank Hodges, assuring him
of the government's earnest sincerity:

> Dear Sir,
> . . . I have pleasure in confirming, as I understand you wish me to
> do, my statement that the Government are prepared to carry out in
> the spirit and in the letter the recommendations of Sir John
> Sankey's report.
> Yours faithfully,
A. Bonar Law

Of course, once the emergency had passed, the government quietly for-
got its promises. The recommendations of Mr Justice Sankey suffered
the same fate as those of the National Industrial Conference. Both had
served their purpose; now the talking could stop. As the new relationship of class forces developed, the government felt confident it could
deal with any group of workers. In rapid succession, it crushed the
miners, railwaymen and engineers. The British ruling class again asserted
its supremacy; the period in which its dominance could be seriously
challenged was over.

The crucial question is: was the restoration of capitalist normalcy
inevitable? With greater foresight and knowledge, could socialists have
conquered power and created a new society? An examination of the
SLP, the largest of the revolutionary groups, suggests that broadly
speaking it pursued the correct policy. Its inadequacies did not arise
from policy blunders; rather they resulted from lack of members
and resources. In 1917, as the wave of discontent was rising, the SLP
only possessed 15 branches. This meant that in many parts of the
country where crucial battles were being fought, it had no chance of
participating. Even where it was fortunate enough to have a branch,
the SLP monthly journal could not hope to be topical, commenting
on day-to-day events in the struggle.

Yet, despite these handicaps, the SLP's voice frequently did secure
a hearing. Because its line fitted the needs of the time, militants flocked

into its ranks. In three years, the number of branches had more than trebled. At the same time, the membership had risen to 1,258, almost a third of whom had joined in 1919.[27] Still small, the SLP nevertheless was a force to be reckoned with. Its journal, *The Socialist*, had been made into a weekly in 1919, with a circulation of about 20,000 copies, and as a consequence, could have a bigger impact on industrial affairs.

The SLP's growth helped to change the nature of the Party. In its early days, it had possessed an overwhelmingly Scottish membership. This is probably the basis of the myth, still widely held among students of labour history, that the SLP was largely confined to skilled engineers on the Clyde. But this no longer was true by 1910 and, as the influx of new recruits occurred in the immediate post-war period, it became even less true. Probably, by 1920 four-fifths of the SLPs membership lay South of the Border.

The expansion of the SLP generated tensions inside the Party. The new members brought new experiences and a new outlook into its ranks. Unlike the old-timers, they had not received years of tuition in Marxism at SLP classes and many of them had never read the works of Daniel De Leon. Instead of joining after profound theoretical study, as was the usual practice in the SLP before 1914, these new members' decision to join arose from their experiences in the heat of class conflict. Not generally as theoretically sophisticated, many of them still carried the intellectual baggage from the positions they previously held. Even as thoughtful a man as J.T. Murphy illustrates this point: joining the SLP in 1917, at the age of 29, he had previously been a syndicalist and had imbibed the traditions of the SLP but imperfectly. Murphy's book, *Preparing for Power*, is strewn with factual inaccuracies about the Party.[28] This was not to say that he did not make an important contribution to the SLP — indeed, during his time in the Party he was one of its most talented and hard-working members.

Facing unprecedented situations, with opportunities for intervention not previously known by British revolutionaries, the SLP probably gained through being an admixture of old and new and the tension it generated helped the Party between 1918 and 1920, its most fruitful and creative period.

Typical of its style of working was its participation in the 1918 khaki election. The SLP fought three constituencies — Gorton, Halifax and Ince near Wigan. At one time, it was hoped also to fight Nottingham with Tom Bell, and Camlachie in Glasgow, but in the pre-election rush this idea had to be dropped. Haste, however, had not prevented a careful choice of targets — each constituency was chosen for a purpose.

At Gorton, the sitting MP was the Minister of Pensions. His SLP opponent, J.T. Murphy, had made a special study of the pensions. His pamphlet, *Equality of Sacrifice*, contrasted the vast wealth accruing to arms manufacturers and other industrialists as a result of the war with the scant provisions made for the widows of servicemen and for soldiers permanently disabled. The grim harvest of the conflict, the vast numbers killed and injured, meant that millions of people's lives would be affected by whether or not they obtained pensions and, if they did, how much. As J.T. Murphy saw it, they would only get what they were prepared to struggle for: in his pamphlet he recommended the formation of ex-servicemen's organisations to fight on this issue.

At Halifax, the sitting Member was J. Whitley, whose name is still remembered because he presided over the committee that led to the creation of the Whitley Council, the body that determines pay and conditions in the civil service. Precisely for this reason the SLP decided to fight the seat. It had repeatedly attacked Whitleyism in *The Socialist*. As well as epitomising class collaboration, the Whitley Council by its composition had a built-in bias against the workers.

At Ince, the sitting Member was Stephen Walsh, one of the most right-wing members of the Labour Party. Having held a minor position in the Coalition government, he was reluctant to fight the 1918 general election under the banner of the Labour Party. This incensed many members of the Lancashire & Cheshire Miners' Federation, which sponsored his candidature. At a meeting just before the general election, a resolution calling for his expulsion from the union was narrowly defeated by 868 votes to 853. The SLP put forward a candidate to expose this particular labour lieutenant of capitalism and to appeal to disgruntled miners. Its candidate, William Paul, stated the aim of his campaign:

> I don't know how many votes will be cast for me, and I don't care. The fight as a piece of revolutionary propaganda, is the greatest educational campaign the SLP has ever undertaken. The effect of the great enthusiasm of our meetings, together with the distribution of our literature, must lower the prestige of capitalism and its parliamentary institutions. To have accomplished that is a victory in itself.[29]

Under the pretext of fighting the election, the SLP produced 100,000 copies of its manifesto, calling for the formation of workers' and soldiers' councils. Many found their way to soldiers serving overseas.[30]

In normal circumstances, the distribution of anti-militarist and pro-Soviet Union literature to members of HM Forces would probably have led to prosecution.

The result of the Ince election was that Walsh obtained 14,882 votes as against Paul's 2,231. No Tory or Liberal candidates stood, and their supporters were advised to support the official Labour candidate. As for Paul, he received help from the local ILP and BSP, whom he subsequently thanked. This did not happen at Halifax, where the local ILP refused to campaign for Arthur MacManus. Nevertheless, he gained 4,036 votes. At Gorton, J.T. Murphy did less well, polling 1,300, and again having no help from ILP or BSP.

Throughout the election campaign the SLP suffered from the handicap of being without its printing presses. These had remained immobilised since the police raid on 6 July 1918 (see Chapter eight). The suppression of a socialist paper had caused embarrassment, particularly for Labour members of the Coalition government. In October 1918, when George Barnes tried to justify the ban before the Glasgow Trades Council, he came under heavy fire. As the act of suppression had not been effective — *The Socialist* continued to appear — it was decided, once the war was over, not to stop the SLP from replacing those parts of the two linotype machines that the police had taken away. In January 1919 the presses were once more in working order. Within two hours of the replacement parts arriving, they began printing 20,000 copies of the Clyde Strike Bulletin daily.[31]

The SLP aided the Clydeside struggle for the 40-hour week in other ways. It saw that its one chance of success depended on extending the strike to other parts of the country. So it sent comrades to try and do this. David Ramsay, an Edinburgh engineer, went to London. He was charged with 'preaching sedition and sowing disaffection among the civilian population' while making a speech at the Croydon Cinema. Conducting his own defence, Ramsay claimed words had been added to his speech. The court did not accept this plea and he was given a five-month sentence.[32]

No action, however, was taken against William Paul, who went to South Wales, presumably because the authorities did not wish to anger further the people there. (A secret report to the cabinet, which mentioned Paul's activities, said that 'The main storm centre at the moment is South Wales'.)[33]

In his speeches, Paul constantly referred to the need to link the struggle of the miners with that of the Clydeside engineers: together they stood a very much greater chance of wresting shorter hours from the employers. But he also gave another reason: if the Clyde strike spread 'the government, instead of sending a few thousand soldiers to Glasgow, would be compelled to withdraw all the British soldiers from Russia and Germany, and this would help the Bolsheviks and our German comrades.'[34]

The defeat of the 40-hour strike was regarded by the SLP as a temporary setback. Discussing the lessons to be learnt from it, *The Socialist* said: 'it proved that the government stand behind the ruling class with the whole power of the armed forces to fight Labour'; 'it proved that the trade union leaders in London, who control the large unions, are prepared to betray and blackleg their own members.'[35] Principal culprits were the leaders of the Amalgamated Society of Engineers, who played a vital role in defeating the strike. They suspended the Glasgow and Belfast district committees for supporting the strike and the London district committee for backing attempts to spread it.

Underlying these two lessons of the 40-hour strike was a third, the defects it revealed in revolutionary ranks, which severely disturbed leaders of the SLP. Disunited, belonging to various small groups, the militants were unable to make their potential impact upon events. J.T. Murphy alluded to this in a leading article entitled 'Appeal for a United Effort', which said: 'Strikes are threatening of a magnitude which alarm the governing class . . . and still the socialist movement flounders about and allows petty things to obscure the demands of the international situation.'[36] Arthur MacManus was even more forthright in his criticism:

> With the passing of each succeeding ferment is recorded a loss of opportunity. To make the most of a crisis, the main point of action must be controlled by, and in the hands of, revolutionary socialists. Theoretical differences, so far as discussion is concerned, are of little moment, in this intense dynamic surge, the extent of each particular school's success being ultimately determined by the actual amount of work done.[37]

Mindful of the need for left unity, the SLP had held a special conference at Glasgow on 11-12 January 1919. The delegates unanimously agreed to suspend the Party constitution so that none of its provisions could impede unity negotiations. The conference also endorsed 'A Manifesto: A Plea for the Reconsideration of Socialist Tactics and Organisation'. This document declared that the aim of socialists should be to achieve working class unity, both industrially and politically, but to be truly socialist this could only be done on a revolutionary basis. With that important proviso, the SLP were prepared to join with comrades with whom it had theoretical differences: 'The organisation should be all-embrasive.'

The spirit in which this manifesto was compiled was explained by an editorial in *The Socialist*:

> Four years of world war and one year of revolution in Russia have taught the SLP many things. It has revealed the weakness of the organisation of the revolutionary movement in this country. Our manifesto indicates where the weakness lies, and seeks to outline a new basis of organisation. It is neither issued as a bigoted cate- chism nor as a dogmatic pronouncement. It is placed before the movement to provide the basis for discussion.[38]

Copies of the manifesto were sent to the BSP and ILP, as well as to socialist journals. The tortuous negotiations over unity which finally led to the formation of the British Communist Party will be discussed in a later chapter. But what is worth considering here is whether there was potentially a revolutionary situation at that time. Had a Commu- nist Party existed at that time and seized the opportunities, could capitalism have been vanquished?

Definitely, Gallacher thought there was:

> We had possibilities of winning great new forces to our side if we had only the necessary revolutionary understanding and audacity. Revolt was seething everywhere, especially in the army. We had within our hands the possibility of giving actual expression and leadership to it, but it never entered our heads to do so. We were carrying on a strike when we ought to have been making a revolution.[39]

In retrospect, the SLP made rather a different analysis. Writing in *The Socialist*, of 3 January 1922, James Clunie said:

> According to Sir Basil Thomson, the most critical period in this country after the war was the beginning of 1919. Caused by the delay in demobilisation, the insufficient aftermath preparation, and the general temper of the soldiers and sailors. That it was a critical period let us further agree. But do not let us be carried away with the idea that the situation was one that could have given rise to revolutionary change.

In my opinion, the weight of evidence tends to confirm the view of James Clunie. It would appear to have been objective conditions that were responsible for no revolution occurring in Britain, the comparative lack of severity of the crisis of British capitalism and therefore its failure to be reflected in an acute form *inside and throughout* the working class. Even had an active and vigorous Communist Party existed, it would have been unable materially to have altered the situation. The reasons for holding this opinion are:

1. Economic conditions in Britain were not as bad as those in countries where revolutions did break out. In 1917 the Russian economy ground to a halt, in 1918 the Germany economy collapsed exhausted. No similar strains were felt in Britain, which emerged from the war as one of the victors.

2. The workers' rank-and-file movements were relatively weak. The shop stewards' movement had major deficiencies: (i) it was largely confined to skilled men; (ii) many industries and many areas were without shop stewards' committees altogether; (iii) where they did exist, they were often small and ineffective; (iv) they were usually preoccupied with local issues; (v) the leadership of the various committees, as well as their memberships' were at various stages of development. The overall effect of these shortcomings was to make joint action difficult and sustained action impossible. As an independent industrial force, the shop stewards' movement ceased to exist by 1920.

3. The ability of the official trade union leaders, who never lost control, to divert working class militancy into channels that were harmless to the system. Their policy of class collaboration, the traditional policy accepted by the British working class, still possessed powerful appeal. Once the class action initiated by flimsy unofficial committees petered out, it tended to discredit the notion of class action altogether. The TU leaders were able to sell the way of caution and compromise as the most sensible to follow.

4. The political immaturity of the working class. By relatively tranquil progress, continued virtually for three-quarters of a century, the British proletariat had been steeped in evolutionist, reformist ideas; a belief in modest gains made under the aegis of that venerated institution, Parliament. Significantly, a sizeable proportion of working people still enthusiastically supported the Tory and Liberal Parties, the open and avowed advocates of capitalism. Even the one party that, albeit timidly and hesitantly, criticised a few aspects of the

existing system — the Labour Party — secured very little support from the working class. At the 1918 general election, the Liberal-Conservative coalition under Lloyd George romped back to power with 478 MPs; the Labour Party obtained a mere 63 seats. Significantly, on the 'Red Clyde', only one of the fifteen Glasgow constituencies was won by a Labour candidate. The overall evidence does not point to class consciousness being deeply and widely rooted in the British working class at the end of the First World War.

5. Although there were undoubtedly grumblings within the armed forces, the main body of the military remained loyal to the State. Against the disaffection, mentioned earlier in this chapter, which at the outside involved a quarter of a million men, it must be remembered that the overwhelming majority of the 3½ million soldiers did not mutiny. Moreover, the most extreme acts of defiance could be construed in a different way: when sailors hoisted the Red Flag, it may have been not so much a sign of political commitment as simply a gesture of defiance, an expression of disgust about demobilisation delays. In the opinion of the Home Office, one of the influences dampening revolutionary enthusiasm in 1919 was the troops returning home. Most of them, it was claimed, came back with a feeling of antagonism towards those whom they thought had been troublemakers and shirkers during the war.[40]

6. Last, but most important of all, the British working class failed to develop workers' and soldiers' councils. These were the pre-requisite of a revolutionary transformation: only if they existed would there be an alternative power-base to capitalist rule. In Russia, the workers spontaneously created their own workers' and soldiers' councils, the soviets, without any instructions coming from the Bolsheviks. The task of Lenin and his comrades was to raise the demand 'All power to the soviets'. In Britain, such a call hardly had a realistic ring about it. The workers' committees went out of being or became hollow shells soon after the war ended. The London Workers' Committee's influence can be gauged, to some extent, by the support given its journal. In 1918, *Solidarity*'s circulation was 10,000 copies, hardly an impressive figure, but by 1919 it had shrunk to a mere 3,000 copies.[41] As we have already seen, the Clyde Workers' Committee, which had been the strongest in the country, never recovered from the débâcle of the 40-hours strike.

For these reasons, I do not consider a revolutionary situation existed in Britain after the First World War. There must, however, be an important proviso made: had the German Revolution been successful, it would have altered the entire relationship of class forces. The position of the British left would have been much stronger. But at the time socialists thought that other events might have given them an opportunity. They envisaged the possibility of Ireland going socialist or the possibility of British involvement in the war of intervention against Russia leading to extensive disaffection among the troops and heavy expenditure that proved too great a burden for this country's economy. The solidarity shown by socialists for events in Ireland and Russia will be dealt with in the next chapter.

Notes

1. Basil Thomson, *The Scene Changes*, p. 410.
2. R. Higham, *Armed Forces in Peacetime* (1962) p. 21.
3. CAB. 44 GT 3838.
4. CAB. 24/57 GT 6603. I.P. Hughes, among the first batch of organisers appointed by the Communist Party, remained active in politics throughout his life. In his later years, he became a member of the International Socialism Group. He died in 1972.
5. A useful account of events in Sheffield is contained in Bill Moore's pamphlet, *Sheffield Shop Stewards in the First World War*, published in the Our History series, No. 18. Also, Dr J. Hinton, *The First Shop Stewards' Movement* (1974) pp. 162-77 which gives a more analytical account.
6. *War Memoirs of Lloyd George* (1933-6) p. 1149; J.T. Murphy, *New Horizons*, pp. 54-5; J.T. Murphy, *Preparing for Power*, pp. 135-7.
7. W. Kendall, *The Revolutionary Movement in Britain*, p. 371.
8. At first, Arthur MacManus refused to sign. When all the other imprisoned shop stewards agreed, he fell in with the majority opinion.
9. Air Ministry Weekly Orders for 7 November 1918, 1380-1433; *Aeroplane,* 13 November 1918.
10. *Glasgow Evening News*, 8 March 1919.
11. *Sheffield Telegraph*, 16 March 1919.
12. War Cabinet, 31 January 1919. CAB.23/9.
13. *The Times*, 30 January 1919. According to Cole and Postgate, the Red Flag was also raised by servicemen stationed at Kinmel Park, near Rhyl.
14. *Glasgow Herald*, 28 and 29 January 1919.
15. *The Socialist*, 16 October 1919. Other committees were suffering similar financial difficulties. The *Workers' Dreadnought*, of 17 January 1920, cites one workers' committee that contributed £88 to headquarters in 1918, but only £4 the following year.
16. CAB.77 GT 7254. 14 May 1919. Also H. Pollitt, *Serving My Time* (1940), p. 107.
17. James Hinton, op. cit., pp. 226-8.
18. *The Socialist*, 17 July 1919.
19. CAB.96 CP.462. 'Survey of Revolutionary Feeling 1919', p. 4. The other steadying influences cited were (i) the Royal Family, (ii) workers' pre-occupation with sport, (iii) the poverty of revolutionary organisations, (iv) soldiers returning from the armed forces, (v) disunity inside trade unions,

and (vi) increases in wages.

20. CAB.24/118. CP.2455. 'A Survey of Revolutionary Movements in Great Britain in the year 1920', by The Directorate of Intelligence (HQ) p. 11.
21. Letter from James Messer to Herbert Highton, 15 October 1917.
22. *Railway Review*, 13 June 1919.
23. Lloyd George's comments were made at cabinet meetings on 4 April and 5 April 1921.
24. Aneurin Bevan, *In Place of Fear* (1952) pp. 40-1.
25. CAB.23/9.
26. G.D.H. Cole, and R. Postgate, *The Common People*, p. 550.
27. Report of SLP Carlisle conference, 3-4 April 1920.
28. Among the errors in J.T. Murphy's book are: (i) that the SLP was centred on Scotland (p. 87), (ii) that the SLP accepted the pseudo-syndicalist ideas expressed in Connolly's pamphlet, 'Socialism made Easy' (pp. 87-8), (iii) most SLP members became conscientious objectors in the First World War (p. 106), (iv) the SLP pursued a purely sectarian policy (p. 208).
29. *The Socialist*, December 1918.
30. Tom Bell, *British Communist Party* (1937) pp. 49-50.
31. *The Socialist*, 20 and 27 February 1919.
32. Ibid.
33. CAB.77. GT 7091.
34. William Paul's speech aroused the wrath of Robert Blatchford, the editor of *Clarion*, who denounced him in the *Sunday Pictorial*, 23 May 1919.
35. *The Socialist*, 20 February 1919.
36. Ibid, 5 June 1919.
37. Ibid, 6 March 1919.
38. Ibid, January 1919.
39. W. Gallacher, *Revolt on the Clyde*, p. 221.
40. See Note 19.
41. *Workers' Dreadnought*, 17 January 1919. It is worth comparing the puny circulation of British left-wing journals with the position in Russia before the October Revolution. There were six socialist dailies being published in Petrograd alone.

10 LENIN AND THE BRITISH COMMUNIST PARTY

The October Revolution endowed its custodians with immense prestige. In British left-wing circles, the majority of comrades hung on every word issuing from Moscow. Lenin, in particular, had an opportunity to exert great influence on the socialist movement. He was not, however, in a position to use his chances to the full. The exigencies of the Revolution, the attempts by armies of intervention to overthrow the Soviet State, as well as the multifarious problems associated with the building of the new international, all resulted in great demands on Lenin's time. He was not able to study the British political scene in depth, to acquire a thorough grasp of the subject on which to base his analysis. So his remarks should not be regarded as pronouncements of the Revolutionary Almighty, handed down from some red Mount Sinai, but subjected to critical scrutiny. When this is done, many of them are shown to be inaccurate or — perhaps more important — based upon inadequate information.

In a sense, Lenin was a victim of his own success. Throughout his life, he applied the Marxist method with consummate skill. He understood completely that the truth was concrete. His colossal literary output indicates that he studied Russian events in tremendous detail and sought to relate them to socialist theory and practice. This was an arduous task. Yet it was vital if the Bolsheviks were to be able to make those penetrating analyses that, by clearly showing what was to be done, guided Russian workers along the road to revolution. Other things had to be subordinated to this overriding objective. The comprehensive study of Russian affairs necessarily meant that Lenin had less time to devote to developments elsewhere, and his references to Britain are few and usually perfunctory. Even before the October Revolution made such inordinate demands upon him, Lenin never got the feel of the British working-class movement. It was as if he had adopted a self-denying ordinance not to become involved in what, at that time, he saw as a peripheral issue, but to husband all his resources for the job of smashing capitalism in Russia.

In 1902-3, Lenin lived in London, producing Numbers 22 to 38 of the journal *Iskra,* The Spark, from the offices of the SDF in Clerkenwell Green. Although this was a period of great discussion inside the Social Democratic Federation, Lenin makes no mention of it in his writings.

He appears to have been quite content to share a room with Harry
Quelch and to remain on friendly personal terms with his SDF hosts.
The fact that Quelch was Hyndman's hatchetman, responsible for the
expulsion of James Connolly and the left wing of the SDF, seems to
have escaped his notice. Likewise Lenin did not appear to know that
Quelch, like the rest of the SDF leadership, had a weakness for unprincipled electoral alliances, a penchant he displayed during the
Dewsbury bye-election, or that Quelch thought that strikes were super-
fluous and largely irrelevant to the struggle for socialism. So, when
Quelch died in September 1913, Lenin wrote a warm tribute to him,
recalling their friendship, and saying: 'Quelch was in the front ranks of
those who fought steadfastly and with conviction against opportunism.'[1]

An equally strange use of the term opportunism comes in Lenin's
references to the *Daily Herald*. In his report on the Labour Party conference of 1912, he talks about 'the opportunist *Daily Herald*' whereas
in November 1914 he refers to it as 'the organ of the opponents of
opportunism'.[2] This inconsistency is made less explicable by the change
of attitude of the *Daily Herald* during these two years: in 1912, it
wholeheartedly supported, albeit in a confused way, the massive
strikes that were taking place; by contrast, in 1914 the paper no longer
advocated industrial action but supported industrial peace in the
interests of the war effort.[3] Lenin's statement on 1 November 1914
creates further problems. He declared:

> With the British, the Hyndman group (the British Social Democrats
> – the British Socialist Party) has completely sunk into chauvinism,
> as have also most of the semi-liberal leaders of the trade unions.
> Resistance to chauvinism has come from MacDonald and Keir Hardie
> of the opportunist Independent Labour Party. This, of course, is an
> exception to the rule.[4]

While it is debatable whether Lenin was correct to identify 'the
Hyndman group' with the entire membership of the BSP or to say that
the BSP had *completely* sunk into chauvinism', there can be no doubt
that his characterisation of MacDonald and Keir Hardie's attitude to the
war was factually incorrect (see Chapter Six). Only a few months
earlier, Lenin had made an evaluation of the left in Britain. He has said
that the BSP alone had 'been carrying on systematic propaganda and
agitation in the Marxist spirit.'[5]

His inconsistencies and inaccuracies ranged from matters of theoretical principle to points of trivial detail. In her autobiography of her

father, Nan Milton points out that Lenin usually referred to John
Maclean as 'John Maclean of England' — a description that may well
have irked a man so proud of his Scottish heritage.[6] Similarly, in the
following quotation there is a hint that Lenin thought the SLP in Scotland was separate and distinct from the SLP in England instead of being
part of the same organisation:

> Of the three socialist parties in England, only one, the independent
> Socialist Labour Party, is openly becoming an ally of the Bolsheviks,
> while the Socialist Labour Party in Scotland definitely declares itself
> to be an adherent of the Bolsheviks. Bolshevism is beginning to
> spread in England also.[7]

This statement was made at a time when the Bolsheviks were trying to
get a regrouping of revolutionary forces in Britain. It was during this
period that Lenin's influence in this country was at its greatest and also
had its most disastrous effects on the development of revolutionary organisation in Britain.

As parliamentary illusions were deeply embedded in working-class
consciousness, Lenin rightly saw that it was vital for the newly-formed
British Communist Party to differentiate itself clearly from reformism.
At the same time, it had to wean the masses away from their beliefs in
constitutionalism and the traditional parties and this, claimed Lenin,
could only be done if the CP established a meaningful dialogue with the
class. This theoretical position seems acceptable; where it fell down was
in practical, tactical application. Lenin linked it with a faulty analysis
of the Labour Party, situated in British conditions he did not really
comprehend. Erroneously, Lenin believed that the Labour Party was a
mass party, a party with millions of worker-activists; that the Communist Party would be freely permitted to join it; and that belonging to the
Labour Party would enhance the Communist Party's influence and
growth. All these contentions are wrong. Let us examine more fully in
turn.

Speaking about the Labour Party at the Second Congress of the
Communist International, Lenin declared:

> The members of the Labour Party are all members of trade unions.
> The structure of this party is a very peculiar one and is unlike that in
> any other country. This organisation embraces from six to seven
> million workers belonging to all the trade unions. The members are
> not asked what political convictions they adhere to.[8]

Actually, Lenin's figures were two to three million out. The Labour Party claimed a membership of 4,360,000 in 1920.[9] By far the major portion were trade unionists, paying the political levy. As nobody of significance on the Left advocated contracting out of this levy, all were agreed that communists should participate in any political debates within the trade unions, discussing how their unions should cast their votes at Labour Party conferences. Communists could even be elected as delegates to the Labour Party conference, or be union-sponsored election candidates fighting on a Labour ticket. Until revisions of the Labour Party constitution were introduced, nothing stopped CPers from being individual members of the Labour Party, and at the 1923 Labour Party conference there were 30 communist delegates. In the December 1923 general election, the CP put forward nine candidates, seven of whom stood under the Labour Party banner. Indeed, the Party even had two Members of Parliament, Saklatvala and J.T. Walton Newbold, returned as Labour MPs.

So the issue of formal affiliation would not have made an appreciable difference to the position of the Communist Party in relation to the Labour Party, and it is difficult to understand why Lenin attached such great importance to it. All it would have meant would have been that a handful of delegates, bearing the communist label, would have been allowed to attend Labour annual conference and cast a derisory number of votes for their organisation.

Lenin's position becomes more inexplicable when the record of communists operating within the Labour Party is examined. Their lack of success would tend to suggest that the Labour Party was not a particularly fruitful field for recruitment of new CP members. Nor were there any perceptible signs that, under communist pressure, the Labour Party was moving in the direction of being a fighting socialist organisation. In these circumstances, it is difficult to see why Lenin regarded it so vital to acquire affiliation. Perhaps he confused paper membership with active membership. Most local Labour Party branches were tiny cliques, preoccupied with elections, not centres of mass struggle involving large numbers of workers. To enter their dismal committee rooms and become involved in the routine of electoral intrigue would merely waste revolutionaries' valuable time and energy, which could be better spent elsewhere.

Then, to turn to Lenin's second contention, he appears to have had an exaggerated idea of the freedom of expression the Labour leaders permitted. Politicians like Henderson and MacDonald were not exactly overflowing with brotherly toleration. Yet Lenin told delegates to the

Second Congress of the Communist International that the Labour Party
'is a very peculiar party . . . (It) allows sufficient liberty to all political
parties to affiliate to it.' No shadow of doubt existed in Lenin's mind
that a newly-formed British Communist Party would be allowed to bask
in this liberty:

> Comrades Gallacher and Sylvia Pankhurst cannot deny that. They
> cannot deny the fact that while remaining in the ranks of the Labour
> Party, the British Socialist Party enjoys sufficient liberty to write
> that such and such leaders of the Labour Party are traitors, cham-
> pions of the interests of the bourgeoisie and their agents in the
> Labour movement; this is absolutely true. When Communists enjoy
> such liberty, then, taking into account the experience in all coun-
> tries, and not only in Russia (for we here are not a Russian but an
> international congress), it is their duty to affiliate to the Labour
> Party.[10]

Of course, it *was* possible for Gallacher and Pankhurst to deny Lenin's
assertion. Indeed, the passage of a few months proved them correct.
The Labour Party National Executive Committee turned down a CP
application for affiliation. When this decision came before the Labour
conference for ratification, Emmanuel — now Lord — Shinwell
pointed out what it should surely have been the job of the communists
to stress, namely, that fundamental issues of principles divided social
democracy from communism, while Henderson warned that CPers
could not be expected to adhere to the Labour Party constitution. The
conference rejected the application by 4,115,000 to 224,000.[11]

In Lenin's speeches there was no mention of the fact that in 1918
the Labour Party's constitution had been drastically changed, that the
hitherto federal structure had been replaced by a much more tightly-
controlled set-up, eventually compelling the mildly leftish ILP to realise
that even it could not function properly and remain affiliated. For a
genuine CP, affiliation was never on. Lenin had, moreover, a highly
romanticised conception of how the BSP had operated in the pre-1918
period: it never attempted to mount an organised and concerted campaign against the Labour Establishment, and had it done so, it would
almost certainly have been expelled. Even with a federal structure, such
conduct would not be admissible.

On Lenin's third contention, that affiliation to the Labour Party
would enhance the CP's influence and growth, it becomes more difficult
to give a definite answer. As it did not happen, then it must remain a

matter for speculation. Nevertheless, it is worth pointing out that the Labour Party has always contained some members closely connected with the CP, who have put forward CP policies at every opportunity. These 'fellow-travellers' have never met with much success — indeed, over the years their influence has tended to wane — and it seems probable that the same fate would have befallen the Communist Party had it ever affiliated.

What is less open to conjecture is the effect of raising the question of affiliation on the infant Communist Party. 'Comrade Gallacher is wrong when he says that by advocating affiliation to the Labour Party we will repel the best elements of the British workers,' claimed Lenin. 'We must test this by experience.' And so it was, with disastrous consequences. It alienated the overwhelming majority of potential members. The SLP, in the forefront of the organisations wanting regroupment, immediately withdrew from negotiations. The WSF also stood aloof, as did most of the shop stewards, including the Scottish Workers' Committee.

But Lenin appears to have remained oblivious to what was happening. On 8 July 1920, he wrote a letter to British communists that indicated he still believed the SLP were taking part in unity negotiations. On 18 July 1920, *L'Humanité*, official organ of the French CP, built on this error with a statement, later quoted in the British Press, to the effect that 'Lenin considers that Sylvia Pankhurst and the Workers' Socialist Federation are wrong in refusing to link up with the Socialist Labour Party.' Since the SLP had said categorically that it did not want to belong to a Communist Party which was affiliated to the Labour Party, the quote from Lenin was tantamount to an incitement to form a revolutionary organisation outside the Communist Party — that is, if Lenin really knew what he was saying. A more likely explanation is that he was totally out of touch with what was happening in Britain. A sign of this is the way he consistently over-estimates the strength of the BSP and other groups. Referring to the last BSP conference in April 1920, he wrote: 'The latest Congress of the British Socialist Party, held in London three or four days ago, decided to assume the name of the Communist Party . . . 10,000 organised members were represented at this conference.'[12] Apparently, Lenin was unaware that the sole commitment required for BSP membership was the payment of a shilling a year to the party's national funds. Probably far fewer than 10,000 people did that. The figure of 10,000 was the number on which the BSP affiliated to the Labour Party, and it seems likely that the party leaders, conscious of the weakness of the BSP, deliberately inflated its numerical strength. And even of those who held membership cards, many were 'sleepers', not activists in the BSP or subsequently in the Communist Party. Referring to the mysterious 10,000, Bob Stewart, the first Scottish organiser of the CP, remarked: 'There were thousands I never saw, and I very much doubt if anyone else ever saw them.'[13]

Besides exaggerating BSP support, Lenin was equally mistaken about the strength of Gallacher's Communist Labour Party in Scotland. In the already-quoted speech, Lenin goes on to say that a further 10,000 would join the new organisation when the Communist Labour Party fused with it. In reality, Gallacher brought in only one or two hundred.[14] From all sources, the CPGB started off with a membership of around 3,000, which dropped to 2,000 by mid-1922. This is the estimate of James Klugmann, who wrote the official history of the CPGB and must have had access to confidential party membership records. Tom Bell, who, since he played a leading part in the formation of the CP, was well-placed to make a judgement, puts the figure slightly lower — 2,000 to 2,500 were, according to him, represented at the founding conference.[15] So it would seem that total membership was only slightly over a tenth of what Lenin estimated. We can accept that Lenin was misinformed, but equally inescapable is the conclusion that a large proportion of militants shunned the affiliationist Communist Party.

The unpopularity of the Communist Party stemmed from several sources. From the outset, it did not look as if it was a natural growth, springing from the experiences of the British working-class. Instead, it appeared to be under Russian domination, which raised issues at the behest of Moscow rather than having its ear to the grievances of workers in this country. Suspicions were further heightened because the old BSP, an organisation discredited in the eyes of many militants, formed its nucleus.

It is in this context that the issue of affiliation to the Labour Party must be viewed. Many of the BSP, with deeply engrained reformist illusions, wanted the Communist Party to continue in the old ways of the BSP. They did not want to be in the Labour Party to fight an unremitting battle with the right-wing leadership, but to maintain their position as the left wing of social democracy. In April 1920, at the BSP's final conference before it merged into the CP, delegates debated their attitude to parliamentary and local elections. A resolution was moved that 'this conference considers the time ripe when all candidates should stand as socialists based on the class war.' This was defeated by 48 votes to 26. As J.T. Murphy pointed out:

The BSP takes pride in the election of members to the Municipal Councils; but their election is not a signal for revolutionary agitation therein. They accepted departmental office and become part of the administrative machinery of capitalism.[16]

The newly-formed Communist Party continued this practice (and has done so to the present day). It was proud when its members were elected to local authorities. As Mayor of Bethnel Green, Joe Vaughan of the CP flaunted the mayoral regalia and behaved like any other worshipful first citizen. He made pious speeches at municipal functions, not militant speeches at strike meetings. Some other communist councillors behaved even worse than Joe: Edgar Lansbury and A.A. Watts, mindful of the need to keep down the rates, voted for a 10 per cent cut in outdoor Poor Relief. For good measure, they also voted for cuts in the wages of local authority workers. When Sylvia Pankhurst criticised their conduct, the secretary of the Bow Communist Party wrote to rebuke her and remind her of party discipline. Strangely in a party of the workers, there was no suggestion of disciplining Lansbury and Watts.[17]

A similarly indulgent attitude was adopted to the solitary Communist MP. Lt.-Col. Cecil John L'Estrange Malone had been elected on a Lloyd George Liberal ticket at the 1918 general election. After visiting Russia a year later, he moved leftwards and became a founder of the Communist Party. A small but significant incident occurred at a meeting of ex-servicemen in his constituency. The chairman asked all those assembled to salute the Union Jack. Everybody, with the exception of W.H. Bain, did so. Then a Red Flag was held up, and the chairman asked the meeting if the meeting would like to salute it. Nobody, except Bain, did so. Some ex-servicemen then set upon him, and the disturbance led to Bain, in the true tradition of British justice, being fined by local magistrates. As the incident happened in his constituency and he was an ex-serviceman himself, Colonel Malone was asked to comment. Whereupon he expressed surprise 'that anyone should object to the Union Jack.'[18]

It may well be that the behaviour of the BSP and, later, Communist Party representatives on local councils and in Parliament contributed to Sylvia Pankhurst's change of mind. She did not always oppose the contesting of parliamentary elections. In the 1918 general election she called upon people to vote Labour and went out of her way to applaud the SLP for using the electoral opportunity to propagate revolutionary ideas.[19] What she objected to was the primary orientation of the organisation becoming the battle for votes, instead of industrial work being given pride of place. In a letter to Lenin, she explained:

> The Labour Movement in England is being ruined under my eyes by
> parliamentary and municipal politics. Both leaders and masses are
> only waiting for elections, and, while preparing for the election
> campaign, are quite forgetting the socialist work. Nay, they totally
> suppress all socialist propaganda in order not to frighten the
> electors.[20]

This subordination of all other considerations to electoral advancement
was made all the more pitiful by the pathetic performance of the handful of candidates returned. Sylvia Pankhurst thought their existence
could only be justified if they attempted to build fortresses of local
resistance to the capitalist state. Replying to a councillor who thought
this impractical, she wrote:

> But perhaps the unemployed will urge: do something illegal; do not
> wait for government sanction; defy the government . . . Set us to
> build houses to replace the slum property that ought to be pulled
> down; seize the pits that have been closed down and let us work
> them; seize the land lying idle; open boot and clothing shops.[21]

Sylvia Pankhurst went on to contrast communist councillors quietly
obeying the law with the Sinn Fein in Ireland setting up its own illegal
administration in defiance of the British state. Pointing to the failure
of communist councillors even to make socialist speeches, she asked:
'Where, indeed, are to be found Communist Party representatives on
local bodies using their position on the bodies in a revolutionary way?
Where are those communists? Let us hear of them. Echo answering
"where?" has long given the only response to that urgent question.'[22]
Sylvia Pankhurst continued with a denunciation of existing CP representatives for their failure to implement the thesis of the Communist
International on the conduct of members elected to public bodies.

She was never a theoretician, with a firm grasp of Marxism; her
significance came from a tremendous courage and dedication, a total
commitment to the struggle of working people, particularly working
women, in the East End of London. Therefore, while her criticism of
the practices of CPers on local councils and in Parliament had considerable validity, she nevertheless drew false conclusions from sound criticisms. She went so far as to call for, as a matter of principle, the abstention of the Communist Party from the electoral struggle. At that

particular time, it might, posed as a tactic, have been a tenable position. It could be argued that the CP of the early 1920s, small in membership and influence, had many more pressing calls on its limited resources. In a similar way, organisations like International Socialism in the late 1960s, which probably had a membership roughly equal to that of the CP forty years earlier, did not contest elections: they devoted their meagre resources to the industrial struggle, whereas the CPGB in that period, having a fetish about 'the parliamentary road to socialism', squandered energy and money to prove its diminishing support among the voters.

Because Sylvia Pankhurst raised the issue of electoral abstention as one of principle rather than merely a tactical question, she exposed herself to unnecessary political attacks. Lenin concentrated his fire on her demand for abstention; he did not deal with the underlying reason for her making it. Lenin's role can be seen as one of fighting the tendencies towards ultra-leftism in the British movement, while having far less to say about those towards reformism, which were much stronger and more dangerous.

In politics, it is important not only to say the right thing but to say it at the right time. Lenin's call for affiliation to the Labour Party, coupled with his criticism of leftists like Gallacher and Pankhurst, must be in its setting: given that the BSPers predominated in the Communist Party, it merely tended to reinforce the right-wing within the organisation. True, that had not been Lenin's intention, but, as he did not possess firm knowledge of the British political scene, this was the unintentional effect of his intervention.

Ideas must always be considered in their political context. The ideas of De Leon had a differing impact in America and in Britain: the same theories which remained politically sterile when espoused by German emigrés living in the United States had a seminal influence on the British labour movement when propagated by Clydeside engineers. Unlike those of De Leon, Lenin's ideas had an exceedingly mixed influence in this country. Of course, there is no doubt of his greatness – genius – as a theoretician. In the Britain of 50 years ago, the study of his writings brought new vigour to the socialist movement. Yet, at the same time, there were two sides to the statement of accounts: debits as well as credits.

We have already seen that the incisiveness of Lenin's critique was blunted, to some extent, because he did not possess either a detailed knowledge of British politics or a feel for the working-class movement. Adding to these problems was the fact that his writings were frequently badly translated. J.T. Murphy raised this point with him, and Lenin readily acknowledged the deficiency.[23] But it does not appear to have been rectified. What was even more serious was that, as Lenin was otherwise engaged, with little time to study British affairs, his mantle fell upon men of much lesser calibre. Claiming to speak for the Communist International, these emissaries from Moscow frequently gave garbled versions of what were Lenin's views and, whenever possible, gave their own right-wing interpretations of what should be done.

This was a period of grave emergency, when the existence of Soviet power was threatened by enemies at home and abroad. Obviously, in these circumstances, the dedicated Russian communist was likely to feel that he was most needed at home. With the necessity of safeguarding the revolution paramount, it is hardly surprising that men of lesser consequence tended to be sent as representatives of the Comintern to such countries as Britain.

A Comintern agent with a big influence on the CPGB in its formative years was D. Petrovsky, who worked in Britain under the alias of Bennett. According to Trotsky, he was 'a Bundist-Menshevik of the American, i.e. the worst, school', who had returned to Russia from the United States in 1917. Only then did he become a Bolshevik and, for a while, was employed on military work. Trotsky described Petrovsky's dominant characteristic as 'organic opportunism'.[24] Presumably, he was sent to Britain because he was one of the few English-speaking operators who could be spared.

Of much more importance than Petrovsky was the Comintern's first representative in Britain, Theodore Rothstein, who played a leading role in the creation of the Communist Party. It was largely under his guidance that the unity negotiations took place. He possessed the funds, the much-vaunted 'Russian Gold', to distribute among the various left-wing organisations. While it may be that a historian like Walter Kendall attaches too much importance to the influence of money, there can be no doubt that financially hard-pressed socialist groups in Britain must have been sorely tempted to toe the line and get the cash.

How Theodore Rothstein used his position can best be understood through an examination of his political principles. Although born in Russia, he had lived in Britain for many years and had been active in the SDF and, later, the BSP. When the James Connolly-Hyndman dispute led to the formation of the SLP, Rothstein sided with Hyndman and the right-wing of the Federation. It was he who dubbed Connolly and his followers 'the Unholy Scotch Current'. In 1907, when the Russian

Social Democratic Party held its congress in London, Rothstein again
sided with the right-wing and against the Bolsheviks. He wrote in
Justice:

> A portion of the Social Democrats, the Lenin section, say that the
> proletariat has to go hand in hand with the revolutionary peasantry
> and fight the treacherous bourgeoisie. This sounds very plausible and
> very revolutionary since the proletariat, together with the peasantry,
> would probably be able to bring the revolution to a victorious issue,
> even without the assistance of the bourgeoisie. Unfortunately, not
> everything which sounds plausible and revolutionary is in reality so,
> and in our opinion the other section of Russian Social Democracy,
> that under Plekhanov, is nearer the truth . . . Is there any sane man
> at the present who doubts that the present Revolution in Russia
> cannot lead to socialism, but must end in the substitution of a bour-
> geois regime for the present autocracy?[25]

Rothstein's disagreements with Lenin continued. During the First
World War, he never adopted the revolutionary stance of the Bolsheviks.
In a letter written in early 1916, Lenin had occasion to write: 'We are
naturally in full agreement with Ornatsky in his polemic with T. Rothstein, a correspondent of *Kommunist*, who takes a Kautskyite attitude.'
Lenin went on to say that Rothstein still supported the Second International and did not see the necessity for the creation of a new international.[26] In a pamphlet, *Essays on War and Peace,* published by the
BSP in 1917, Rothstein reveals that he had not advanced any further
towards a Leninist position: instead of calling for an end of the war
through socialist revolution, he wished to see a negotiated peace.

It is instructive to read Rothstein on the situation in Russia during
1917. Writing in *Plebs* (August 1917), he described the Russian revolutionaries as being characterised by 'jealousy, quarrelsomeness, and
excessive predilection for theoretical niceties.' He backed the entry of
the Mensheviks into the Provisional Government, describing it as 'a
great step which marked the official triumph of the revolutionary proletariat.' By contrast, he criticised the 'violent opposition of the
Leninites.' Clearly, Kendall is correct in his opinion that 'Rothstein
does not seem to have declared for Bolshevism until after the October
Revolution.'[27] And it is legitimate to question how deep the conver-
sion actually was.

In forming the Communist Party, Rothstein naturally looked first to
those who had been his comrades for many years in the BSP. Most of

the financial subvention from Russia went to them, and it was around them that the new party was formed. This was at variance with the original intention of the Communist International. In its manifesto, published in April 1919, it invited forty organisations throughout the world to join in forming the new organisation. Of these, five were British:[28] the BSP, 'particularly that tendency represented by Maclean',[29] the Socialist Labour Party,[30] the IWW of England,[31] the International Workers of Great Britain, and the Shop Stewards' Movement.

While it must remain a matter for speculation as to the exact extent to which Rothstein himself was responsible for the outcome, the strange fact is that none of the above organisations, with the exception of the BSP, actually came into the Communist Party. And even in this instance, the group specifically mentioned, that around John Maclean, appears to have been debarred. In his 'Open letter to Lenin', Maclean alleged that Rothstein arranged his secret expulsion from the BSP.[28] When the last BSP conference was held, Maclean tried to attend as the delegate from Tradeston branch, but Ernest Cant and the conference arrangements committee would not accept his credentials. From then on, Maclean was effectively debarred from participating in the negotiations that led to the formation of the Communist Party. This may well have been because of Rothstein's influence behind the scenes.[29]

In the spring of 1920, John Maclean had journeyed to London to meet Rothstein, then the Comintern's official representative. A quarrel had broken out between the two men. Ostensibly, it was caused by Maclean's refusal to accept the job Rothstein had allocated to him. (It is interesting to note that Rothstein had the power to appoint people in this way). According to both the Gallacher and McShane reports of the meeting, Rothstein wanted Maclean to devote all his energies to the 'Hands Off Russia' campaign.[30] Though not averse to participating in this campaign, Maclean refused to accept a full-time post; he believed that to continue lecturing on Marxism and building a revolutionary organisation would be more valuable.

Underlying this disagreement about what may, at first glance, appear a comparatively trivial tactical point lurked conflicts of a personal and political character. Rothstein and Maclean even appear to have been in dispute about how the new Communist Party should be built. Rothstein, with more rightist conceptions, wished to open the floodgates as wide as possible. Into the party would come many politically confused and naive individuals. These, in the course of time, would either develop sounder ideas or, by a winnowing process, fall by the wayside.

Maclean, on the other hand, in his 'Open Letter to Lenin', complained that

> those who are coming together are a heterogeneous mixture of anarchists, sentimentalists, syndicalists, with a sprinkling of Marxists. Unity in such a camp is likely to be impossible; but should unity lead to any menace, then the 'leaders' will conduct surplus energy through 'safe' channels — safe for Lloyd George.

At the beginning of his 'Open Letter', Maclean forecast that the maturing crisis of British capitalism would force the ruling class to place greater reliance upon social democracy:

> A sham Labour government with our beloved friends MacDonald and Snowden (and ethereal Ethel, too)* in it, will be formed, although the real work will be done by the 'Old Gang' under the guise of the Privy Council.

In Maclean's eyes, reformism would never overthrow the existing system, but Theodore Rothstein took a much more optimistic view. He backed left reformists in the Labour Party and trade unions in the hope that he would eventually win them over. Criticism became muted or was dropped altogether. Instead friendly offers of financial assistance were made. While the precise figure remains uncertain, it appears that the *Daily Herald* was offered between £75,000 and £125,000.[31]

Such assistance would seem to be at variance with usual Bolshevik practice. Admittedly, Lenin himself paid little or no attention to left reformism in Britain. Nevertheless, from polemics with Kautsky in Germany and Martov in Russia, Lenin's general position on left reformism cannot be in doubt. It is exceedingly improbable that he would have favoured giving financial support, thereby strengthening political tendencies which he regarded as obstacles to revolutionary change. Almost certainly, Lenin would have taken the same line as Trotsky adopted a few years later. In his book, *Where is Britain Going?*, (1925), Trotsky launched into a furious attack on left reformists like Lansbury, Kirkwood and Wheatley.

But in the early 1920s it is doubtful whether Lenin even attempted to keep abreast of political events in Britain. In a letter to Tom Bell, written in August 1921, he says: 'I have read nothing concerning the

*A reference to Ethel Snowden.

English movement last months because of my illness and overwork.'[32] (The faulty English in this sentence may be indicative of Lenin's imperfect command of the language.) But, having little or no time to read about Britain for himself, Lenin would be dependent on scraps of information gleaned from others, and the role of advisers on British affairs — men like Rothstein and Petrovsky — became crucial. Inevitably, they had to sift and select data and, in the process, transmit their own interpretation. Indeed, it may well be that the influence that Rothstein had indirectly on Britain, through providing the Communist International with 'information' on which it based its decisions, was far greater than his direct influence in the formation of the CPGB. The British comrades invariably carried out the orders made in Moscow.

It is significant that John Maclean thought the question of advisers was of vital importance. In his 'Open Letter to Lenin', he clearly expressed the opinion that Lenin was not getting an accurate picture of what was happening in Britain. He suggested that the man with the greatest knowledge was Peter Petroff, who spent many years in the struggle alongside Maclean before he returned to Russia. There is no evidence that Maclean's message had any effect.

There appears to have been a decided (and decisive) lack of rapport. Quite serious theoretical contributions, stating deeply held criticisms of the line proposed by the Comintern, went unanswered. Indeed, they may not even have been read. And this attitude has tended to be self-perpetuating: while almost every student of British revolutionary movements will be acquainted with, for example, what Lenin wrote about the need to work within the Labour Party, the vast majority will not be aware that strong arguments were expressed against this tactic. They will have read the booklet, *Left-wing Communism: an Infantile Disorder*; they will not know the objections to some aspects of it advanced by socialists like Maclean, Pankhurst and J.T. Murphy.

Probably the most cogent and powerfully argued article putting the case against Lenin's tactic of Labour Party affiliation came from J.T. Murphy.[33] He examined ten reasons given for adopting it. To each, he provided a rebuttal. Some of the points he made are questionable, perhaps invalid. Yet others show Murphy still had a strong case — one which was never properly answered.

1. The first argument advanced by those favouring affiliation was that the Labour Party represented the organised working class; it was essential for the Communist Party to be within the Labour Party to maintain contact with the working class.

Murphy replied: 'The Labour Party is not the working class *organised as a class*, but the political reflection of the trade union bureaucracy and the petty bourgeois. Contact with the working class is not, and never has been, dependent upon contact with the Labour Party.

2. The second argument was as Lenin said – and what has already been quoted in this chapter – namely, that the organisation structure of the Labour Party differed from that of other social democratic parties. Murphy's answer to that was that the only difference was that the Labour Party contained a more federalist structure and federalism was an anathema to communist principles.

3. Then, it was suggested that affiliation to the Labour Party was analogous to the Bolsheviks being in the Soviets when they were dominated by the Mensheviks.

   'In no sense is there a parallel in the two situations,' wrote Murphy. 'The Soviets are the instruments of revolution, the future governmental machinery of the proletariat. The Labour Party is a parliamentary party, an instrument of reaction, a body to be destroyed. The Soviets were created in the heat of revolutionary struggle. The Labour Party is a product of counter-revolutionary conciliation with capitalism.'

4. The advocates of affiliation thought belonging to the Labour Party would provide the CP with a public platform.

   But Murphy replied: 'The workers are always accessible in the workshops, the streets, the unions, and the creation of an independent communist platform is better than going cap in hand to the Labour Party for a hearing.'

5. Then, it was argued affiliation would provide the Communist Party with a fine opportunity to influence the Labour Party through participating in its annual conferences and getting socialist resolutions passed.

   Murphy answered: 'This implies that the Communist Party is either intent on capturing the Labour Party or passing revolutionary resolutions for the reactionaries to carry out. If the first, the policy is fundamentally wrong because the Labour Party, in composition and form, is not a revolutionary organisation; its members are neither communists nor revolutionaries, and it is structurally incapable of mobilising the masses for revolutionary action. It is a product of capitalism, and is to be used only for the maintenance of capitalism. If the second, then the masses are betrayed and their revolutionary fervour used to strengthen the forces of reaction. This proposition also indicates that the BSP does not clearly understand the functions of a Communist Party in the struggle for power. It is evidently content to be a spur to another party for whose actions it refuses responsibility instead of being a strong revolutionary party leading the masses into action.'

6. A further argument used by those favouring affiliation was that Trades and Labour Councils constituted the nuclei of Soviets.
But Murphy denied this: 'The Trades Councils are not the nuclei of Soviets. Their ineptitude in industrial disputes provides ample proof of this. They possess no executive power over the unions and action comes either through delegates from the workshops, etc., or the local district committee of the unions, which improvise strike committees composed of stewards and district committees, leaving the Trades Councils in the background or playing a reactionary part. It is in such a manner that the Soviets will be formed and not through Trades Councils as suggested.'

7. But affiliation may provide a chance for electing communist MPs on the Labour Party ticket.
'This is sheer parliamentary vote-catching opportunism,' replied Murphy, 'and a repudiation of independent political action. It is also confusing the masses. The Communist Party must go into elections not on vote-catching excursions, but for revolutionary agitation and to familiarise the masses with itself as the Party of Revolution.'

8. Affiliation to the Labour Party, it was sometimes argued, may lead to the overthrowal of Ramsay MacDonald.
Murphy's answer was that, even if true, this was irrelevant. Given conditions inside the Labour Party, were MacDonald overthrown another MacDonald would arise and take his place. The task was to destroy the Labour Party, not to capture it.

9. Those supporting affiliation contended that it would involve accepting Labour Party policy.
Murphy retorted: 'This is an argument of political tricksters. The masses do not follow the winding paths of politicians and are con-fused by such practices. The masses reason more simply, and think that those in the Labour Party are of the Labour Party and re-sponsible for its deeds. The Communist Party can best make its antagonism to the policy of the Labour Party clear to the masses by being neither in it or of it.'

10. Finally, in mitigation, some of those favouring affiliation suggested it might only be a temporary tactic.
To this, Murphy replied that sudden shifts of policy were liable to confuse and lessen the confidence of the masses in the Communist

Party.

Others advanced arguments like those of J.T. Murphy. Tom Bell, for instance, argued that it was imperative for the newly-formed Communist Party to have a clear, separate identity. Nothing would be gained by affiliation; the CP could appeal directly to the masses, many of whom were disenchanted with the Labour Party.[34] Like John Maclean, William Paul appears to have thought the Russian leaders did not have a sufficiently thorough grasp of the British scene. He told the Communist Unity Convention:

> There is not one in this audience to whom I yield in admiration for Lenin, but, as we said yesterday, Lenin is no pope or god. The point is that, so far as we are concerned on international tactics, we will take our international principles from Moscow, where they can be verified internationally; but on local circumstances, where we are on the spot, we are the people to decide. Not only so, but our comrade Lenin would not have us slavishly accept everything which he utters in Moscow. The very warp and woof of our propaganda is criticism and, as we believe in criticism, we are not above criticising Lenin.

Turning to the BSP delegates, who favoured affiliation, Paul went on to point out that 'they had to admit so far as the Labour Party and its structure was concerned, Lenin was a little vague.'[35]

All these arguments proved of no avail: by a narrow margin, the Communist Unity Convention resolved to apply for affiliation. On 7 July 1920, the Party's provisional committee formally wrote to the Labour Party. The letter, couched in firm, uncompromising language, received a flat rejection from Labour's National Executive Committee.

We have seen that this was a situation never envisaged by Lenin. He thought affiliation to the Labour Party would be there for the asking. Admittedly, Lenin did think problems might arise once the CP was inside:

> If the British Communist Party starts out by acting in a revolutionary manner in the Labour Party, and if Messrs. Henderson are obliged to expel this Party, it will be a great victory for the communist and labour movement in England.[36]

This remark led nimble-minded left-wingers, like MacManus and Paul, to devise an ingenious strategem. They saw a means of complying with

Lenin's advice, achieving his 'great victory' (if that were not a chimera), and doing so without having to endure the discomfiture of belonging to the Labour Party. If the object of the exercise was to get the Labour leaders to slam the door in the Communist Party's face, then this could be accomplished merely by knocking at the door; there was no need to enter the room. Any clear, forthright declaration of communist principles was sure to arouse the wrath of Ramsay MacDonald, Henderson & Co. So the Communist Party included a statement of these principles in its first application for affiliation, thus courting rejection. When the inevitable reply came, MacManus said it was their funeral, not ours.

The attitude adopted in this initial approach subsequently came in for considerable criticism, though it would still have been possible for MacManus and his friends to have justified the style used. Many statements of the Communist International employed much more fiery language. In fact, Lenin himself had said he would support the Labour leaders as a rope supports a hanging man. Paraphrasing this remark, Tommy Jackson said that CPers should take the Labour leaders by the hand 'as a preliminary to taking them by the throat.'[37]

The problem was that the Labour leaders heard all this and had no desire to occasion their own early demise; they did not desire to become closely acquainted with their would-be assassins. Far from sanctioning affiliation, they sought to impose further safeguards. Successive annual conferences introduced new restrictions: communists could not be delegates to Labour organisations, stand in the name of the Labour Party at elections, or even belong to the Labour Party as individual members. By 1925, the separation had become complete.

For the leaders of the Communist Party, this was all very frustrating. As more and more restrictions were imposed, there was no signs of 'the great victory' Lenin forecast would come if the Labour leaders took action against the communists. Generally speaking, Labour's rank-and-file seemed to endorse the Henderson attitude. The prospect of gaining affiliation receded further and further. What were they to do? If affiliation was the supreme goal, then other considerations should be subordinated to it. The Communist Party should minimise its differences with the Labour Party and tone down any criticisms. As most of the CP's membership came from the BSP, this was not a particularly difficult task. Most of them, anyway, were hazy about the distinction between reformism and revolutionary socialism.

Matters of principle were deliberately blurred. Reassuringly, Gallacher explained in 1924: 'The Communist Party does not attack the Labour Party. The Communist Party strives all the time to make the

Labour Party a useful organ of the workers in the struggle against capitalism.'[38] At the 1922 general election, when Gallacher unsuccessfully stood at Dundee, he gratefully received the assistance of prominent left-reformist politicians and trade unionists.[39] Lieutenant-Colonel L'Estrange Malone MP took the process of accommodation a stage farther. 'There are still a few differences between the Communist Party and the Labour Party,' he declared. 'I am glad to realise, however, that these will soon be settled by affiliation.'[40]

The ideological backslidings of the British Communist Party did not always gain approval from communists abroad. In 1924 Ruth Fischer, the German CP leader, came to the Communist Party congress as a fraternal delegate. She detected in its proceedings 'the loyal attitude of the Left-Wing within the Labour Party itself rather than the attitude of a Communist Party really fighting against the government.' She went on to say that the attempt to secure the election of communist MPs, with tacit or open Labour backing, was necessarily compromising.'[41] Reporting on her visit to the Comintern, Ruth Fischer sardonically remarked 'every English comrade has two party tickets in his pocket, the Labour Party ticket in his right pocket, the Communist Party in his left; they were members of the Labour Party on weekdays and communists in a mild way on Sundays for recreation.'[42] In his reply, Gregori Zinoviev, chairman of the Communist International, admitted that the members of the British Left were 'no revolutionaries' and were 'at present no better than the Left German Social Democrats.'

Certainly, Zinoviev exaggerated the position. Nevertheless, his view contains more than an element of truth, and it is relevant to ask why the British Communist Party was so lacking in revolutionary ardour. The reasons are varied and complex. Undoubtedly, the formation of the CPGB at a time when the tide of working-class discontent was receding was partly responsible. Likewise the failure to get the majority of the members of Left groups — the SLP, WSF and the shop stewards' movement — into the Communist Party had an effect, as did the exclusion of John Maclean and Sylvia Pankhurst. That the core of membership came from the BSP also helped to give the new party a right-wing bias. The removal of the handful of SLPers who did come in — for example, MacManus and Paul — from positions of influence helped to reinforce this trend. Even more important was degeneration of the Communist International as Stalin's influence asserted itself: since the CPGB was more dependent than most sections on Moscow for finance and in other ways, the British party was especially vulnerable.

But, when all these factors are added up, another one must be mentioned: the intervention of Lenin. The manner in which he posed the issue of Labour Party affiliation gave aid and comfort to the right-wing of the CP as well as alienating many good revolutionaries from it.

Notes

1. Lenin, *Collected Works* (Moscow, 1961), vol. 19, p. 370. Andrew Rothstein's pamphlet, *Lenin in Britain,* gives a reasonable factual account of his stay in this country.
2. V.I. Lenin, op. cit., vol. 18, p. 467 and vol. 21, p. 156.
3. Raymond Postgate, in his biography of George Lansbury (1951, p. 153), wrote, 'The *Herald*, like nearly all the rest of Britain, assumed at first that nothing else could have been done but to declare war and fight it to the end.'
4. V.I. Lenin, op. cit., vol. 21, p. 36.
5. Ibid, vol. 19, p. 370.
6. Nan Milton, *John Maclean,* p. 243.
7. *Lenin on Britain* (1941 ed.) p. 201.
8. Ibid, p. 265.
9. D. Butler and J.Freeman, *British Political Facts, 1900-1968* (1969 ed.) p. 108.
10. *Lenin on Britain* (1941 ed.) p. 269.
11. Labour Party Annual Report, 1921, pp. 158-167.
12. V.I. Lenin, *Collected Works*, vol. 31, p. 259.
13. Bob Stewart, *Breaking the Fetters* (1967) p. 101.
14. Interviews with S. Pankhurst, J.T. Murphy and Dick Beach made by S.R. Graubard, quoted *British Labour and the Russian Revolution, 1917-1924* (Oxford, 1956) p. 137. Also, Tom Bell, *Pioneering Days,* p. 195.
15. J. Klugmann, *History of the Communist Party of Great Britain,* vol. 1, p. 331 and Tom Bell, ibid.
16. *The Socialist,* 22 April 1920.
17. *Workers' Dreadnought,* 2 and 30 July 1921
18. *The Socialist,* 14 April 1921.
19. *Workers' Dreadnought,* 7 December 1918.
20. *The Call,* 22 April 1920.
21. *Workers' Dreadnought,* 8 October 1921.
22. Ibid, 24 September 1921.
23. V.I. Lenin, Collected Works, vol. 24, p. 399.
24. Trotsky's Archives T 3129, p. 12, cited by E.H. Carr, *Socialism in One Country, 1924-1926,* (1972) ed.) p. 131.
25. *Justice,* 30 March 1907.
26. V.I. Lenin, op. cit., vol. 22, p. 180.
27. W. Kendall, *The Revolutionary Movement in Britain 1900-21,* p. 388.
28. *The Socialist,* 3 February 1920.
29. *Vanguard,* August 1920.
30. H. McShane in the *New Edinburgh Review* (1972), p. 9, and W. Gallacher, *Last Memoirs,* p. 141.
31. W. Kendall, op. cit., pp. 254-6.
32. *Lenin on Britain,* p. 271.
33. *The Socialist,* 6 May 1920.
34. *The Communist,* 26 November 1921.

37.   *The Communist,* 24 December 1921.
38.   Sixth conference of the CPGB, 1924. p. 11.
39.   J. Klugmann, *History of the CPGB* (1968) vol. 1, p. 189.
40.   *Workers' Dreadnought,* 28 January 1922.
41.   *Die Internationale,* vii nos. 10-11, cited by E.H. Carr, op. cit., p. 132. Also R. Fischer, *Stalin and German Communism,* (Harvard, 1948) p. 400.
42.   *Protokoll: Funfter Kongress der Kommunistischen Internationale (n.d.)* vol. 2, p. 913, cited by E.H. Carr, op. cit., p. 134.
35.   Communist Unity Convention Report, p. 35.
36.   *Lenin on Britain,* p. 271.

11 THE FORMATION OF THE COMMUNIST PARTY

Two concepts of unity crystallised in the period before the London
Unity convention. The first emphasising continuity, desired merely a
re-shuffling of existing furniture, a re-groupment of organisations still
retaining social democratic principles and outlook. But the second tendency regarded this as inadequate: it sought a unity on a clear revolutionary basis. The October Revolution (the argument ran) had not
merely established the first workers' state, bringing a new force into
international affairs, but had also provided a fund of new theory and
practice which could be of great utility to the workers of every nationality. The lessons of the Russian Revolution demanded that a radical
change of approach be made.

These concepts came into collision in March 1919. The BSP provided the arena for combat, organising two conferences to explore the
possibility for greater unity. The BSP envisaged making progress by
adopting the same path as before. Three years previously, it had formed
the United Socialist Council with the ILP, which had sought to be an
all-embracing body, including everyone who had the least socialist pretensions. In the same way, the BSP strove in 1919 to collect all
strands of left-wing opinion under one roof. It hoped, ingenuously,
that this would provide an opportunity for differences to be resolved,
but, instead of conflicts vanishing, they became even more apparent.
An unbridgeable gulf existed between the reformism of the ILP and
the revolutionary standpoint of the SLP. The second meeting, as Tom
Bell described, ended with the two main protagonists having a heated
exchange:

> This conference turned into a dialectical skirmish between Mac-
> Manus and Philip Snowden on industrial unionism versus trade
> unionism; Soviets versus parliamentary democracy; and the role of
> violence in the social revolution. I never saw a man look so dejected
> as Snowden when Mac was finished with him. As a last word
> Snowden said: 'Well, you are asking us to give up all we have stood
> for these thirty years. The past thirty years' work of the ILP is good
> enough for me.' And we broke up.[1]

That Snowden aroused the ire of the SLP was understandable. Only two months before, the German Social Democratic leaders had connived in the murder of Karl Liebknecht and Rosa Luxemburg, whom the SLP regarded as their comrades. The ILP leaders, like Snowden, were suspect. because they held similar political principles to the German Social Democratic leaders. *The Socialist* declared: 'Ramsay MacDonald, like Noske in Germany, would butcher workers quite mercilessly.'[2] For this reason, the SLP envisaged not a unity with MacDonald but against MacDonald. It aimed at convincing any militants within the ILP that their duty was to work towards a split, bringing the left out of the Party.

In its manifesto to the conference in May 1919, the SLP's declared intention was to stimulate rank-and-file discontent in the bigger, reformist organisation and direct this against the old guard who were in control:

> We must set up a revolutionary organisation, for both the changing historical situation and the era of revolutionary action on the part of the proletariat demand it. But such a transition is possible only over the heads of the old leaders, who strangled revolutionary energy — over the head of the old party and along the path of its destruction.[3]

The SLP had basically the same attitude to the BSP as it had to the ILP. Its disagreements were manifest on two issues of immediate relevance. The first was its line on the Labour Party. The BSP was affiliated to the Labour Party, loyally working within it and striving to push the Labour Party in a leftward direction. In the SLP's view, this was a sign of the BSP's essentially reformist outlook. It also led to another error: because the BSP was concerned to gain the trade union block vote at Labour conferences, it was reluctant to criticise union leaders who uttered left phrases but failed to match their words with deeds. Not wishing to antagonise the Bob Smillies and Ernest Bevins, the BSP was never officially in favour of building rank-and-file organisations within industry to challenge the union bureaucracy. To the SLP, this was a vital, an integral, part of the struggle.

The BSP's assessment of union leaders, its refusal to realise that in any serious crisis they would strive to dampen down discontent, led the BSP to have a totally false picture of how socialism could be achieved. If one of the BSP's faces was reformist, the other was syndicalist. In a leftish mood, as at its final conference in 1920, the BSP called upon all trade unions to strike together to overthrow capitalism.

J.T. Murphy sought to explain the error of this line of argument:

It implies that the overthrowal of capitalism can be attained by the
general strike alone, a further proposition repudiated in history. No
finer example of a general strike can be cited than the recent strike
in Berlin. But it did not achieve the social revolution. More than a
strike was required — real communist leadership, the seizure of arms,
an open united military struggle for power. The repeated limitation
of mass action to direct action (a syndicalist limitation) by the BSP
is either an indication of lack of insight into the needs of revolution
or moral cowardice expressing itself in a fear of an open declaration
that revolution cannot be carried through without a resort to arms.[4]

In the same article Murphy outlined the fundamental differences he
saw between the two parties:

It should be observed that the Russian Revolution has affected the
SLP and BSP differently. The Communist programme of the Third
International partly accepts and partly supplements the principles
and programme the SLP has fought for since its inception. Its uncompromising waging of the class war, its advocacy of industrial
unionism, and its insistence on the impossibility of using the parliamentary state to accomplish the revolution, and the realisation of
the need for an intermediate Soviet state with the dictatorship of the
proletariat. This is a development of first principles. The BSP, on the
other hand, in adherence formally to the Communist International,
has had to reverse its former policy. Trailing with all the traditions
of the SDF, its opposition to industrial unionism, its reformist parliamentarianism, it has had to pass through a process, and it has still
to pass through a further process of internal change.

In Murphy's opinion, the BSP simply gave formal adherence to the
Third International: it remained, in essence, true to its reformist spirit.
He saw the path to unity through the fusion with the South Wales
Socialist Society and Workers' Socialist Federation, not with the BSP:

There must be no compromise with the BSP. Better a Communist
Party without the BSP than a party including the BSP, trailing with
it the spirit of compromise to hamper the party in its revolutionary
practice.

The majority of the SLP accepted the Murphy line. They saw unity not as a short battle but a protracted war, slowly won as more and more militants came to realise the efficacy of the revolutionary standpoint. They would come, it was envisaged, not only from other left groups but also from the large number of good socialists who remained outside all political parties. It was a characteristic of this period that a sizeable proportion of class-conscious workers belonged to no party. Jack Tanner, a shop stewards' delegate to the Communist International, tried to explain this by saying that disenchantment with the BSP had led workers to shun political parties generally.[5] Perhaps this is too severe on the BSP: the antics of the Labour Party and the ILP also helped to swell the ranks of the disgruntled and unattached. The SLP believed it could attract many of these people, thereby mobilising fresh forces in the struggle. But this could only be accomplished so long as the SLP was not tainted by the 'old corruption' of the Labour Party.

In pursuance of its objective, the SLP made small, yet significant, strides. The 17th annual conference, held in Carlisle at Easter 1920, heard that the party had 48 branches, an increase of six on the previous year. The figure did not include the South Wales Socialist Society which, on 28 March 1920, decided to dissolve into the SLP. The influx of new blood from South Wales, an area in which the SLP had hitherto had a scanty membership, added to the party's industrial credibility — many of the new recruits had played a prominent part in industrial battles since the Cambrian Combine strike. The entire membership of the Aberdare ILP joined the SLP following this development.

A similar process was going on in Scotland. As we have seen in the last chapter, John Maclean drew closer to the SLP. He frequently spoke from its platforms, and early in 1921, *The Socialist* announced: 'Comrade Maclean is now a fighting member of the fighting SLP.'[6] Along with his closest collaborator, James D. MacDougall, he joined the party's executive. Obviously, to have enrolled the man who epitomised, perhaps more strongly than any other man, the spirit of revolution gave the SLP a great boost.

But there was a crucial influence militating against the SLP in the form of agents who purported to act on behalf of Moscow. In mid-1919, the Communist International decided to exert all its authority to gain a unification of left groups in Britain. The formation of a single British Communist Party was seen as the supreme task; everything else was subordinated to this aim. The fact that many of the group were confused theoretically, had definite tendencies to reformism, or did not relate themselves to the industrial struggle was of little consequence.

Disregarding the inner laws of motion of British left politics, the evolutionary process that was slowly leading to revolutionary re-groupment, the Comintern leaders were prepared to wrench bits off existing organisations and forcibly bring them together, irrespective of the effect.

The Comintern's main agent was Theodore Rothstein. There can be no doubt that he played a vitally important role: he had at his disposal 'Moscow Gold'. His ability to bestow largesse upon pliant individuals and organisations gave him immense influence in British left-wing circles, where money was scarce. However, as already stated, some historians probably exaggerate the importance of the economic factor. Of much greater significance was that, for many British socialists, Rothstein was the living embodiment of the first successful workers' revolution. This gave him tremendous moral authority. Whenever he spoke or wrote, as he did frequently, his words were seen as the genuine expression of Russian Bolshevism.

The problem was that Rothstein's connection with Bolshevism could be described, at best, as tenuous. He thought of building the new party around the BSP. He had been one of its executive members, at times a not particularly left-wing one, and he almost automatically looked to his former colleagues to form the nucleus of the Communist Party. All the financial resources at his disposal were channelled, as J.T. Walton Newbold observed in his autobiography, into the BSP.[7] Even police agents, operating inside working-class organisations, knew this. The Directorate of Intelligence (HQ) survey of revolutionary movements, produced in January 1921 for the Cabinet, observed that the Russian representatives were dealing exclusively with the BSP and shop stewards; other groups, such as the SLP, were left out in the cold.[8] There was even a degree of selectivity here — only those shop steward groups clearly backing the BSP line received support.

This represented a complete change of policy. At one time, Moscow had rated others much more highly than the BSP. In March 1919, when the Communist International was formed, its international executive committee looked primarily to the WSF and SLP for support in Britain. Sylvia Pankhurst had been exceptionally prominent, not only liaising with the Comintern in Britain but travelling over Western Europe to establish links on its behalf. She went to Italy to attend a conference of the Italian Socialist Party, where the seeds of the future Italian Communist Party were sown, and then on foot, illegally, crossed the frontier into Switzerland and, subsequently, Germany. In Frankfurt, she was the British representative at an international communist conference. Sylvia Pankhurst was probably the foremost British contact of the International. As one historian stated:

> During the first five months of the Communist International's exis-
> tence, her interpretations of the British scene were accepted as
> authentic by the ECCI and by Lenin. Her articles appeared in the
> first five numbers of the *Communist International* in its various
> language editions.[9]

Lenin's great respect for her was shown by the remarks he made after
her arrest:

> Comrade Sylvia Pankhurst represents the interests of hundreds upon
> hundreds of millions of people that are oppressed by the British and
> other capitalists. That is why she is subjected to a White terror, (and)
> has been deprived of her liberty.[10]

Although Lenin was exaggerating, there can be little doubt that,
through her years of struggle, Sylvia Pankhurst had built up a reputation in the British working class much more impressive than the
reputations of many of those who were later to control the British
Communist Party.

Lenin made similar flattering references to the SLP. He declared
that 'of the three socialist parties in England, only one, the independent
Socialist Labour Party, is openly becoming an ally of the Bolsheviks.'[11]
This was said at a meeting of the Moscow Soviet on 22 October 1918,
and, a few months later, *Pravda* carried an article on Britain which
described the SLP as the British Bolshevik Party.[12]

But a completely different approach became discernible later in
1919. This can be attributed to two things: first, the BSP agreed to
apply for affiliation to the Communist International in October 1919;
and, second, Theodore Rothstein was on hand to maximise the influence of his long-standing friends. Quickly, it became obvious that
unification would be based upon the BSP, with other groups playing a
subordinate role and merging with it.

This placed revolutionaries in a predicament. Should they accept this
plan, hoping after unification to push the newly-created organisation in
a leftward direction? Or should they ignore the Russians and continue
with their own moves towards re-groupment? The question threw the
SLP into turmoil. Bell, Paul and MacManus led the faction in favour of
unity at all costs; Clunie, Mitchell and Murphy headed the group who
believed that principles should not be lightly dropped.

It should be remembered that the SLP initially entered the unity negotiations with the intention of prising the more revolutionary members from the BSP and ILP. Now, ironically, it was within the SLP itself that the split occurred. At the centre of the argument was the BSP's reformist attitude and its unwillingness to budge on the issue of Labour Party affiliation. In discussion, Tom Bell, who was one of the SLP's specially appointed Unity Committee, made a concession. He suggested that the issue of affiliation should be shelved until a year after the formation of the Communist Party, and then a referendum of the members taken on it. This proposal angered many members of the SLP. Bell, supposedly speaking on their behalf, had exceeded his brief. Within a unified organisation, containing all the membership of the BSP, the SLP would be swamped. It would lose its identity. Just as important, it would lose control of the SLP press and publishing business, which sold more Marxist literature than any other concern in Britain. But Bell's proposal was not accepted by the unity conference, which resolved that organisations participating in the conference should simply hold a referendum on whether their memberships wanted to belong to a unified Communist Party. The resolution said that the issue of affiliation to the Labour Party should be decided by referendum three months after the new party had come into existence.

The unity conference's motion provided the Clunie faction with a useful stratagem. Having majority of one on the SLP executive, they resolved to put both questions to the membership ballot: whether the SLP was prepared to join a unified Communist Party, and whether this party should be affiliated to the Labour Party. As generally anticipated, the ballot revealed a majority in favour of fusion but against affiliation, which the executive interpreted as giving it a free hand in any future negotiations. Bell resigned from the editorship of *The Socialist* as a protest against this decision, and on 22 January 1920 Dr Tom Estermann took his place.

It appeared that ultimate victory would go to Bell and his comrades, who over many years had developed into hard cadres, skilled debators and tacticians, as well as being the main spokesmen for the SLP. But they do not seem to have taken the factional struggle seriously, being more concerned about bringing the broader unity to fruition. So they formed their own organisation, the Communist Unity Group, and while remaining members of the SLP, turned their backs on its internal politics. This move may well have been a tactical blunder: their opponents only had a small majority, many of the membership were undecided and, with sustained debate, Bell and his comrades might well have won.

An event which swung many SLPers against Tom Bell and his friends was the Paisley bye-election. The local branch of the party planned to contest it, adopting William Paul as the SLP candidate. But at the last moment, on 28 January 1920, when it was impossible to find a replacement, Paul sent a telegram saying he was not prepared to stand. It was generally assumed that the reason for his unwillingness was that he did not want to stand against a Labour candidate and thereby antagonise members of the BSP. Many SLPers saw it as a betrayal, the placing of considerations of unity with the BSP before the need to expose reformism. The Labour Party's candidate at Paisley was J.M. Biggar, a notorious right-winger. What worsened the situation was that, although William Paul and his associates were still prepared to use the facilities of the SLP, speaking from SLP platforms, they did not encourage people to join the party. At Leigh Socialist Club and at Horwich in Lancashire, Paul even went so far as to dissuade workers from joining the SLP, saying that they should wait to join the soon-to-be-formed Communist Party. Of course, when this became known, it only served to antagonise the SLP membership further.

Even so, the Communist Unity Group would probably have taken a few more members out of the SLP had it bothered to attend the party's annual conference at Carlisle during Easter 1920. Instead, it held a rival conference at Nottingham. Besides giving the damaging impression that they were shying away from debate, Bell and his friends revealed their own weakness when they published a list of those attending the Nottingham gathering. Of the 22 people there, only 14 were actually members of the SLP.[13] The failure of their enterprise can be judged in another way. The ostensible reason for the Nottingham conference had been to rally support among disaffected SLPers for the forthcoming Communist Unity Convention in London, where the Communist Party of Great Britain was officially to be formed. Yet in the Communist Unity Group's delegation to the London Convention only one delegate, Tom Bell himself, represented a group in Scotland. When it is remembered that most of the very hard work by Bell, Mac-Manus and Paul had been done in Scotland, the extent to which they had detached themselves from their former supporters becomes apparent.

The London Convention met while the Second Congress of the Third International was in session. It may seem an oversight, or bad organisation, that the organisers of the London conference allowed the two events to clash. Much of the Second Congress's time was spent dis-

cussing Britain. Had the Communist Unity Convention been held a few
weeks later, delegates would have been able to benefit from hearing
about the deliberations of the Second Congress. There was, moreover, a
strong British contingent in Moscow. They included John S. Clarke,
Helen Crawfurd, William Gallacher, W. MacLaine, J.T. Murphy, Margery
Newbold, Sylvia Pankhurst, Tom Quelch, Dave Ramsay and Jack
Tanner. Admittedly, some of these may not have wanted to attend the
Communist Unity Convention, but the Convention was surely that
much poorer because of the non-attendance of the rest. One would have
thought that, at the inaugural conference of the CPGB, every effort
would have been taken to secure the presence there of those who had
gained prominence in the working-class movement.

Another mystery associated with the Convention was the publication
of Lenin's pamphlet, *Left-Wing Communism: an Infantile Disorder.*
Lenin finished this on 27 April 1920, and three months elapsed before
it appeared in English. Then, only extracts were printed in the BSP's
journal, *The Call,* on 29 July 1920. This was just at the crucial moment:
the Communist Unity Convention was a mere two days away and the
main issue to be discussed would be affiliation to the Labour Party.
Lenin came firmly down on the side of the BSP's position, while the
individuals whom he attacked — in particular Gallacher and Pankhurst
— would be unable to reply as they were in Moscow. Indeed, with three
exceptions, all the delegates in Moscow opposed affiliation to the
Labour Party, and many of them disagreed with using the BSP as the
nucleus of the new party. Certainly, things went very well for the right
wing. They narrowly won the vote on the Labour Party by 100 votes to
85. Had it not been for convenient absences, and the equally convenient
publication of extracts from Lenin, the vote might well have gone the
other way.

It *may* have been accident rather than design that produced these
absence conditions for the right wing. But it does seem strange that
in the period before the October Revolution, when obstacles to communication were very much greater, Lenin's articles could appear in *The
Socialist* without a three-month delay.

Another mystery of the Communist Unity Convention was the
absence of John Maclean. As we saw in this last chapter, his quarrel
with Theodore Rothstein in the spring of 1920 appears to have been a
personal turning-point. From then on, he considered himself banished
by what is referred to as, 'the London gang'. In May 1920, he resumed
publication of his monthly journal, *Vanguard.* Not being *persona grata,*
it was no use him going to the Unity Convention: he had already had

the door slammed in his face at the final conference of the BSP; there was no reason for making it happen again.

Of course, we only have John Maclean's own word that he was debarred from helping in the formation of the Communist Party. He claimed he was denied access to the final BSP conference by 'the trickery of the Cockney, Cant' — Ernest Cant, chairman of the conference arrangements committee — who, according to Maclean, was acting at the behest of Theodore Rothstein.[14] If this claim was untrue, then one would have expected a public denial. The leaders of the newly-formed Communist Party could have said that there had been a slight misunderstanding and Maclean would be welcome in the fold. Yet no such statement was made.[15]

Interestingly, in the period immediately before the Communist Unity Convention, Ernest Cant, the former London district secretary of the BSP, was despatched to Scotland to arouse support. His efforts do not seem to have been crowned with much success. Only ten out of the 155 delegates attending came from Scotland.[16] Included in the ten was Cant himself who, somehow or other, came as the delegate for Paidley BSP. It seems highly peculiar that Cant, with such limited associations with Clydeside, could obtain conference credentials while the same appear to have been denied to Clydeside's most famous revolutionary. One might have thought that with Scottish representation at the Unity Convention so weak, the services of so influential a socialist as John Maclean would have been eagerly sought. But no letters appealing to him to assist by joining the Communist Party are contained in Maclean's papers, deposited in the National Library of Scotland. Nor did anyone dispute the claim made in his 'Open Letter to Lenin': 'I myself was automatically excluded from the London show.' Clearly, CP leaders were not over-keen to have him.

The differences went much deeper than allegations of trickery. As shown in the previous chapter, Maclean and Rothstein had fundamental political disagreements. Intertwined with these, as so often happens, was personal hostility. According to Gallacher, who was there when the fateful quarrel occurred, Maclean accused Rothstein of being a police agent.[17] But Harry McShane, admittedly only on the basis of second-hand information — Maclean's version of the quarrel — had claimed that no such accusation was made; he said Maclean simply had an intense dislike for Rothstein.[18]

This arose largely because Rothstein had enjoyed a comfortable job during the war, while many British socialists were enduring hardship, imprisonment and even death. In fact, Rothstein had served on the

staff of the War Office. His work entailed being confidential adviser to
Lord Balfour on Russian affairs.[19] To reach that exalted position, it
would appear reasonable to conclude, Rothstein would have been subjected to rigorous security checks, and the authorities would be aware
of his political activities. Definitely, when he began operating as the
Comintern's main agent in Britain, the Special Branch kept close tabs
on him. There are copious references to his activities in the Home
Office papers. They became acquainted with his financial disbursements
down to the exact penny.[20] Sylvia Pankhurst considered him 'much
too talkative for a conspirator'. She cited an instance where he talked
quite freely to a man, Jacob Nosovitsky, who she had already warned
him was a police spy. Presumably, the authorities allowed Rothstein to
function for so long because he provided them unintentionally with
much useful information. Clearly, John Maclean was wrong if he
accused Rothstein of being a police spy, although all socialists would
have been well-advised to treat him with extreme caution.

Since January 1918, Maclean had been the Scottish Consul for the
Soviet government, but, after his quarrel with Rothstein, he ceased to
use the title. Did this mean that he had been deprived of the post?
Having been given it by Litvinov, was it taken away by Litvinov's
successor as the chief Soviet representative in Britain? The answer to
this question remains a matter for conjecture. What is certain, however,
and of much greater significance, was that, after his quarrel with Rothstein, Maclean returned to Scotland determined to continue revolutionary activity, but to do so outside the Communist Party's ranks.

With Maclean in full spate, and the SLP's strength not seriously
dented, the prospects for the newly-formed CPGB in Scotland, the
most militant part of Britain, did not look particularly bright. *The
Worker,* organ of the Scottish Workers' Committee, gave a singularly
unenthusiastic report of the proceedings of the Communist Unity Convention in London. It regarded the decision on Labour Party affiliation
as an 'unpardonable mistake', adding that 'communists in Scotland are
nine-tenths anti-Labour Party.' The paper went on to declare there was
'not the slightest prospect of the Communist Party in its present form
making any headway north of the Border.'[21]

As if to underline the point, one of the handful of Scottish delegates
to the Unity Convention wrote in the next issue of *The Worker* that he
had changed his mind. Alex Geddes, of the Greenock Workers' Committee, now no longer favoured the CPGB; he thought a Scottish Communist Party should be built. His initiative met with a response from
those who disagreed with the decision of the London Convention on

Labour Party affiliation as well as those with nationalistic leanings. These included John Maclean and the Scottish Workers' Committee. A preliminary conference, held in Glasgow on 18 September 1920, was attended by representatives of 21 groups. It was agreed officially to form a new party, to be known as the Communist Labour Party, at a special conference on 2 October 1920.[22]

These developments had been watched with friendly interest by the SLP. A close similarity of views existed: John Maclean wrote to Tom Mitchell, SLP general secretary, urging co-operation, and the SLP appointed delegates to the inaugural meeting.[23] They wanted to suggest that exploratory talks take place with the aim of effecting a merger. In the meantime, however, a complicating factor had arisen: on 27 September 1920, Gallacher, returning from the Second Congress in Russia, arrived in Glasgow. His influence was to have a decisive impact on the unity negotiations in Scotland.

To understand Gallacher's role, which was quite different to that depicted in his various autobiographies, one has first to examine his political development. A person with sound class instincts, a first-class militant, he never had theoretical depth or profundity. Therefore, his political course was very erratic. During the First World War, which he did not oppose, he belonged to the BSP. However, by 1928 he had become an anarcho-syndicalist. But this did not stop him, as a gesture of personal friendship and solidarity, deputising for John Maclean as parliamentary candidate in the 1918 general election. Maclean was in prison almost up until polling day; it was Gallacher, not believing in parliament, who urged workers to vote for him.[24] The two men were, in that period, close companions. When Maclean came out of prison, they went for a short holiday together. Soon after that, in February 1919, came the forty-hour strike. When the police began batoning demonstrators in George Square, he showed his tremendous courage by rushing up to the chief constable, who was standing on the steps of the City Chamber, and punching him in the face before policemen knocked him into insensibility. At the ensuing trial, he stoutly defended his action, accusing the police of a brutal assault on peaceful demonstrators.[25] To Red Clydesiders, this made Gallacher a hero. It enhanced his influence considerably, and was the main reason why he could play such an important role in the unity negotiations.

But for a fiery rebel like Gallacher, the thought of accomplishing unity around the BSP was an anathema. Early in 1920, he denounced this idea in *Solidarity*, organ of the London Workers' Committee. After accompanying Maclean to his stormy meeting with Comintern adviser

Rothstein, he seems to have been even more firmly convinced of its futility. Having shaken off the last traces of anarchism, he moved towards the SLP in the spring of 1920. Writing in *The Socialist* on 'Communism and Fusion', he denounced the idea of the inclusion of the BSP in any unity scheme: 'Their inclusion in a Communist Party would sooner or later spell disaster . . . If real unity is to be obtained, there must be unity of theory and action.'[26] In the period immediately before going to the congress of the Communist International in Russia, he was regularly writing and speaking for the SLP. For example, on 24 June 1920, the Vale of Leven SLP reported it had had 'a very successful week with Comrade Gallacher as speaker.'[27]

The Second Congress had a profound influence on Gallacher's political development. In his discussions in Moscow, he still denounced the plans for unity around the BSP. But Lenin disagreed with him: 'When in speaking of the British Socialist Party Comrade Gallacher said that it is "hopelessly reformist", he is undoubtedly exaggerating.'[28] Eventually, in private conversation, Lenin convinced him. Gallacher later admitted that he accepted Lenin's criticism 'as a child takes the rebuke of a father.'[29] He promised Lenin that, on his return to Britain, he would do everything within his power to get all communists to join the CPGB.

This was tantamount to a complete *volte face*. And, to make matters worse, on his arrival in Glasgow Gallacher found that plans to build a rival to the CPGP, the Communist Labour Party, were well advanced. In the circumstances, he had no alternative but to go along with his comrades. He attended what was to be the inaugural conference of the Communist Labour Party on 2 October 1920. His aim was to steer the new organisation into harmless channels. Opposition came from Maclean's chief lieutenant, J.D. MacDougall, the SLP representatives, and from many of the other delegates. But Gallacher had three important advantages: first, his leadership of the Clyde Workers' Committee gave him an influence on key positions; second, his heroism on a number of occasions helped to create a fund of goodwill for him among activists; and, third, and most important, he had the added distinction of being just back from Moscow, carrying the instructions of the Communist International.

As a result of Gallacher's intervention, the inaugural conference adopted an equivocating position. On the one hand, it formally asserted its independence, proclaiming itself the Communist Labour Party. On the other, it agreed to enter into unity negotiations with the CPGB. Given the committee elected, this amounted to a victory for Gallacher.

It saw its function as being that of a staging-post for people en route to Communist Party membership.

The change of direction led both the SLP and John Maclean to make a reappraisal. They did not agree that, under the pretext of building a Scottish organisation, individuals should be inveigled into the CPGB. Maclean denounced the Communist Labour Party as 'a shameful bewilderment of the best fighting elements in Scotland.'[30] He regarded it as a sign of the deviousness that his namesake, John Maclean of Bridgeton, had been appointed secretary. It conveyed the impression that he gave his support whereas, in fact, the Communist Labour Party sought to undermine his influence and that of the SLP in Scotland.

A few months earlier, Maclean had formed the Tramp Trust Unlimited. This was a small group, all of whom were unemployed, who trekked around Scotland spreading the socialist message.[31] Wherever they went, their activities were supported by SLP branches. In the aftermath of the 2 October conference, with J.R. Campbell, Gallacher and others exhibiting hostility towards them, the SLP and Maclean drew closer together. *The Socialist* proclaimed: 'In Comrade Maclean we find the revolutionist, the tactician, the educationalist, the organiser and administrator — in every way the one man worthy of the fearless trust of the revolutionary masses.'[32]

After receiving such wholehearted praise, John Maclean decided to make his own attempt to form a new organisation. He aimed his appeal at all revolutionaries who accepted the 'Twenty-one Points' of the Third International and wanted a specifically Scottish party. The inaugural meeting was to be in the SLP's Glasgow headquarters on 25 December 1920.

Maclean's move represented a definite threat to Gallacher's strategy. There was the danger that Maclean would attract disgruntled members of the Communist Labour Party, not prepared to join a London-based organisation. Moreover, were his scheme to get the support of the Socialist Labour Party, the largest left-wing body in Scotland, it was liable to make the CPGB's efforts North of the Border puny by comparison. So Gallacher and some of his colleagues decided to gatecrash the conference. They constantly heckled the speakers. At one stage, Gallacher left his seat and strode towards the platform while Maclean came forward to confront him, and it seemed likely that the two men would come to blows. The danger of a fight was temporarily averted, and order was restored. But Gallacher and his clique resumed their interruptions, and proceedings came to an end, amid a cacophony of abuse, when Gallacher became involved in a violent scene with James

MacDougall, the chairman.[33]

This disruption was not responsible for the failure of Maclean's plan
– that was due to the SLP's unwillingness to participate in it. Maclean
had hoped that the nucleus of his new party would be the SLP, but an
SLP spokesman made it plain that they would not be prepared to co-
operate in such a definitely nationalistic venture. Confronted with this
declaration, Maclean changed his tactics. In his last contribution to the
conference, he urged all non-committed revolutionaries to join the SLP.
In the columns of *The Socialist,* Maclean explained his position in an
article headed 'Rally to the SLP':

> Subtle attempts having been made to destroy the SLP, now the sole
> clean Marxian organisation in Britain, I have thought it opportune to
> fuse with the SLP rather than form a new party for Communism
> inside Scotland, especially as Glasgow is the centre of the SLP and
> the Clyde is the area where most of the best work has been done . . .
>   The SLP has at least to its great credit the printing of the finest
> Marxian literature in the world. To allow the SLP to be crushed
> would be a crime to Marxism, upon which alone a successful revolu-
> tion can be based. It is the duty of all determined Marxists to rally
> to the SLP.[34]

These attempts to destroy the SLP became none too subtle. Socialist
Labour Party speakers began to encounter opposition, led by J.R.
Campbell and Gallacher, at their meetings. James Clunie, editor of *The
Socialist,* had his Fife class on Marxism broken up, and Maclean's class
at Shotts was destroyed. Most of the venom, in fact, was reserved for
him. J.R. Campbell tried to take control of a meeting of the
unemployed being addressed by Maclean in Glasgow on 27 December
1920. 'He was voted down,' wrote Maclean later, 'and would have been
struck down but for my intervention.'[35] Undeterred, Campbell also
tried to gatecrash a meeting of the Miners' Unofficial Movement, where
Maclean was the invited guest.

The reason why Gallacher and his comrades resorted to such tactics
can be understood when considered in context. As the London Communist Unity Convention had been so dismal a failure, it had been
decided to hold a second convention, this time at Leeds, on 29 January
1921. Gallacher wanted to mobilise maximum support for this
gathering, and to smash all rival centres of attraction. His efforts' most
immediate effect was not to rally great support, but to cause socialists
to remain outside both contending camps. The Communist Labour

Party claimed a membership of 4,000.[36] Almost certainly, this was a gross exaggeration. Even so, many of its members voted against fusion with their feet: at the most, 200 of them entered the CPGB.[37]

The same dismal picture was repeated elsewhere. The Workers' Socialist Federation, not prepared to accept the BSP-dominated unity, rather presumptuously resolved to call itself the Communist Party (British Section of the Third International) in June 1920. A small organisation, it appeared to be making reasonable progress, but then in the autumn a *diktat* came from Moscow: the executive of the Third International instructed it to unite with the organisation created as a result of the London Unity Convention. Sylvia Pankhurst, just back from Moscow, suggested the CP (BSTI) should comply. She had never been as strongly in favour of parliamentary abstentionism as some of his followers.[38] So, presuming that there would be internal democracy and having faith in her own ideas, she advised her comrades to join the CPGB and struggle inside it to win the majority to their viewpoint. A CP (BSTI) conference, held in Cardiff, considered her plea. Sylvia Pankhurst herself could not attend as she was serving a six-month sentence for sedition. The whole situation was further complicated by the ineptitude of the Comintern. It expected the CP (BSTI) to accept the Theses, Statutes, Resolutions and Conditions of the Third International without the majority of delegates having an opportunity to read them. As the secretary, E.T. Whitehead, remarked, 'this made things undoubtedly very difficult.'[39] But the majority of the CP (BSTI) agreed to this demand for blind loyalty. Yet the manner in which unity was achieved only served to alienate some of the members. Four CP (BSTI) Manchester branches refused to go along with the merger and resigned in disgust.[40]

Very much greater casualties were sustained in the operation to pull the left wing from the Independent Labour Party. Had the object been to gain the greatest possible number of members, then the split should have come in 1920, when revolutionary influence in the ILP was at its peak. Before the 1920 conference, the Lancashire, Cheshire, North-East, Yorkshire and Welsh divisions had all come out in favour of disaffiliating from the Second International and joining the Third. At the conference, Ramsay MacDonald had to use all his oratorical skill to prevent this happening. Nevertheless, a resolution was carried by 529 votes to 144, taking the ILP out of the Second International, although another resolution calling for immediate affiliation to the Third was defeated by 472 votes to 206. Essentially, MacDonald and the right wing played for time. They managed to persuade conference to enter

into negotiations with the Swiss Socialist Party to discuss the possible
formation of an intermediate body between the two Internationals.
Their tactic paid off. The decline in revolutionary fervour throughout
the working class was reflected inside the ILP. The tight control over
the party apparatus, and especially the party press, by MacDonald
insured that the members were continuously confronted by the official
viewpoint. At the same time, their opponents, by their own actions,
demonstrated that they were not wanting to improve the ILP but to
wreck it. When the average party member realised the left's loyalty lay
elsewhere, he became thoroughly disenchanted with it. The left split
from the ILP in March 1921. Once more, the grandiose vision of
thousands of workers clamouring for admission to the Communist
Party did not materialise. Klugmann says 'several hundred joined'
whereas Tom Bell says it 'only added one or two hundred.'[41]

It is interesting to note how the Communist Party fared through the
various fusions. Klugmann, the CP's official historian, claims that at the
London Unity Convention (August 1920) there were between 4,000
and 5,000 members represented on paper. By the time of the Leeds
Unity Convention (January 1921), when the Communist Labour Party
and the CP (BSTI) joined, the total number had shrunk to 3,000. However, at the 1922 Congress, after the ILP Left united with it, the Communist Party membership had dwindled to 2,000. A cynic may be for-
given for wondering whether the CPGB could have survived another
merger.

But behind paucity of recruitment lies an important question: why
did so many fish get away? We have already seen that Lenin had much
more optimistic forecasts of CPGB strength. It is one of the few
opinions he shared with the Special Branch: in a report to the Cabinet,
dated 13 January 1921, the Special Branch estimated the number of
active communists at 20,000, but thought that five times that number
favoured communism.[42] How was it, then, that so small a proportion
joined the Communist Party?

The reasons, I think, are numerous and complex. First and foremost
among them is that the party failed to relate itself to the prevailing level
of working-class consciousness. In part, this was associated with another
handicap: the Communist Party was not seen as a genuine, indigenous
group but as a Russian agency, prepared to twist and turn as its masters
decreed. What worsened the CP's plight was that its masters were so ill-
informed. John S. Clarke, the editor of *The Worker,* considered himself
to be a Bolshevik, but still felt obliged to report to the Clydeside
workers about the illusions he found prevalent among the leaders of the

Comintern:

> Sylvia Pankhurst was believed to be lying in a dungeon undergoing
> the tortures of Rosa Luxemburg. John Maclean was thought to be
> the particular personality around which rallied the Communist
> movement of Great Britain (they discovered he wasn't just before we
> arrived). The Guild Socialists had virtually captured the trade unions,
> and the unofficial Workers' Committee were endeavouring to smash
> the unions and had rejected political ideas, like the IWW.[43]

As well as failing to understand the experiences of the British proletariat, the Russians may also have failed to translate their own experiences into terms that made sense and were helpful to British workers.
Lenin himself appears to have perceived this latter point. Speaking at
the Fourth Congress of the Communist International in 1922, he said:

> I have the impression that we made a big mistake with this resolu-
> tion, namely, that we ourselves have blocked our own road to
> further success. As I have said already, the resolution is excellently
> drafted; I subscribe to every one of its fifty or more points. But we
> have not understood how to present our Russian experience to
> foreigners. All that has been said in the resolution has remained a
> dead letter. If we do not realise this we shall make no progress.[44]

Whether Lenin was correct or not, the British Communist Party failed
to make progress.

Notes

1. Thomas Bell, *Pioneering Days*, p. 180.
2. *The Socialist*, 15 April 1920.
3. Ibid, 15 May 1919.
4. Ibid, 6 May 1920.
5. *Report to the Second Congress of the Third International*, pp. 65-6.
6. *The Socialist*, 24 February 1921.
7. J.T. Walton Newbold, Unpublished Autobiography, no pagination (Rylands
    Library Manchester).
8. CAB 24/118/CP2429, *A Survey of Revolutionary Movements in Great
    Britain in the Year 1920*, by the Directorate of Intelligence (HQ), p. 11.
    Also J.T. Walton Newbold, op. cit.
9. J.W. Hulse, *The Forming of the Communist International* (Stanford, 1964)
    p. 117.
10. V.I. Lenin, *Collected Works*, vol. 31, p. 143.

11.   *Lenin on Britain,* p. 201.
12.   *Pravda* article quoted in Home Office papers CAB 77 GT7254, 14 May 1919.
13.   L.J. MacFarlane, *The British Communist Party* (1966) pp. 51-2. Bell, Paul and MacManus were the only prominent SLPers at Nottingham. Quite incorrectly, James Hinton, in his preface to J.T. Murphy's *The Workers' Committees* (1972 ed.), says on p. 5 that Murphy belonged to the Unity Group.
14.   *The Socialist,* 3 February 1921; *Vanguard,* August 1920.
15.   Several historians have criticised John Maclean for not belonging to the CPGB – see, for example, Terry Brotherstone, *Fourth International,* summer 1974. This begs the question of whether he could actually belong to the Communist Party.
16.   *Communist Unity Convention Official Report,* pp. 71-2. The Report gives the number of delegates as 152, but this was faulty arithmetic.
17.   W. Gallacher, *Last Memoirs,* p. 141; Nan Milton, *John Maclean,* pp. 227-8.
18.   Interview with Harry McShane, 8 August 1972.
19.   Pankhurst Papers, Amsterdam. Also *New Edinburgh Review,* No. 19, 1972 'Remembering John Maclean', by Harry McShane.
20.   Examples of the authorities' knowledge of Rothstein's activities can be seen from the frequent references in the reports from secret agents of the Home Office to be found in Cabinet Papers. For example, 544 of 2 February 1920; 791 of 4 March 1920; 1039 of 8 April 1920; 1355 of 27 May 1920; 1743 of 5 August 1920; 1772 of 12 August 1920; 1804 of 26 August 1920 – to cite a few.
21.   *The Worker,* 14 August 1920; *The Communist,* 16 September 1920.
22.   *The Worker,* 25 September 1920.
23.   Letter from J. Maclean to T. Mitchell, secretary of the SLP.
24.   Tom Bell, *John Maclean,* p. 79.
25.   W. Gallacher, *Last Memoirs,* pp. 118-25.
26.   *The Socialist,* 22 April 1920.
27.   Ibid, 24 June 1920. To have spent an entire week campaigning for the SLP indicates some commitment on both sides.
28.   *Lenin on Britain,* p. 268.
29.   J. Clunie, *The Third International,* p. 23. Also, W. Gallacher, *Revolt on the Clyde,* pp. 251-3.
30.   *Vanguard,* December 1920.
31.   Nan Milton, op. cit., pp. 234-277.
32.   *The Socialist,* 14 October 1920.
33.   *Daily Record,* 27 December 1920, carried the sensational headline, 'Angry Scenes: Maclean and Gallacher Duel'.
34.   *The Socialist,* 13 January 1921.
35.   Ibid. As Hugh MacDiarmid correctly points out in *The Company I've Kept* (1966) p. 125, the Communist Party have continued to use Maclean's name although it was hostile to him.
36.   *The Worker,* 4 December 1920.
37.   Tom Bell, op. cit., p. 195.
38.   *Workers' Dreadnought,* 7 and 14 December 1918.
39.   Ibid, 27 November 1920.
40.   *Workers' Dreadnought,* 27 November 1920.
41.   Tom Bell, op. cit., p. 195; J. Klugmann, op. cit., pp. 197-8.
42.   CAB 24/118/CP2452.
43.   *The Worker,* 2 October 1920.
44.   V.I. Lenin, *Selected Works,* vol. 10, p. 322. It may be significant and a sign

of Russian domination of the International, that Lenin has to remind his
audience that they are at a Comintern meeting, not simply a Russian
gathering.

12 THE REVOLUTIONARIES' LAST STAND

The end came unexpectedly: in 1921 the SLP did not realise that its demise was near. Its Easter conference, held at Dewsbury, was reported to be 'the most enthusiastic and successful ever held.'[1] The annual report said that the SLP press was working overtime, producing books, pamphlets and leaflets. The Party still had a large number of people on the periphery, ready to read and sell its literature. Admittedly, there were some setbacks, reversals that seemed of a minor nature. In 1920-1, the SLP had lost 12 branches, mainly to the CPGB. On the other hand, it had created six new ones, so the Party had a total of 42 branches. . Similarly in membership, the figures had taken a slight downward turn: 796 had been lost while 434 members had been gained. Looking at these statistics, it is perhaps surprising that so few had succumbed to the lure of the CPGB, and that MacManus, Paul and Bell had so few followers when they left the SLP. Their loss, it could be argued, was more than compensated for by the recruitment of John Maclean, who undoubtedly had great popularity among the masses. When he did a speaking tour of Lancashire, Maclean secured audiences that were twice the size of other speakers', according to Home Office spies.[2] In Scotland, his power to draw crowds was sure to be much bigger.

The formation of the Communist Party left most SLPers undismayed. It seemed to them that it was not based on firm theoretical and organisational principles, and so would not survive the test of events. This was the opinion expressed by Maclean in a letter to his friend James Clunie: 'The CP is going "rocky", and as it fades the ground will be cleared for a real fighting party, independent of outside dictation of finance.' He went on to describe two packed meetings he had addressed in St Mungo Hall the previous Sunday and concluded with the opinion that 'a real mass movement is simmering in Glasgow, despite every mode of repression or treachery.'[3]

The SLP seemed to have definite advantages in comparison to the Communist Party. True, the CPGB had more money to splash about, but money was not everything. As *Solidarity,* the London journal, pointed out: 'It is possible to buy an organisation, but not a social revolution.'[4] When it came to industrial work, the SLP was at a definite advantage. Its members had traditionally devoted themselves to this sphere of activity, whereas many CPers, coming from the BSP, had been orientated to the electoral scene. Of course, this is a generalisation. There were many exceptions: often it was merely a question of chance, depending upon which party had a branch in your particular locality, that determined the organisation to which you belonged. But there appears little doubt that the SLP, with more experience and attaching more importance to it, worked in industry in a more systematic way.

The haphazard approach of the Communist Party was criticised by Karl Radek, one of the leaders of the Comintern. In particular, he attacked the CPGB's failure to give a coherent lead during the miners' strike of 1921:

> We discovered that meetings took place in the mining districts, but they were in no way arranged or co-ordinated by the Party.
>
> One of the comrades said: 'When I get on the platform at the meeting, I know as much as the Man in the Moon what I'm going to say on these points, but I give them Communism.
>
> What slogans do you go to the meeting with? What do you say to the masses is your attitude to nationalisation? What does this mean? The Party is in the midst of a terrific struggle of the workers, and has no plan for directing its own forces. This is the first point: the less the strength, the more it must be directed to its aim, and, in addition, to what forces it set in motion it gave no slogan. Nor does it tell the comrades what they should say to the miners on the problems of today and tomorrow. And still further: the Party appeared in many places under the guise of 'Workers' Committees' and as far as this agitation has effect it does not bind the masses to the CP. Comrades, it is our duty to tell even the smallest Communist Party that you will never become a mass party if you busy yourselves only with the propaganda of the theory of Communism.[5]

In contrast, the SLP's position was clear. It anticipated the betrayal of the Triple Alliance, and argued that no faith should be placed in the union leaders, including those who mouthed leftish phrases. It was up to the workers to spread the strike to other industries. The miners could sharpen the conflict by seizing the mines and working them for themselves. It was necessary to call upon the soldiers for support. Victory in such a significant struggle could be of inestimable value to either the capitalist state or to the creation of socialism, so it was important to raise the slogan: 'All power to the workers'.[6]

The Communist Party adopted a less hostile line towards union leaders. In part, this arose because many of its members were less clear

about the role of the union bureaucracy and did not see the need to
build rank-and-file organisation. But it was also due to pressures arising
from the 'Hands Off Russia' campaign. While Harry Pollitt, who directed the campaign, did not like SLPers appearing on its platforms, he
went out of his way to encourage respectable and influential members
of the Labour Movement. These included A.A. Purcell, of the TUC,
C.T. Cramp (NUR), W. Straker (MFGB), Ben Turner (Textile Workers),
Ernest Bevin and Robert Williams (Transport Workers). Looking at the
list of speakers, one sees many leaders who later betrayed the General
Strike of 1926. In fact, a foretaste of this came in 1921, when the
Triple Alliance failed to come to the assistance of the hard-pressed
miners. In view of his conduct on 'Black Friday', the CPGB could not
permit one of the main culprits — Robert Williams, general secretary of
the Transport Workers — to remain a member of the Party. Yet they
still remained on friendly terms with him. Palme Dutt permitted
Williams to explain and try to justify his apostasy in the *Labour
Monthly,* a journal which the CPGB controlled, and he also remained
active in Communist-front organisations.[7] Given this kind of close
association, it becomes impossible to make a thorough-going criticism
of the man or a serious attempt to unseat him from his union position.

Dissatisfaction with trade union leaders provided an impetus to the
development of rank-and-file movements. This had already been recognised to happen: cabinet papers reveal that inefficiency of ASLEF and
NUR officials was the reason for grassroots organisation emerging on
the railways. And similar moves occurred in other parts of industry. In
the Northumberland and Durham coalfields, the Northern Miners' Unofficial Reform Committee was formed on 19 February 1921, with
George Harvey as secretary. Likewise in Lancashire, an unofficial organisation, closely assisted by Maclean and MacDougall, was very
active. In April 1921, the Stirlingshire Miners' Reform Committee was
created, with Patrick Lafferty as secretary.[8]

While the coal industry was to the fore when it came to the development of the unofficial movement, even there it was patchy. Many coalfields remained with little or no rank-and-file organisation. Nor should
the strength of those that did exist be exaggerated. It may appear impressive at first to hear that 24 lodges, with 30,000 members, were
represented at the Northern Miners' Unofficial Reform Committee
conference, but when it is remembered that there were 400 miners'
lodges in Northumberland and Durham, these numbers can be seen in
true perspective.

This is not to deny that there was very considerable discontent, at times even hatred, of union officials and union policy. The problem was that the passionate outbursts were prone to be transitory. Disgruntled workers, after making a protest, would sink back into apathy. It became exceedingly difficult to sustain a rank-and-file organisation, particularly with a shortage of finance and facilities. Whenever a serious threat emerged, the united efforts of employers and trade union leaders, aided if necessary by state repression, were usually sufficient to smash it. As a consequence, most rank-and-file organisations, whatever their grandiose plans, operated on a modest scale. Generally, they would devote themselves to propaganda activities rather than to attempts to supplant, or by-pass, the official negotiating channels. They might also, like the AEU group, attempt to co-ordinate activity within the union, sending information from one part of the country to another, hoping to overthrow the official bureaucracy.

Recognising its own weaknesses, the SLP sought to garner its industrial forces, helping to give them direction and purpose. In February 1921, a conference was held in Glasgow on Socialist Industrial Unionism. This stated its broad agreement with the method of working proposed by the Comintern. The conference report started with a quotation from Zinoviev, chairman of the Third International, which stressed the need to belong to organisations that had the allegiance of the workers and to win them over to a revolutionary standpoint:

> Everywhere where there are workmen, there must be communists.
> We cannot abandon several millions of workmen to the influence of
> social traitors and stand aside ourselves. The social traitors, who
> have been thrown out of the political parties, have now surrounded
> themselves with the thick walls of trade unions.
>
> We must get hold of this fortress; we must conduct a regular,
> systematic, patient siege; we must expel the traitors of the working
> class from their refuge; we must exterminate their defences between
> us and the bourgeoisie; and then we shall stand face to face with the
> capitalists, who will have a hard time then.[9]

Delegates at the Glasgow conference saw two issues as paramount. First, they wanted to transform the unions, giving them a revolutionary outlook, so they would affiliate to the Red Trade Union International. The situation in the AEU looked promising. Delegates wanted to mobilise AEU members to bring pressure to bear on the reluctant leaders to allow a vote on the affiliation question. The second matter that concerned delegates was that of educational provisions. The

Labour College movement was then at its height. It provided a wide variety of classes to trade unions and other working-class organisations. All told, it constituted a formidable means for developing socialist consciousness and militancy.

The authorities appreciated that the Labour Colleges were a threat to capitalist stability. The Home Office papers are strewn with reports from its agents on the damaging effect of tuition from this source. The following illustrative quotations are taken from the Directorate of Intelligence's reports on revolutionary movements for the years 1919 and 1920:

(i)   class prejudice and ignorance of elementary economics has a firmer grip upon the working class than ever before . . . Unfortunately, almost the only agency is the Labour Colleges, which are imparting instruction in false economics.   (1919, p. 18)

(ii) Revolutionary classes were increased and well-supported, and lantern lectures became a successful feature of Bolshevik propaganda. The cost of living lent impetus to the propaganda of Marxist economics, which were eagerly absorbed by the younger trade unionists.   (1920, p. 7)

(iii) The College [i.e. the Central Labour College-RC] is the fountain-head of Marxian teaching in this country and is responsible for the training of more dangerous revolutionaries than all the communist parties put together.   (1920, p. 40)

Naturally, the government were concerned about these classes. Equally alarmed were the moderate union officials, whose class-collaborationist policies met abrasive criticism from union members who had attended Labour College courses. So it was resolved, despite the country's financial difficulties, to fling more money into adult education: the Government decided to increase its grant to that rival of the Labour College Movement, the WEA. When the Cabinet considered the matter, it had before it a covering note in the form of a letter sent by a former leader of the engineering union, G.N. Barnes, to the General Secretary of the WEA:

The only effective method of counteracting the educational side of the movement [i.e., the Labour College movement-RC] is to cater for the intellectual hunger which has undoubtedly been stimulated by the war in a broader and better way — in other words, to provide increased facilities for lectures, classes and study groups where subjects of interest can be thrashed out under university guidance.[10]

It is in this context that the decision of the Glasgow conference must
be viewed. Trade Unionists there were facing an immediate threat:
education facilities within the unions were being taken out of their
hands, Marxism was to become a forgotten subject, and control was to
be vested in university lecturers, including orthodox capitalist principles.
For these reasons, the call went out to rally to the defence of IWCE —
Independent Working Class Education.

The Labour College Movement possessed a sizeable number of active
adherents, its greatest strength probably existing in Scotland. When, in
May 1919, the Scottish Labour College held its conference, 571 delegates attended. They represented the impressive total of 222 trade
unions and branches, 70 socialist organisations, 40 Co-operative
Societies, 15 Co-operative Educational Committees and 11 Trade and
Labour Councils.[11] John Maclean and William McLaine, a leading shop
steward, became full-time tutors, while there was also a large body of
part time voluntary lecturers. The prospects for the Labour College
Movement appeared bright. But by 1921 its position had somewhat
darkened. The Scottish Labour College's income had dropped by half
on the previous year.[12] Even so, it maintained its two full-time tutors,
now John Maclean and A.M. Robertson, and had 1,800 students,
mainly in Edinburgh and Glasgow, studying Marxism. The Labour
Colleges still remained a force of some significance.

The decline of the movement can be attributed little, if at all, to
Government sponsorship being given to the WEA. Far more important
were changes taking place within the working class. A succession of
defeats, of which that of the miners in 1921 and of the engineers in
1922 were the most damaging, helped to transform the industrial
scene. The AEU paid out £2 million in unemployment benefit in a year
while the miners' union doled out £7 million. All trade unions discovered their outgoings had drastically increased while their incomes
had declined. In 1922, the NUR reported it was £250,000 in debt.
Quite correctly, the situation was assessed in an article by J.T. Murphy
when he declared: 'The trade union movement of Britain has received
within the last 12 months the severest hammering of modern history.'[13]
In the wake of the employers' offensive came demoralisation among
workers, as they were forced to endure round after round of wage cuts
combined with mounting unemployment. In essence, the difficulties
facing the Labour College arose from a waning of class consciousness.

Of course, the SLP suffered also as a consequence of these calamities.

Many sympathisers, who sold SLP literature in Labour College classes, discovered their market much reduced. Among workers in general, both the ability to afford socialist pamphlets, as well as the inclination to buy, accentuated the trend to falling sales. Then, again, the SLP found itself hard hit by unemployment: its members, usually the active shop stewards, were the first to go when redundancy came along. Hence factory sales also declined.

Mass unemployment, a feature that characterised almost the entire period between the wars, presented socialists with a profound problem. Many of their former strongholds had become industrial graveyards. Not only were people out of work, there were no prospects of work. Widespread misery and demoralisation inevitably ensued. R.M. Fox cited a typical example of what happened, when he described the fate of many of those who had joined him in resistance to the First World War and now found themselves on the scrap-heap:

> Ostracized during the War, they had no jobs to turn to. I saw them then, tramping the streets of London in threadbare clothes and broken boots. I met them then, these courageous comrades I had known who stood steadfast through the prison years, selling boot polish or insurance at the doors. Men will always be found to endure martyrdom confidently, if not with exultation. To live for a purpose — it is a grand thing, the best that life can offer. But the aimless, fruitless, worthless sacrifice of ordinary life, that is the bitterest draught.[14]

What was to be done? It was easy to say that mass unemployment constituted a sign of British capitalism's decline and to argue that the answer was to introduce socialism, but this did not help people in the here and now. After considerable discussion within the SLP, its policy appeared to be based upon two main principles. The first was the reiteration of the right to work: if a man was unemployed, he should either be provided with work or — as the misfortune was not of his but the system's making — he should be provided with an amount equivalent to a wage. The slogan 'Work or full maintenance' was seen as the demand which would unite the unemployed in struggle. At the same time, it was preferable not to become unemployed in the first place. Therefore, the second principle enunciated to fight for a cut in hours without a reduction in pay. Should this not be attainable, then workers should strive for work-sharing, even if it meant smaller pay packets, rather than accept redundancy.

The disintegration of working-class power made it impossible to prevent unemployment growing. With the shop stewards' movement seriously weakened, resistance to sackings rarely occurred. Those militants still with jobs were inclined to keep their heads down, avoiding trouble, rather than disputing the boss's right to hire and fire. In these conditions, it was not possible even to build effective links between the employed and the unemployed. If those who had jobs were unable to prevent wage cuts and deteriorations of conditions being imposed on them, how could they hope to help those out of work? In January 1921, John Maclean, backed by the SLP, proposed that a general strike should be held as a protest against mounting unemployment. He failed to secure a response. Similarly, on 23 February 1921, when Maclean held a conference in Glasgow to build an all-Scotland movement of the unemployed, James Clunie in *The Socialist* described the attendance as 'a very sad affair'.[15] In most towns, the unemployed remained unorganised. In the few places where organisations existed, funds were virtually non-existent, quite inadequate for sending delegates to conferences and maintaining regular contact with groups elsewhere. But even more important as a cause of fragmentation was that responsibility for poor relief stayed with local authorities. Initially, therefore, the struggle was seen in a parish pump, not a national, context.

It was on this local level that John Maclean secured his greatest degree of success. He led countless demonstrations to the Glasgow council. He accused the Labour councillors of playing politics, of 'sympathising' with the unemployed while doing little or nothing to ameliorate their conditions. In January 1921, 200 policemen barred entrance to the council chambers to Maclean and other protesters. Inside, a handful of the Labour group contented themselves with trying to suspend standing orders and, when this failed, simply allowing proceedings to continue. 'Meantime, the unemployed are being insulted by food tickets to the value of £1 a week,' complained Harry McShane.[16] Ultimately, a meeting with the Labour group was arranged. From the chair, Shinwell agreed that more money should be given. But when the motion was brought before the council by Wheatley, it was defeated. This merely served to reinforce Maclean's low opinion of Labour representatives. He considered Labour politicians looked upon the unemployed from a vote-catching angle. They were not genuinely concerned about the plight of people out of work. When one delegation met Labour councillors, some of them were absent making a tour of inspection of local public houses, and on another occasion David Kirkwood, instead of being there, was speaking for Ramsay MacDonald in the Woolwich bye-election. They greeted the demand from Maclean that the Labour Party should call for a general strike as a protest against the mass unemployment with the reply that it might damage their prospects at the next elections.[17] Underlying this lay a further point – the acceptance by Labour, with a few minor reservations, of orthodox capitalist economics. As a result, the supreme importance of increasing profitability, as a means of restoring the economy to health, was acknowledged. This could not be accomplished if public expenditure, including expenditure on the unemployed, was permitted to rise.

The net result of Maclean's Glasgow campaign was small. Perhaps the furore of mass demonstrations prodded the city fathers into granting a few more crumbs of relief, it is difficult to say. What is more certain is that Maclean gave to the Glasgow unemployed organisation an ideology: the reserve army of labour in Central Scotland spoke with a Marxist voice. Yet, for all his tireless efforts, Maclean had not achieved much among the unemployed. Preoccupied with their personal problems, with the day-to-day struggle to survive, men who were out of work did not have the money or energy to help build a revolutionary party. This lesson, experienced by Maclean in Glasgow, was learnt by SLPers and others elsewhere. Few, if any, recruits would come from the dole queues.

Almost as barren from a recruitment standpoint was the solidarity campaigns. As already shown, the 'Hands off Russia' campaign, controlled by the CPGB, sought to entice the respectability of the working-class movement to participate; it did not want the assistance, at least in a leading way, of Marxists who remained outside its ranks and were critical of its policy. So the SLP was virtually excluded. The Communist Party, however, was not in the same position to place an embargo on the campaign over Ireland, an issue that had a direct effect on large numbers of people. It must be remembered that, unlike the Irish troubles today (1977), the disturbances spread throughout the whole of Ireland in the 1916-22 period. Large numbers of Irish in Britain were first generation immigrants, people who still retained their links with relatives and friends at home, and, at the same time, a larger proportion of British people than now had sons or husbands fighting in the army in Ireland. As a consequence, whenever the Irish question was raised, it was sure to kindle the passions of the British public.

At the Third Congress of the Comintern, two Irish delegates pointed to painful inadequacies in the approach of British left-wingers to the problem of Ireland. 'The attitude of the British workers towards Ireland,' one of them declared, 'is the barometer of social revolutionary feeling in Britain.' He called upon his comrades to show solidarity by blacking the transport of arms and by spreading anti-imperialist propaganda among the troops. He continued:

> With regard to the statement that the British workers will regard as treason to England the support of the colonial revolutionary struggle against British imperialism, the sooner the British workers get familiar with treason to the bourgeois state the better for the revolutionary movement.[18]

He also referred to Irish railwaymen and engineers, who had disaffiliated from the British-based NUR and engineering union, because they had failed to receive assistance with stopping the manufacture and despatch of weapons to be used against Irishmen.

These strictures from the Irish delegate could be accurately applied to the BSP and, subsequently, with lesser justice, to the CPGB. Instead of trying to arouse disaffection in the armed forces, they tended to confine themselves to the less dangerous activity of calling attention to the need to stop the war. The BSP, in particular, did not visualise its task along class lines; rather it sought to exert an influence through changing public opinion. But to many revolutionaries, whether they were in the SLP or other left groups, this approach appeared inadequate and wrong. *The Socialist* was very scathing about this approach:

> The old game goes merrily on. On the same boat as the resolutions of sympathy come 10,000 bombs, made by British Labour and fired by British Labour into Irish Towns, to kill Irishmen and destroy Irish homes. Resolutions on paper won't do.[19]

The SLP argued that the treacherous role of the British Labour Party, making a few noises for peace while doing nothing effectively against the British government's repressive policy, needed to be exposed. The demand needed to be raised for self-determination for the Irish people. The SLP regarded Ireland as the Achilles heel of British capitalism, where defeat for the imperialist forces would so weaken the general position of the ruling class as to open exciting revolutionary possibilities. Hence a high priority was given to the work.

Foremost in the struggle was a remarkable man, rarely mentioned in history books, called Sean McLoughlin. Although still young, he had had an eventful career: he became interested in Larkinism during the

Dublin lock-out of 1913; he participated in the 1916 Easter Uprising, taking a leading part and being known as the 'boy commander' after Connolly had been seriously wounded; and in 1919 he organised volunteers in the south of Ireland.[20] But McLoughlin gradually became convinced that Sinn Fein would never create a workers' republic. He therefore left the IRA and joined the Socialist Party of Ireland. He spoke alongside John Maclean, who visited Ireland in May 1919. When the issue of affiltion to the Third International arose, the Socialist Party split and McLoughlin became secretary of the newly-formed Irish Communist Party.[21]

Instead of using all his energy in trying to build up the tiny Irish CP, McLoughlin spent considerable periods on speaking tours of Britain. He did this because he believed the struggles in the two countries were inextricably linked. 'If once a workers' republic were established in Ireland,' he declared, 'the effects in Britain would be tremendous.' A workers' state in Ireland, however, would not survive long were Britain to remain capitalist. The question of revolution in Britain, he argued, would then become paramount: 'There must be unity of action between the conscious Irish and British workers.'[23]

Wherever McLoughlin went in Britain, he addressed large and enthusiastic meetings. It was frequently reported that these were the biggest ever held in this or that town. In Yorkshire, he addressed nine meetings, attended by 20,000 people. An old ex-SLPer, C.H. Burden, recalls two of McLoughlin's meetings in the Dewsbury-Batley area: 'He was the greatest propaganda speaker I have ever heard. He was able to draw the largest crowds and hold them. I think he outshone A.J. Cook, who, too, was a mass orator of the biggest calibre. I heard McLoughlin say he was sentenced to death for his part in the Easter Uprising but was amnestied because he was under 16 years old.'[23] Usually McLoughlin spoke under the auspices of the SLP, probably because he thought the CPGB line too mild, and the Communist Party retaliated by telling its members to boycott McLoughlin's meetings.[24]

Many other socialists campaigned alongside McLoughlin over Ireland. Perhaps some indication of the strength of feeling that prevailed among sections of the working class can be judged by the fact that John Maclean, assisted by his four companions of the Tramp Trust, sold 20,000 copies of a pamphlet on this issue. *Ireland's Tragedy: Scotland's Disgrace* is not one of Maclean's better works, being marred by a nationalistic outlook, yet undoubtedly it evoked a responsive chord among workers, especially those of Irish descent.

But, although welcome, the combining of industrial militancy with involvement over Ireland did create problems. It gave an opportunity for agents provacateurs to try to discredit the workers' struggle by a few carefully-timed bomb outrages. Also, there was the danger that Sinn Fein and its supporters, who operated in Scotland, would oblige the authorities with a firework display all of their own. In the 1921 miners' lock-out, John Maclean went out of his way to ask pitmen of Irish extraction 'to stand steady and calm'. He went on: 'This is no plea for passive starvation, but the refusal to resort to childish displays of petty force when the Government is ready to give us a deluge of blood.'[25]

Notwithstanding the absence of any large-scale disturbances, the authorities still resorted to repressive policies. They arrested key people, thereby hoping to disrupt working-class organisations and intimidate them. Support for the Irish struggle provided a convenient handle with which to beat the left. Likewise involvement in the wave of industrial struggles was another.

The SLP lost a number of important comrades through imprisonment and the functioning of its headquarters was affected. One of the worst examples of persecution occurred to William Hedley, of Sheffield SLP. An ex-soldier himself, he was accused of causing disaffection among the British army in Ireland. He was arrested at Rotherham and taken over to Belfast. When last mentioned in *The Socialist,* he was on his fourth hunger strike in twelve months.[26] In Glasgow, Thomas McGregory received a three-month sentence with hard labour for speaking outside the Bath Street recruiting centre about 'the atrocities committed by our own Government in India, Egypt and in Ireland.'[27] Then on 6 June 1921, Tom Mitchell, SLP general secretary, and Sam L. Smith, of the SLP Press, were charged with writing and publishing 'an article likely to cause sedition and disaffection amongst Her Majesty's Forces and among the civilian population.' After having their appeals rejected, they also served three-month sentences with hard labour.[28] John Maclean suggested that another reason for this prosecution, which lessened the efficiency of the SLP, was that presses were used to print the Sinn Fein journal, *Dark Rosaleen.*

Inevitably Maclean himself, being the foremost revolutionary, was a prime target for the authorities. He appeared to spend his time going in and out of prison, interspersed with fiery defences of his revolutionary politics in court proceedings. Typical of this was his prosecution, along with his comrade Sandy Ross, in May 1921. Arraigned under the Emergency Regulations Acts, some of the charges took on a faintly humorous aspect. The first was 'that you had told your audience that if

they had given their money to revolutionary agitators instead of book-
makers, they would have had a much better return.' While the eleventh
charge, one made against Sandy Ross, was that in a speech during the
1921 lock-out he had said

> if any of the miners expected a decent settlement from David Lloyd
> George, that they might as well expect the truth from a policeman in
> the witness box, and they would be lucky if they did not get their
> heads knocked off by "dirty Davie's" defence force.

In the course of cross-examination, Maclean was asked what he meant
by revolution. Maclean held out both hands, one above the other. He
said they represented the two classes in society, the top being the
capitalist class. Then he swung his hands round to the reverse position,
and said that was revolution. The alarmed Fiscal inquired, 'You want
workers to seize other people's capital?' To which Maclean tartly
replied, 'The workers will seize the world.'[29]

John Maclean received a three-month sentence. In prison, in protest
at being denied the rights of a political prisoner, he went on hunger
strike. Although he must have been weakened by the ordeal, within two
hours of leaving jail on 17 August, Maclean was in court again — this
time as defence witness for his comrade, Harry McShane, prosecuted
for selling socialist literature.[30] Not for a moment did he have a respite:
throwing himself back into the struggle, he was re-arrested on 31
August, charged with sedition, and sentenced to a year's imprisonment.
Once more he went on hunger strike.

Inevitably, this kind of treatment — the frequent imprisonments,
deprivations, hunger — took its toll. Maclean who prided himself on his
constitution, was nevertheless gravely weakened. But he disregarded his
physical condition; to him, politics were paramount.[31] So he continued
until the final collapse came, and died in 1923 at the age of 44.

In a sense, the fate of John Maclean exemplified the fate of the
entire Movement. State repression, a receding tide of militancy, victimisation all hastened the end of the SLP and other revolutionary groups.
Even where opportunities at first appeared bright, as in the case of Ireland, demoralisation ensued. The partition of 1922 and the creation of
Ulster established the conditions, as Countess Markievicz foresaw, for
the continued economic domination of Ireland by British capital.[32]
Despite all the sacrifices, Connolly's vision of a workers' republic had
become by 1922 remote and unrealisable — at least, for the foreseeable
future.

In the aftermath of intense class conflict it is quite customary to experience a period of demoralisation. After 1848, 'the year of revolutions', Marx and Engels found themselves isolated, with no influence whatsoever, during the 1850s. Similarly, Lenin's support virtually vanished, the Bolsheviks being reduced to a very tiny sect, in the reaction that followed the 1905 Revolution. So it is not surprising that, after the quasi-revolutionary situation in Britain of 1919-20, left-wing organisations like the SLP should go through a decline.

What made the 1920s difference was the existence of the Communist Party. This constituted a serious rival, a competitor for the dwindling pool of potential recruits. Bolstered up from abroad, the CPGB could expect that, regardless of how uncongenial conditions became, the Comintern would do everything within its power to see that the party survived. Moreover, as the prospects for a British revolution grew dimmer, the triumph of the Russian Revolution grew more impressive. The CPGB, basking in the reflected glory, gained thereby. It was the sole publisher of Bolshevik literature. Naturally, this meant that all people on the British left, interested in what Lenin and his comrades had written, needed to contact the party. And then, of course, there was the vital question of financial aid. J.T. Murphy, who became a leading CP functionary in the late 'twenties, confessed that 'had the Communist Party not received big financial shots in the arm, it would have been reduced and probably gone out of existence within a year or so of formation, just as Sylvia Pankhurst's organisation and its paper died when they got no money from external sources.'[33] Like Sylvia Pankhurst, the SLP was also without any outside aid.

Financial assistance gave the CPGB many advantages over rival groups. It provided victimised militants who had lost their jobs and had no prospects of gaining others, the possibility of joining the payroll of the Communist Party or one of its front organisations. This prospect must have been appealing to people faced with the likelihood of indefinite unemployment. Then, having greater manpower, the Communist Party's apparatus could function with reasonable efficiency, and quickly dominate broad movements of the working class. When the Depression worsened and these lost their substantial support, among the masses, they became easier for the CP to secure control over.

The Shop Stewards' and Workers' Committee Movement was a case in point. By the early 1920s the flesh had dropped off, leaving merely a skeleton — and the Communist Party to manipulate the bones. In Liverpool, shop stewards, who had years of struggle behind them, complained that none of them had been consulted before Liverpool's delegates to the Shop Stewards' and Workers' Committee conference were appointed. One of the complainants, Wilf Braddock, went so far as to say he did not know the gentlemen who had been appointed as 'their' representative.[34]

Still more strange was the appointment of J.R. Campbell to the chairmanship of the Shop Stewards' and Workers' Committee Movement. His sole qualification would appear to have been that, as a close friend and colleague of Gallacher, he would carry out any order given him by the Communist Party. In his *Last Memoirs,* Gallacher mentioned J.R. Campbell's background: he worked in a grocer's shop, volunteered for the army in the First World War, and 'had never been in a factory.'[35] Can anyone imagine a thriving rank-and-file organisation being led by somebody with no industrial experience whatsoever? That the Shop Stewards' and Workers' Committee Movement *was* merely indicates that it had degenerated into a CP-dominated rump. Quite logically, in 1922 it dissolved itself in the Communist Party.[36]

When not in control of other organisations, the Communist Party usually attempted to capture or destroy them. In Chapter Eleven, an account was given of how Campbell and Gallacher tried to disrupt John Maclean's meetings with the Glasgow unemployed. A much more serious situation arose in the East End of London. In 1921 the Poplar Board of Guardians had been in the vanguard of the struggle for more adequate provisions for the workless. Led by George Lansbury, it defied the courts and the councillors went *en bloc* to jail rather than apply iniquitous regulations. All this is well known, and has been mentioned by many historians. What is less well known is certain events in 1923, when the ardour of the Poplar Board of Guardians had somewhat cooled.

On 26 September 1923, the unemployed demonstrated at the Board of Guardians. They wanted the coal allowance, which had been taken away, restored for the winter months. They also asked for increased allowances to be given to single persons. In reply, Edgar Lansbury, a member of the CP who was chairman of the Board, rejected both demands and said the Board was even considering reducing the existing scale of relief. Whereupon the unemployed, angered by his answer, locked the doors of the building, saying the Guardians could only leave when they re-considered their decision. After some altercation, a Guardian who belonged to the Communist Party, A.A. Watts, moved (and was seconded by the Mayoress) that the police be called. Then proceedings came to an abrupt and violent end. According to the *Workers Dreadnought*:

A terrible scene ensued. The police fell upon the unarmed people in the building, beating them cruelly with their truncheons. Not only members of the Unemployed organisation were beaten, but also individuals who had come independently on their own special cases. Numbers of men were felled to the ground bleeding. Men rushed to Mr. George Lansbury, crying: 'Can't you stop it?' Mr. Lansbury spurned them: 'They have asked for it, and now they will get it. It will give a lesson to them,' he answered.[37]

Almost 40 people were badly hurt and many more were slightly injured.

Nationally, the Communist Party justified what had happened at Poplar. The demonstration was called by the Unemployed Workers' Organisation, which did not belong to the CP-dominated National Unemployed Workers Committee. It would have looked bad if this rival had won concessions. Failing to win higher allowances, the demonstration had developed into a protest against left Labour councillors, again something the Communist Party could not tolerate since the pivot of their policies was to achieve an alliance with the Labour left.

Shortly afterwards, when the memory of the police action at Poplar was still fresh in people's minds, George Lansbury was billed to address a meeting on unemployment in Glasgow. But he failed to turn up and Wal Hannington, the Communist Party's chief spokesman on unemployment, deputised for him. For the meeting, John Maclean and his comrades published a leaflet, deploring the use of police at Poplar and referring to the political inadequacies of the stand being taken by Lansbury and Robert Smillie, who was also speaking at the meeting. Forbidden by the Glasgow police to hold a counter-demonstration, Maclean entered the Hall. When Wal Hannington tried to justify the use of police at Poplar, the audience erupted and the meeting ended abruptly.[38]

From the Communist Party's standpoint, such confrontations were to be avoided. It sought, therefore, to restrict the contact of its members with the dissident left. Before the CPGB had been formed, MacManus had argued that this would lead to a strengthening of the Labour College Movement.[39] However, once the Communist Party had been created, the Communist Party's attitude was somewhat different. It did not want its members subjected to alien influences. The Dutt-Pollitt Report on Party Organisation (1923) claimed that the NCLC was 'hostile or indifferent to the Party'.[40] It argued that CPers should concentrate on building the CPGB's own educational facilities, not those of the Labour College, except for classes where Communist Party members were in control and could therefore determine the lecturers.[41]

Despite this attempt at sterile thought-control by the CPGB, the Labour College remained an aggravating sore about which the scions of King Street could do little. When, early in 1925, *Plebs* commented on the internal situation in Russia, it came down in support of Trotsky and against Stalin. On the other hand, the CP apparatchiks could take action against Sylvia Pankhurst. In the *Workers' Dreadnought*, she had sought to stimulate thought by publishing various Russian viewpoints, not simply the official one. This was heresy and had to be stopped. When Sylvia Pankhurst was in jail, she was instructed to hand over her journal to the Communist Party — as a private individual, it was argued, she should not own her own political paper. Because she refused, Sylvia Pankhurst was expelled from the CPGB. This explanation would be plausible were it not for the fact that, in the same month as she was thrown out of the Party for having her own paper, R. Palme Dutt started his own paper, *Labour Monthly*. Clearly, the underlying principle, nothing to do with ownership of papers, was plain: put forward, through thick and thin, the line as dictated from Moscow and get it accepted; but encourage workers to think for themselves, by confronting them with the variety of views expressed on a given topic, and, like Sylvia Pankhurst, one is asking to be purged.[42]

The Communist Party sought to prevent its members, and those in front organisations which it controlled, from reading the publications of the dissident left, such as the SLP. This represented a new departure for British politics: traditionally, while the various left groups disagreed with one another, there was no attempt to stop members from reading rival publications. The new restriction hurt the SLP in particular. Although with a small membership, it had been accustomed to selling its publications through the many channels of the Socialist Movement. Understandably, *The Socialist* denounced the prohibition. It said the Communist Party executive was guilty of 'intellectual dictatorship', telling the party's members that they were not to read *The Socialist, The Spur* or the *Workers' Dreadnought:*

> Primitive mythological conceptions of 'taboo' are small compared to that superstitious dictatorial expression of the narrow-minded prejudice by a set of persons who have small confidence in the views they profess to hold.[43]

Members of the Communist Party, not supposed to read the publications of rival tendencies, therefore were dependent upon the CP's own press for accounts of what these other organisations' policies happened to be. A distorted or totally false picture could be given to the faithful: the SLP could be described as 'anti-working class', John Maclean's sanity could be brought into question and Sean McLoughlin could be called a police agent. The techniques of Stalinism, later developed by the Communist Party against the Trotskyists, had their first trial run in the early twenties. Against this onslaught, the left opposition succumbed.

The Socialist Labour Party rapidly disintegrated. The first sign, not important in itself, came at the 1921 conference. Leonard Cotton, Frank Budgen and a handful of others left the SLP to form the Socialist Propaganda League. The schism was largely inspired by the American SLP which, over the years, had become increasingly uneasy about its British counterpart's departure from De Leonite orthodoxy.[44] While the Americans were unlikely to have much impact so long as the SLP floated on an expansive wave, with the first signs of a setback their criticism had greater force.

A much more serious defection came with the departure of John Maclean, who set up the Scottish Workers' Republican Party in October 1922. Distinctly nationalist in orientation, the SWRP's line could not be reconciled with that of the SLP, still taking an inter-nationalist position. Yet the new body does appear to have attracted some recruits from the SLP, particularly from Clydeside. Probably many other SLPers became demoralised, dropping out of activity, as a result of this split with Maclean. Sales of *The Socialist* and other publications drastically dropped. A 19-hour meeting of the SLP national executive, held on 26-7 August 1922, were informed by T. Mitchell, that, at the present rate of losses, the deficit would be £544 in a year.[45] Cuts were, therefore, made. *The Socialist* appeared monthly instead of weekly, but this did not halt the decline. Although no longer a member, John Maclean saw the importance of keeping the journal going. In a letter to James Clunie, he wrote:

I am writing to *The Socialist* to prevent it going under altogether. The SLPers, whatever our quarrels and misunderstandings may be, must be saved for Marxism if possible. You know I'm out of the SLP, and yet I see in the press a mighty engine for the development of Scotland.[46]

The efforts of Maclean and others proved to be in vain. By December 1922, *The Socialist* stopped regular publication. Sporadic attempts to revive it continued for many years. From time to time, it appeared in duplicated form, uttering a few sectarian pronouncements and collapsing after a few issues. The circulation always stayed miniscule; the influence was even less. Effectively, the Socialist Party was dead but would not lie down.

It could be argued that the SLP was tactically wrong, that it should have joined the Communist Party and then it would have stood a greater chance of maintaining its influence. Evidence does not bear out this contention. Had the SLP entered the CPGB, determined to be a left faction within it, then it would merely have been doing exactly the same as Sylvia Pankhurst and would have suffered the same fate. The Communist leadership, rapidly developing Stalinist characteristics, would not brook internal opposition. A second possibility would be to have joined the CP, hoping gradually to bend its policy leftwards. But the chances of this succeeding were equally remote. Talented ex-SLPers, MacManus, Bell and Paul, started out with this idea. They held influential positions in the Communist Party's formative period. However, they were elbowed out as the party bureaucracy became firmly established. Far from shifting the Communist Party to a revolutionary position, in most instances they only succeeded in losing their own.

The fact was that from 1922 onwards was the Ice Age of British socialism. Small groups operated on the fringe of politics without any impact whatsoever upon events. Obviously, their dogmatism and sectarianism further restricted their already very limited influence. But even without such handicaps, it is difficult to believe their success would be significantly greater. For two monsters, social democracy and Stalism, barred the way forward.

Today the situation is beginning to change. No longer do these two tremendous impediments have the same force as they have possessed for half a century. Revolutionary politics again becomes a possibility in Britain. And, as this occurs, the new generation is likely to look back to the Socialist Labour Party, not slavishly to copy it, but to learn from the experiences of the last truly revolutionary party to fight in the arena of British politics.

Notes

1. *The Socialist*.
2. CAB. 24/57. GT. 6713
3. J. Maclean to James Clunie, 24 November 1922. (Maclean Papers, National Library of Scotland). Also, all Maclean's letters to Clunie

reprinted in James Clunie's book *The Voice of Labour* (Dunfermline, 1967) pp. 81-101.

4. *Solidarity,* 21 January 1921.
5. *The Socialist,* 1 June 1922.
6. Ibid. 7 and 14 April 1921.
7. *Labour Monthly,* August 1921.
8. CAB. 24/57. GT. 6792.
9. *The Socialist,* 10 March 1921.
10. CAB. 24/26. GT. 2073.
11. *The Worker,* 31 May 1919.
12. *The Socialist,* 16 June 1921.
13. J.T. Murphy, *Stop The Retreat* (n.d.) p. 1.
14. R.M. Fox, *Smoky Crusade,* pp. 292-3.
15. *The Socialist,* 24 February 1921.
16. Ibid, 13 January 1921.
17. Ibid, 3 February 1921.
18. Second Congress of the Third International, pp. 145-6.
19. *The Socialist,* 3 January 1921.
20. John M. Henston, *Headquarters Battalion Easter Week 1916* (Dublin, 1958) pp. 35-8; Desmond Ryan, *The Rising* (London, 1962) p. 155; *The Socialist,* 3 June 1920.
21. *The Socialist,* 18 September 1920; *The Worker,* 13 August 1919; also Nan Milton, op. cit., p. 209.
22. Letter from C.H. Burden, 13 May 1973. In a subsequent letter, dated 29 May 1973, Mr Burden says McLoughlin spoke in Batley market place about the year 1930. He was dirty and unshaven. His speech aroused little or no response. That was the last time Mr Burden saw him.
23. *The Socialist,* 27 May 1920.
24. Ibid, 14 April 1921.
25. Ibid, 12 May 1921.
26. Ibid, 6 May 1920.
27. Ibid, 28 July 1921.
28. Ibid, 9 June 1921 and 17 November 1921.
29. Ibid, 26 May 1921.
30 Ibid, 25 August 1921; Nan Milton, *John Maclean,* p. 270.
31. In interviews both Harry McShane and Roy Botchard have made the point to me that John Maclean did not take sufficient care of himself. Roy Botchard said that he came to stay with him near Dundee, immediately after completing a prison sentence, but instead of resting, he addressed a meeting every night.
32. Countess Markievicz, *What Irish Republicans Stand For,* a pamphlet published in Glasgow (1922) forecasts accurately the subsequent development in Ireland.
33. J.T. Murphy, *The New Reasoner,* No. 7, Winter 1958-9.
34. *Workers' Dreadnought* 25 February and 11 March 1922.
35. W. Gallacher, *Last Memoirs,* p. 140.
36. George Williams, *The First Congress of the Red Trade Union International* (Chicago, 1921-2). pp. 25-6.
37. *Workers' Dreadnought,* 6 October 1923.
38. Nan Milton, op. cit., p. 200. John Maclean died a month or so later. Not surprisingly, Hannington does not mention his quarrel with Maclean in any of his books.
39. *Plebs,* October 1920.
40. *CPGB Report on Party Organisation,* 7 October 1922, p. 52.

41. Ibid. p. 54. Box 73 of the NCLC papers (National Library of Scotland) shows that Ilford CP was the only Communist Party branch of the 78 affiliations to the London district of the NCLC in 1924. This is indicative of the extent of the CP's withdrawal.
42. Dave Mitchell, *The Fighting Pankhursts* (1967) pp. 103-6.
43. *The Socialist*, 6 October 1921.
44. *The Weekly People*, 'The Passing of the British SLP', 28 March 1925.
45. *The Socialist*, 10 August 1920.
46. J. Maclean's letter to J. Clunie, 24 November 1922. (Maclean Papers, National Library of Scotland).

13 CONCLUSION

Did the SLP have to die? In the 1920s, there were two courses open to it: either the SLP could join the newly-formed Communist Party or it could endeavour to maintain itself as an independent revolutionary organisation. In a sense, both paths were tried and both failed. Arthur MacManus and a number of other leading members, albeit with only a small section of the rank-and-file, joined the CP. For a time, they held highly influential positions within the CPGB, but gradually they were squeezed out and replaced by apostles of Moscow orthodoxy like Dutt and Pollitt. The second path also led to a dead-end. The task of preserving the SLP as an independent party became increasingly difficult. Support melted away. Only a handful of dedicated socialists remained, ritualistically repeating the slogans of a few years before, which then had inflamed the masses but now did not strike a responsive cord.

Since whichever course it took appeared ill-fated, the question inevitably arises of whether this does not signify the SLP had intrinsic — and fatal — weaknesses. Many historians have arrived at this conclusion. Typical is Walter Kendall. He refers to 'the SLP's slavish adherence to De Leon' stopping 'the springs of natural creativity.'[1] But closer examination shows this is not a tenable position.

From the outset, the British SLP asserted its independence from its American counterpart, using De Leon's ideas critically, not obeying them as if they were the holy writ. At the inaugural conference, delegates incorporated immediate demands in the party programme, a step with which De Leon disagreed. A few months later, *The Socialist* did not hesitate to publish a front page article by Connolly that attacked De Leon's ideas on a number of questions. James Connolly, who, at various times, was active in both the American and British SLPs, thereby became well placed to judge the extent to which the two Parties diverged. In a letter to John Carstairs Matheson, he declared that the British SLP held positions 'widely different from Dan's' — that is, from Daniel De Leon.[2] Indeed, practical proof comes from Connolly's own experiences in the States. In 1904, he was nearly expelled from the American SLP. The British SLP interceded on his behalf, approaching De Leon as he returned from the Amsterdam congress of the Second International to ask him for an assurance that Connolly would not be thrown out. This it appears, was reluctantly given. Although in 1906

278

Connolly was still in bad odour with leading officials of the American SLP, it did not prevent the British Party having a scheme to ask him to return to Britain to be its national organiser. The project fell through at the last moment due to lack of finance. Two years later, Connolly wrote to the British Party for a character reference when he was being accused of disruption. As the forces against him seemed too formidable, he resigned from the American SLP in May 1908 to forestall impending expulsion. Outside the American SLP, Connolly retained his friendly contact with his British comrades. Cooperation after he returned to Ireland was maintained right up to his death in the Easter Uprising.

Allied to his claim that the British SLP had 'almost a theological devotion to De Leon,' Walter Kendall makes a second charge: he says that 'the SLP's sectarian nature' inhibited growth.[3] This would have been quite true if the British SLP had accepted in its entirety a basic proposition of De Leon. In his pamphlet, *Two Pages from Roman History*, De Leon argued that the leaders of the established working-class organisations acted as 'the labour lieutenants of capitalism.' They expressed workers' grievances, at the same time carefully seeing that all protests did not endanger the existing system. From this, he drew the conclusion that it was necessary to build up genuine revolutionary parties and unions, which would ultimately supplant their reformist counterparts.

It was about how this was to be accomplished that the British SLP disagreed with De Leon. While he lumped together both leaders and led, consigning them to the outer darkness, the British SLP sought to differentiate between the leaders, who were, consciously or unconsciously, agents of capitalism, and the mass of their followers, who had to be won over to true socialist policies. Wanting to win over the workers, the SLP realised it could not remain in splendid isolation:

> It [the SLP] is not a cave in the Labour Movement. It does not stand apart from the rest of the working class in remote isolation, suspending action until such time as we have a majority of adherents. It is in the very middle of the Labour Movement, in living touch with the working class, giving and receiving blows in every stage of the combat, striving to repel each encroachment of capital or gain some fresh point of vantage.[4]

This is the complete antithesis of De Leon's position. Realising this, James Connolly explained in a letter to Matheson:

The essence of that difference is that you recognise all the Labour parties and SDF and the rest of the tribe as being part of the *working-class movement,* and their membership as struggling towards the light. Dan would describe them as fake schemes of the capitalist class to down the SLP.[5]

De Leon's erroneous theoretical position condemned the American SLP to sterility and dogmatism. Again to quote Connolly:

Chief among those mistakes was its refusal to recognise the *growth* in the Labour Movement and its consequent absurd insistence that all working class movements which fell short of the cleanest were capitalist conspiracies against the SLP.[6]

Had the British SLP accepted the De Leonite line, it would not have been so effective. Probably more than any other political group, it helped to develop and mould the shop stewards' movement. Seemingly unpromising material, the aristocracy of labour, was transformed into a movement with revolutionary potential that alarmed Britain's rulers. Sectarians, standing aloof, simply mouthing phrases from Marx, would have been unable to accomplish this task. Similarly, the SLPs campaign against the First World War demanded not only courage but flexibility, a preparedness to work with others despite political disagreements. It also could not have been done by a bunch of sectarians.

Yet, nevertheless, there is a need to qualify the above analysis. It views things in a too simplistic, too absolute way. *Some* of the characteristics of sectarianism were present in the SLP *some* of the time. In periods of isolation, they were most pronounced. This particularly applied in the first few years of the Party's life as well as the last few. Unlike Walter Kendall and others, I do not consider that the presence of sectarianism was a cause of its decline; rather it was an effect. Clearly, a complex process of interaction occurred: with the waning of the class struggle, revolutionaries became increasingly isolated. Unable to influence the course of events, they developed sectarian traits which, in turn, merely served to reinforce the isolation.

All revolutionary groups in Britain from 1920 to 1970 have, to varying degrees, suffered from sectarianism. On every occasion, it has been for the same reason: objective conditions have made it impossible for them to participate meaningfully in the struggle. They have been condemned to play the role of spectators instead of being combatants. The reason for this has been that two profoundly counter-revolutionary

ideologies, social democracy and Stalinism, have had a virtual mono-
poly of working-class politics in that period. Only now are there signs
that the Ice Age is beginning to end.

In a period when the fundamentals of capitalism are again starting to
be challenged, the experiences of the SLP acquire a renewed relevance.
Among the principles it introduced into the British working-class movement are some which have gained wide currency whereas others need
to be re-discovered:

First, *the need for serious consistent work within the trade union
movement*. Workers inevitably encountered problems in the course of
their work. Revolutionaries had to relate to them, placing these
problems in a societal context and showing how they formed an integral part of the capitalist process. It also had to indicate the best ways
workers could ward off blows from the employers. This necessitated
the building of rank-and-file organisations. Moreover, since unity is
strength, revolutionaries urged the creation of industrial unions: not
only would these be able to mobilise the maximum strength against the
employing class, they would as well form the basis for industrial democracy in the future socialist society. The SLP was the first to expound
the case for workers' control.

Second, *the need for an independent working-class education movement*. The SLP saw a socialist consciousness could only develop along
with socialist theory. Therefore, it attempted to make as many as
possible of the socialist classics available, either by publishing them on
the SLP Press or by importing them from the United States. At the
same time, the Party realised that, if they were to be utilised to maximum effect, rigorous and hard study was required. The Labour Colleges
provided the framework within which this could be done, and had the
added advantage of bringing together socialists from diverse groups, a
process that helped to break down sectarian mistrust.

Third, *the need to create a new type of working-class party, one that
could act as a vanguard, providng the most dedicated, self-sacrificing
and knowledgeable people for the class battles*. This final point is
related to the fact that, quite independently, the SLP evolved a Bolshevik approach to politics. The Party came to see that the capitalist
state could not be gradually transformed into a socialist one; that the
capitalist state had to be smashed and replaced by a workers' state. It
also saw that, to accomplish the execution of capitalism, a sharp knife
– namely, a revolutionary party – was required. It was equally aware
that this could only be done once the majority of the working-class
found the existing system intolerable and called for a new society to be

created. Self activity oı the working-class was vital for socialism to be achieved.

The SLP approach clashed with those generally held on the left. The ILP looked to Parliament for salvation whereas the SLP thought no fundamental changes could be enacted through an establishment whose function was to assist the smooth running of the existing system. Similarly, the ILP and BSP placed great store by the piecemeal extension of public ownership through nationalisation and municipalisation. In contrast, the SLP thought these hopes were illusory: piecemeal measures did not alter the economic laws that operated in capitalism. Nationalisation did not constitute a step towards socialism. Since the industry was placed in the hands of the state, which represented the employing class as a whole, it would still essentially function in the same way as before. The first nationalisation to be brought before the British Parliament was introduced by a diehard Tory, Lord Palmerston. It was to nationalise the Indian railways. This was done not in the interests of the Indian masses but because the authorities discovered in the mutiny of 1857 that the existence of a number of railway companies, with a variety of size gauges, made it difficult to move troops swiftly from one place to another. Nationalisation of the railways was introduced to make exploitation more secure in India; to eliminate exploitation there would need to be a different type of state in India and industries would have to be under workers' control.

In Britain, the gradualist approach was the traditional one since the decline of Chartism. All sections of society had become inured to accepting capitalist institutions and values. The growth of a comparatively large-scale trade union movement and the election of some of its number to Parliament as Lib-Lab MPs, helped to reveal more clearly than in other countries the limits inherent in this approach. Therefore, the British SLP had practical experience of the nature of reformism. The SLP, unlike Lenin, was not surprised when, at the outbreak of the First World War, the various social democratic parties aligned themselves with their respective bourgeoisies. The SLP could also see more clearly their essentially imperialist role: the close proximity of Ireland did not only show how imperialism exploits colonial people, it revealed as well how labour politicians connived at this exploitation. The close ties the SLP maintained with Irish revolutionaries did not happen accidentally.

Yet, at the same time as the SLP had vision, it did not have power. The economic forces which enabled the ruling class to grant concessions, giving reformists the milieu in which to thrive, simultaneously barred the road to revolutionaries. No enduring discontent prevailed. No opportunity existed for the building of a large-scale revolutionary party.

It is important to realise the handicaps under which the SLP worked. Conditions were far less favourable to them than they are to their counterparts of the present day. The last fifty years has seen the erosion of the faith that workers once possessed in the efficacy of parliamentary action. Few people now believe that the Labour Party will introduce the New Jerusalem. Among militants there is a much greater awareness of the class collaborationist role of union leaders, even when they decorate their betrayals with left rhetoric. While at the present time the obstacles facing the descendants of the SLP are less, the opportunities are far greater. This is because: first, revolutionary groups are much bigger and have more influence; second, the dissemination of Marxist ideas has gone on to a far greater extent; and, third, that rank-and-file organisations within industry operate more extensively and with greater power.

More than 70 years have elapsed since the SLP was formed. In that period a lot has happened. The efforts of James Connolly, Yates and the others in 1903 can be likened to those of pioneers in a different sphere of activity: in 1902 the Wright Brothers were responsible for the first man-made flight. The aeroplane they built was a flimsy, rickety thing, looking as if Heath Robinson had been its designer. Nevertheless, the Wright Brothers' discovery laid the basis for the development of air transport that has led to the super-jets of the present age. In the same way, the principles first enunciated by the SLP still have relevance to socialists involved in current struggles.

Notes

1. W. Kendall, The Revolutionary Movement in Britain, p. 301.
2. J. Connolly to J.C. Matheson, letter dated April 1908 (National Library of Ireland, Dublin).
3. W. Kendall, op. cit., p. 75.
4. *The Socialist*, September 192.
5. J. Connolly to J.C. Matheson, letter dated April 1908.
6. J. Connolly to J.C. Matheson, letter dated 7 May 1908.

INDEX

Ablett, Noah 75, 106, 152
Abraham, W.A. (Mabon) 74-6
Accrington 37
Adams, Mrs Bridges 184, 185, 186
Advocates of Industrial Unionism
 48-9, 51-3, 87-92, 106, 138
Air Ministry 198
Albion Motors 135
Aldred, Guy 77, 86
Alexander, H.W. 162, 164, 165
Allen, E.J.B. 52, 53, 58, 84, 89,
 90-2, 95-6, 98, 106, 113
Amalgamated Engineering Union 260,
 262
Amalgamated Society of Engineers
 58, 78-84, 86, 89, 130-4, 197
Amalgamated Society of Railway
 Servants 59-60, 62, 68-9, 71
American SLP 17, 24-5, 31, 47, 110,
 112, 178-9
Anderson, Alex 19, 44
Anderson, W.C. 161, 180, 181
Anguilly, W.O. 53, 90
Anitchkine 184
Armstrong Whitworth 81
Arnot, Robin Page 85, 86, 148, 180
Ashington 73
Ashley W.W. 129
Ashton 120-1
Ashton, Thomas 75-6, 86
Askwith, Sir George 63, 85
Asquith, H.H. 128, 133, 148

Bain, G.S. 84
Balfour, Lord 247
Barbour, Mrs 133
Naritz, Moses 39-40
Barker, George 118
Barnes, G.N. 80-2, 150, 261
Barrow 159, 197, 201
Bartram, A 105
Bebel, A 110-1
Belfast 50, 63-4, 200
Bell, Richard 60, 62, 69, 93
Bell, Thomas: and Communist
 Party 221, 232, 253, 257, 275;
 and Connolly 41; and education

36, 113, 152; and A. Gordon 146;
 and Lenin 228; and Singers' strike
 104; and SLP 47, 48, 127, 155,
 206, 242-4
Bell, William 140, 156
Berner Tagwacht 151
Bevan, Aneurin 203
Bevin, Ernest 238, 259
Biggar, J.M. 244
Birmingham 17, 18, 53, 87, 89, 138
Blatchford, Robert 20-1, 26
Boer War 14-5, 20
Bow 16
Bower, Fred 66
Bowman, Guy 66, 96
Brace, William 150-1
Bridges, Robert 132
British Socialist Party: and Commu-
 nist Party 233, 237-9, 241, 242-3,
 245, 248, 257; and left unity 190,
 208, 210, 220, 226-7; and First
 World War 160-7, 206; and
 repression 138, 153, 187; and
 Russian Revolution 188, 216,
 219; and SDF 121
Brownlie, J.T. 86, 131, 197
Buchanan, Sir George 174
Budgen, Frank 37, 47, 55, 91, 106,
 111, 119, 274
Burgess, Joe 22
Burnham, Lord 196
Burt, Thomas 73, 74
Bury 108

Cachin, Marcel 162
Call, The 187, 188
Calvinism 35
Cambrian Combine strike 65, 74-5
Campbell-Bannerman, Sir Henry 50
Campbell, J.R. 250, 251, 271
Cannon, Jim 51
Cant, Ernest 227, 246
Carmarthenshire 65
Catholicism 110, 112
Central Labour College 116
Chandler, F.W. 148
Chesterton, G.K. 50, 55

284